HARVARD ECONOMIC STUDIES

HARVARD UNIVERSITY PRESS
CAMBRIDGE, MASS., U.S.A.

HARVARD ECONOMIC STUDIES

VOLUME LVII

AWARDED THE DAVID A. WELLS PRIZE FOR THE YEAR 1935–36 AND PUBLISHED FROM THE INCOME OF THE DAVID A. WELLS FUND. THIS PRIZE IS OFFERED ANNUALLY, IN A COMPETITION OPEN TO SENIORS OF HARVARD COLLEGE AND GRADUATES OF ANY DEPARTMENT OF HARVARD UNIVERSITY OF NOT MORE THAN THREE YEARS STANDING, FOR THE BEST ESSAY IN CERTAIN SPECIFIED FIELDS OF ECONOMICS

THE STUDIES IN THIS SERIES ARE PUBLISHED BY THE DEPARTMENT OF ECONOMICS OF HARVARD UNIVERSITY, WHICH, HOWEVER, ASSUMES NO RESPONSIBILITY FOR THE VIEWS EXPRESSED

LONDON : HUMPHREY MILFORD

OXFORD UNIVERSITY PRESS

STUDIES IN MASSACHUSETTS TOWN FINANCE

BY

EUGENE E. OAKES

INSTRUCTOR IN ECONOMICS IN HARVARD UNIVERSITY

CAMBRIDGE

HARVARD UNIVERSITY PRESS

1937

PRINTED AT THE HARVARD UNIVERSITY PRESS

CAMBRIDGE, MASS., U.S.A.

To

CHARLES JESSE BULLOCK

PREFACE

THIS book is an elaboration of a thesis submitted for the doctorate at Harvard University in 1934. The original version contained five cases. These have been greatly condensed, chiefly by the elimination of all but the most vital of the statistical material, and to them have been added four more cases which present in summary fashion episodes in the financial history of the towns of Millville, Adams, Florida, and Somerset.

While naturally I assume full responsibility for all the conclusions advanced in this volume, I should like to acknowledge the assistance of a large number of people, of tax officials and residents of the towns studied, who have been very gracious in consenting to be interviewed and in several instances in reading and criticizing portions of the manuscript. I wish to thank the staff of the Massachusetts State Library for the courteous treatment I have received at their hands; I am grateful to my mother for the substantial assistance which she has rendered in the preparation of the manuscript; but my primary debt is to Professor Charles Jesse Bullock, at whose suggestion the original thesis was undertaken and whose patient, careful assistance has been indispensable to the completion of this enterprise.

E. E. O.

CAMBRIDGE, MASSACHUSETTS
August, 1936

CONTENTS

LIST OF MAPS

STUDIES IN MASSACHUSETTS
TOWN FINANCE

INTRODUCTION

THE present volume contains a series of studies dealing with certain episodes in the financial history of a group of small Massachusetts towns. The subjects considered were chosen not because of any historical interest they might possess but because they seemed to throw light upon certain important principles of public finance. More specifically, the cases which follow were intended to offer a rather detailed analysis of situations that cannot be explained satisfactorily without a careful study of the relation between the burdens of local taxation and the benefits received from local expenditures. While this is a subject important in itself, it is of even greater interest because of its bearing upon a significant though often neglected aspect of the theory of justice in taxation.

In modern discussions of this larger subject it is usually inferred that a choice must be made between a general system in which the burdens of taxation are distributed in accordance with the benefits enjoyed as a result of public expenditures, and a general system adjusted to the taxpayer's ability to pay. Either proposition, so stated, is dangerously simple. It appears, for instance, that the benefits yielded by government services are usually too intangible, too elusive, to permit anything approaching an accurate measurement. Moreover, in many of the apparently exceptional cases where benefits are roughly measurable, they seem to accrue to people little able to bear the burden of taxation. Consequently, the notion that a general system of taxation can be adjusted to the incidence of the benefits received appears to be useless.[1] Most thinking seems to stop at this point. Hence the widespread acceptance of the generalized ability theory.

[1] This is roughly the argument used by John Stuart Mill in his *Principles of Political Economy*, bk. V, chap. ii, pp. 802–817.

Yet it is also true that the taxpayer's ability to pay cannot be accurately measured by such tangible indices as the amount of property owned or the amount of income received.[2] Consequently, modern ability theories are couched in terms of subjective reactions or "sacrifices,"[3] thus bringing this type of theory beneath the same accusation of vagueness so often directed against the so-called benefit theorists. Small wonder that certain realistic students of public finance have been led to conclude that theories of justice in taxation are nothing more than wishful thoughts reflecting the social leanings of the theorists in question.[4]

This complete cynicism does not seem altogether warranted, however, since many of the difficulties surrounding the discussion of equity are the result of the very general form in which the problem is usually stated. The all-too-frequent failure to bear in mind the distinction between justice in local and in national finance is a case in point. The result of such an omission is an unduly simplified and hence inaccurate theory.[5] Consequently, it is extremely important to call attention specifically to the type of governmental unit to which the theory in question is to be applied. The present volume is concerned, of course, only with the problem of equity in local finance.

The analysis of this complex problem is aided by an explicit

---

[2] It is clear, for instance, that a given income would represent a much greater ability in the hands of a single person owning a substantial amount of property than in the hands of the head of a large family with little or no property to fall back upon if the breadwinner's earnings should cease.

[3] While this approach to the problem of justice in taxation goes back at least as far as John Stuart Mill, it finds a much more sophisticated expression in the writings of one of its outstanding contemporary exponents, Professor A. C. Pigou (*A Study in Public Finance*, 1928, part II, chap. i). The core of Pigou's theory is the notion that economic welfare requires the maximization of an intangible, subjective reaction known as a satisfaction. The pleasurable or at least sense-satisfying responses stimulated in the nervous system or the "mind" of the ultimate consumers of the goods which society produces are to be set off against the distasteful sensations which are supposed to be incurred in the production process. The taxing system is then given the task of assisting in making the difference between these two sets of responses as large as possible. Certainly a theory of this type cannot be advocated on the grounds of its relatively tangible character.

[4] For example, F. W. Taussig, *Principles of Economics* (3d ed., 1921), II, 505–511.

[5] It frequently happens that an author will recognize this distinction when dealing specifically with the problems of local finance only to ignore it completely when treating the subject of equity itself. Here again the result must be an over-simplified and hence inaccurate theory.

recognition of a second distinction, namely, the difference between the propositions that benefits received ought to be used as a
means of determining the *amount* of the tax that is to be levied,
and that at least in the field of state and local finance an attempt
should be made to collect the required revenue from people who
benefit either personally or through their property from the
services provided by the government agencies.[6] Our concern is
mainly with the latter question, for it is the purpose of the
majority of the cases which follow to bring to light situations in
which serious financial difficulties have resulted from a failure to
achieve this reasonable adjustment between the burden of taxation and the benefits received from local governmental expenditures.

Since the understanding of these cases requires the appreciation
of a technical problem of local government, there must be intro-
duced at this point a summary description of the Massachusetts
town, which differs substantially from the primary units of local
government used in other sections of the country. In Massachusetts, although a system of counties has been superimposed, the
towns have retained most of the important local governmental
functions. They provide schools, parks, and libraries; they are responsible for the relief of the poor resident within their borders
and have the power to erect various services in the interest of
public health. They construct and maintain most of the local

---

[6] The possibility of applying the first of these propositions in the field of state and
local finance was explored by Edwin H. Spengler in a paper entitled, "Is the Real
Estate Tax a Benefit Tax?" (Memorandum Number Five appended to *Report of the
New York State Commission for the Revision of the Tax Laws, 1932*. The author's
inference was that the local real-estate tax is largely a payment for services rendered.

The second of the propositions enumerated above is obviously the basic doctrine
contained in the report of the committee appointed by the National Tax Association
to draft a model plan for state and local taxation. Although this report makes no
attempt to propound a theory of justice, its main lines of policy, its insistence that
every person ought to pay a tax to the jurisdiction in which he resides, that tangible
property ought to be taxed where located, and that business enterprises should be
subject to taxation by the jurisdictions in which the business is carried on, reflect
agreement on at least one point. Both persons and property ought to be taxed in
return for general or special benefits received from a governing body. (*Proceedings
... National Tax Association, 1933*, pp. 353–402.) It is interesting to observe that
A. L. Harding in his work on *Double Taxation* has attempted to show that the United
States Supreme Court used similar logic in arriving at a series of apparently contradictory opinions on questions of conflicts in taxing jurisdiction.

roads. They ordinarily furnish fire and police protection if these services are desired by the community. They have been authorized to carry out drainage projects, construct sewers, provide market places, and own and operate utilities.[7] Moreover, it is characteristic of the Massachusetts town that it ordinarily attempts to provide these services for all the groups resident within its borders regardless of the diversity of economic interests existing among them or the varied degrees of urbanization which characterize their members.

Hence the New England town, of which the Massachusetts unit is the prototype, needs to be clearly distinguished from the township found in the central and middle-western states. The powers of the latter are relatively slight, its political importance comparatively negligible. Outside New England the relief of the poor and the maintenance of the more important local roads are usually entrusted to the county, while the latter ordinarily exercises some control over the public schools operating within its borders. The powers of the township have also been whittled away by the incorporation within its limits of special districts assuming responsibility for a portion of the highways, for schools, fire protection, local utilities, or particular improvements of an unusual nature such as drainage projects. Finally, the powers of the township have been reduced by the incorporation of villages within its limits.

Massachusetts, however, has failed to provide for the incorporation of villages within the borders of its towns,[8] and this failure

[7] *Tercentenary Edition of the General Laws*, 1932, c. 40, sec. 5 to sec. 19.

[8] The village has been defined as a special corporation set up to serve the needs of a small, compactly settled area which is semi-urban in character. It differs from a city in size, in the narrower range of its functions, and in the simpler organization used by its government. (J. A. Fairlie, *Local Government in Counties, Towns, and Villages*, 1914, p. 200.) The village was developed in the South because of the absence of a local unit and in the Middle West because of the feebleness of the township (H. G. James, *Local Government in the United States*, 1921, p. 291). But the virility of town government has prevented, to a large measure, the development of the incorporated village in New England.

This statement is not equally true, however, of all the states in this area. Vermont has provided for village government by general law (*The General Laws of Vermont*, 1917, c. 177, sec. 4104) and in 1930 had sixty-six such corporations constituting a fairly complete application of the village system. Connecticut incorporated its first borough (Bridgeport) in 1800 and has continued to set up this type

has produced situations which possess interesting theoretical implications. When a community grows up developing a social and economic structure differing substantially from that existing in the rest of the town, the new settlement is apt to require services not previously provided. It is also apt to place an entirely different estimate upon the desirability of a more highly developed and consequently more expensive system of local government. Provision of the desired services would for the most part be financed out of the general tax revenues of the town; all taxpayers would share in the burden in proportion to the assessed value of their property — a distribution of taxation which is not necessarily adjusted to benefits received.[9] Hence the new expenditures are likely to be opposed by the portion of the community which either is not going to be supplied with the new services or does not approve of the transition to a more expensive form of local government. If the advocates of increased spending are able to control the town meeting, they are in a position to vote themselves the desired services, but if they cannot achieve political dominance, they will be asked to bow to the will of the remainder of the town. The ill feeling generated by the latter alternative is in many cases accentuated by the fact that the developing area, being wealthy, is bearing a relatively large share of the burden of local taxation. In any event, one of the two contending groups will be asked to yield to the wishes of a town meeting which proposes to put into effect distasteful financial policies. The incorporation of a village offers a convenient means of escape. When, however, a state has

---

of government by special act until in 1930 no less than twenty such units were listed by the United States Census. Maine has made no provision for a similar organization in its general laws but has followed the practice of incorporating villages by special act. These numbered twenty-eight in 1930. New Hampshire's general statutes provide for a unit known as the "village district," but the limited powers held by that organization have impeded its development (*The Public Laws of the State of New Hampshire*, 1926, c. 57). Rhode Island, however, has made no progress at all in this direction and the same may be said of Massachusetts. This situation was described by F. G. Bates in an article entitled "Village Government in New England," *The American Political Science Review*, August 1912.

[9] An exception results from the financing of added services by special assessments. The scope of services to which this device can be applied is limited. It offers no solution at all in cases where the dispute arises over the quality of the service required.

not made provision for this type of local government, another solution must be sought. This is the situation in Massachusetts. What, then, are the available remedies?

If the dissatisfied element is large and politically powerful, it is conceivable that it might petition the General Court for incorporation as a city. This, however, is not ordinarily an important alternative in Massachusetts, where even large communities have hesitated to take such a course. The virility of the town meeting has tended to check the incorporation of cities as well as villages, and the larger towns have attempted to avoid municipal organization by adjusting the town meeting to their own peculiar needs. By 1928 a total of fifteen of the largest towns in Massachusetts had turned to the limited town meeting in preference to assuming the status and organization of a city.[10] But neither the grant of a municipal charter nor the adoption of the limited town meeting is a solution for the problem under consideration, since in both cases the area of the town is left unaltered. The conflicts which have caused trouble in the ordinary town meeting will persist in spite of the change in the type of government to which the conflicting groups are subjected.

On the other hand, the incorporation of fire districts does offer some measure of relief. This type of organization enables the inhabitants of one portion of a town to provide themselves with a desired service at their own expense if the town itself is not willing to support that service out of general tax revenues. Such units were at first created by special act, but in 1844 a general statute was passed which, as amended, remained in effect in 1932. This statute provides for the establishment of districts "containing not less than one thousand inhabitants, or not less than five hundred inhabitants in towns the population of which does not exceed two thousand." It stipulates, however, that no such unit may be organized until a petition requesting "the establishment and maintenance of a sufficient fire department for the reasonable protection of the inhabitants and property" within the limits of the proposed district has been refused by the town meeting. If this procedure has been complied with, a district may be organized

[10] John F. Sly, *Town Government in Massachusetts* (1930), p. 179.

having the power to provide fire protection, water, and street lighting within its limits and to raise money by taxation for these purposes.[11]

Further relief was made available in 1870 in the form of a general law providing for the incorporation of "improvement districts." These also are restricted to areas containing more than one thousand inhabitants, and are authorized by the town meeting itself. They are given power to provide street lights, libraries, sidewalks, and police protection.[12]

A third type of special corporation was provided for in 1902, when the statute relating to "watch districts" was enacted,[13] but this law was repealed in 1918.[14] Other units have been set up by special act, most of them being incorporated in order to supply certain particular areas with light and water.[15]

But all these devices offer only a partial solution to the problem under consideration. Both fire and improvement districts are available only to fairly large communities, and both require for their establishment a certain amount of coöperation on the part of the rest of the town. In any event they leave the aggrieved community subject to a considerable amount of interference; they offer no relief at all in cases where the difference of opinion has arisen over the adequacy of the service provided; and they do not touch upon disputes pertaining to the town schools. Under these conditions it is not surprising to find that "in Massachusetts the development of a new center of population in a town has led commonly to a prompt division of the town."[16]

This has been the usual method of adjusting the structure of local government to changes in social and economic conditions, and all but the last two of the sketches that follow deal with cases in which this remedy has been applied. In fact, the group of studies which form Part I is concerned primarily with the financial aspects of such town divisions. These cases have been set forth in

---

[11] *Tercentenary Edition of the General Laws*, 1932, c. 48, sec. 60, 61, and 69.
[12] *Ibid.*, c. 40, sec. 44.
[13] *Revised Laws*, 1902, c. 332.
[14] *Acts and Resolves*, 1918, c. 257.
[15] Bates, *op. cit.*, pp. 382–383.
[16] *Ibid.*, p. 381.

some detail, since in each instance the residents of the complaining area asserted that the services it was receiving were inadequate in view of its needs and the portion of the tax burden which it bore. In short, these cases present the record of a series of determined and successful protests against a failure to bring about a reasonable adjustment between the burden of local taxation and the benefits received as a result of local governmental expenditures.

The miscellaneous studies which make up Part II of this volume are intended to illustrate certain other aspects of the same basic problem, namely, the significance of the relation between benefits and taxation in local finance.

Finally, before proceeding to the studies themselves, it is necessary to point out the importance of the method which has been applied. Case studies of this type have rarely been attempted in the field of local finance, probably because of a general belief that the individual case is unimportant, and of an inclination to doubt the possibility of generalizing upon the theoretical implications of the facts observed. Investigators have chosen, rather, to deal with the combined statistics of a group of local governments, particularly with the totals for an entire state. But this procedure possesses a glaring weakness. The movement of a state total is the net result of a great number of varying and in many cases mutually contradictory changes in the finances of the individual governments. The findings based upon an analysis of such statistical aggregates are abstractions. The results obtained are in the nature of an average; they are not necessarily true of any one of the local units considered; and they gloss over a multitude of individual circumstances which in themselves may possess important theoretical implications.

On the other hand, the separate consideration of the experiences of individual units, especially if those units are small and hence possess a simple economic and financial structure, greatly reduces the number of the complicating factors which make the interpretation of economic history so difficult. By this procedure the picture is simplified and the problems encountered are thrown into sharp relief. The theoretical implications are more easily discerned; the conclusions drawn are less uncertain; and the results obtained are reinforced by the atmosphere of reality which the consideration of actual historical circumstances affords. The present volume has been written in the firm belief that a wide application of the case method to this relatively neglected field of public finance would not only serve to drive home the significance of accepted theory, but, if applied to a sufficient number of cases, would also produce that modification of general principles which is the essence of scientific progress.

PART I

ON THE DIVISION
OF THE MASSACHUSETTS TOWN

CHAPTER I

INCORPORATIONS BASED UPON WEALTH

It is the purpose of this chapter to present the circumstances surrounding two town divisions, both of which involved the separation of relatively wealthy areas from less favored portions of the parent towns. The new units, Hopedale and Wellesley, were so well to do that their finances are interesting in themselves, a fact which further justifies the inclusion of these cases in the present series.

A. HOPEDALE

The territory now occupied by Milford and Hopedale had been set off from the old town of Mendon in 1780 at the culmination of a series of quarrels covering a period of fifty years.[1] The portion of Milford which was to become Hopedale was very sparsely settled and acquired no appreciable population until the appearance, in 1842, of a social-reform group known as the Hopedale Community.[2] The latter's finances, never very strong, collapsed entirely in 1857; its enterprises were liquidated, and its debts assumed by two of its members, Eben and George Draper. Although the community survived as a religious and mutual-

---

[1] In 1730 a dispute arose over the construction of a meeting house. "Inhabitants on the east side of Mill River" objected to contributing towards this project and in 1735 asked to be set off as a separate town. Similar requests were made in 1736, 1739, and 1740. In 1741 the district was incorporated as a precinct and proceeded to erect its own church. Agitation for town status was renewed in 1753, 1766, and 1779. The latter resulted in an unopposed petition which was acceded to in the following year when the General Court incorporated Milford as a separate town. See Adin Ballou, *History of the Town of Milford* (Boston, 1882), pp. 48, 53, 82–87.

[2] This was a "joint stock practical Christian association with a united industrial management." Its original name was the "Practical Christian Republic, Fraternal Community No. I." The story of this experiment is told in Adin Ballou's *History of the Hopedale Community* (Lowell, 1897).

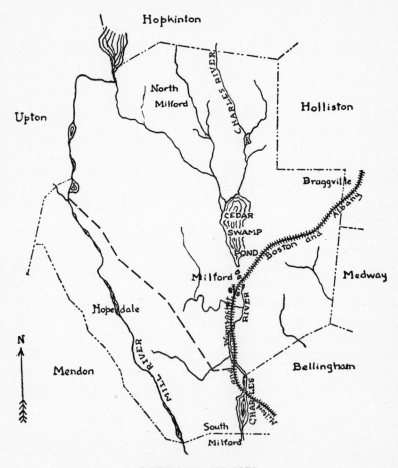

MILFORD IN 1870

SHOWING BOUNDARY BETWEEN MILFORD AND HOPEDALE
AFTER INCORPORATION OF THE LATTER THUS: — — —

guarantee association, it gradually lost its influence in the village of Hopedale, and there is reason to believe that most of the original characteristics of this settlement had disappeared by 1875.[3]

The Drapers, however, continued to operate a machine shop which they had set up independently of the Community, and by 1875 it had developed into a group of mills constituting the largest industrial undertaking in the town of Milford. At this time the Drapers were operating two cotton-machinery plants and two spindle mills with invested capital of $140,000 and $120,000 respectively. The remainder of Milford contained twenty-three small boot and shoe factories with an average capital of about $33,000,[4] but these enterprises were declining in importance as a result of the decay of the shoe industry in this part of the state.[5]

Although the increasing importance of the Draper mills failed to turn Hopedale into an independent community — and the continued development of these enterprises has not done so down to the present day [6] — most of the property in the area had fallen into the hands of the Draper family by 1875 and the village had come to be recognized as the wealthy part of Milford.[7]

There had been no significant change in the latter's boundaries since its incorporation in 1780,[8] and there is no evidence that Hopedale desired separate incorporation until suddenly in 1886 a movement with this object developed under the leadership of

[3] Ballou, *Hopedale*, pp. 291–292; and Ballou, *Milford*, p. 261.

[4] Ballou, *Milford*, pp. 254–255.

[5] The number of shoe factories in Milford dropped from twenty-three in 1875 to seventeen in 1885, and then fell to seven in 1895. The number of persons employed rose from 1,718 in 1875 to 1,812 in 1880 and dropped to 1,016 in 1895. The value of the goods produced fell from $2,800,000 in 1875 to $1,500,000 in 1895. These statistics are from the state census of manufactures. They are not affected by the separation of Hopedale since the boot factories were all located in the Milford area.

[6] In 1875 the town's three railroads had their depots in Milford. Only one of six churches was located in Hopedale and most of the new settlers affiliated with Milford churches. The people of Hopedale village went to Milford for their banking and shopping facilities and for their amusements. The public library was situated there as was also the town high school. (Ballou, *Milford*, pp. 274, 367.)

[7] In the first year after separation the per capita income from bank and corporation taxes was $7.15 in Hopedale and 33 cents in Milford.

[8] Ballou, *Milford*, pp. 87–89.

George and William F. Draper.[9] There was bitter opposition, but the petition of the group was granted in that year by the General Court, and Hopedale was incorporated as a separate town.

The counsel for the opponents of separation had pointed to the common interests which bound the two villages together. He had argued that the division would place an unfair burden on the remainder of the town, since there were about one hundred operatives of the Hopedale mills living in Milford, none of them paying more than a poll tax and all, in the event of accident, sickness, or unemployment, forming a potential burden to the latter town. At the same time the proposed new unit would receive most of the revenue from the state levy on corporate excess and would enjoy a very much lower tax rate.[10]

The reply to these arguments was very largely a complaint about the financial policies pursued by the Milford town meeting. It was alleged that the share of municipal services and improvements allotted to the Hopedale area failed to correspond even roughly with the proportion of town taxes paid by residents of this village. Moreover, it was argued that the people of Hopedale obtained the services which they did receive only after a severe struggle in town meeting. For these reasons separation was believed necessary in order to give Hopedale some assurance of a real return for taxes paid.[11]

In order to check the validity of this complaint it is necessary to review Milford's finances for the period preceding division.

---

[9] J. H. Benton, *The Draper Corporations against the People of Milford: Argument of J. H. Benton* (Boston, 1886), p. 5.

[10] He pointed out also that the Drapers would enjoy complete political control of the new town since the bulk of its inhabitants was made up of their own employees. The counsel concluded that, "There is nothing to justify it [the separation], there is nothing to sustain it, except the personal ambition and self interest of one strong, persistent, and obstinate man."

Substantially the same arguments were presented in a pamphlet entitled *Some Reasons Why the Town of Milford Should Not be Divided, Replied to by a Committee Favoring Division* (George Draper and others, 1886).

[11] *Opening Argument of Nathan Sumner Myrick, Esq.* (Boston, 1886), pp. 11–13. See also the pamphlets entitled, *Reasons Why Hopedale Should be Set off from Milford* (The Committee for Hopedale, 1886) and *Some Reasons Why the Town of Milford Should Not be Divided*, etc.

The record of total and total current expenditures is summarized in the following table:

Year*	Total Expenditures†	Total Current Expenditures‡
	(In thousands of dollars.)	
1872	94.8	79.8
1877	73.1	66.7
1885	101.7	87.1
1886	92.8	78.5

* Year ending February 28.
† Includes capital outlays and net payments on debt.
‡ Total expenditures, less net payments on debt and capital outlays, including such highway expenditures as clearly fall within the latter category.

There is a period of sharply declining expenditures ending in 1877, followed by a slow rise to 1885, in which year expenditures jumped to a point well above their 1872 level. But a substantial drop in the following year left a slight net decline for the entire period under review.[12]

Although there are no data available furnishing a comparison with the expenditures made in the state as a whole, it is possible to compare taxes levied on polls and property, which supplied most of the revenue out of which town expenditures were financed. The Milford levy dropped from $103,600 to $81,000 between 1872 and 1877, and although the state total began to decline after 1875, it showed a net advance from $22,000,000 to $24,800,000 during this same interval. Both town and state totals were higher in 1886, but the Milford levy of $85,600 left a net decline of about 21 per cent for the period as a whole as compared with a 22 per cent advance in the state total.[13] It is apparent that Milford had gone to unusual lengths in her striving for economy during the middle seventies and that her subsequent failure to exceed the level of expenditures present in 1872 was not typical of the state as a whole.

The reduction in the town's current expenditures, which came in the face of an advance in poor relief from $5,500 to $12,500 between 1872 and 1877, was largely the result of a drop from $21,600 to $17,700 in the cost of schools, and a reduction from

[12] This, however, was somewhat less than the accompanying drop in population from 9,874 in 1871 to 9,343 in 1885. As a result per capita current expenditures rose from $8.08 to $8.40.
[13] The total levy for the state was $25,850,317 in 1886.

$20,300 to $9,700 in highway maintenance charges. The large total present in 1885 was the result of expenditures of $31,900 and $12,700 for schools and highways respectively; the decline in the following year was produced by a drop to $24,800 in the cost of town schools.

In 1886, Milford spent only 15 per cent more for schools than it had in 1872. Although there is ample reason to believe that the service furnished at that time had not been very satisfactory,[14] it had been considered extravagant by a group of voters in Milford [15] who seem to have been strong enough to make it difficult to put through any improvements during the period under review.[16]

The road expenditures for 1886 was only 54 per cent of the amount expended in 1872, and this decline was more than sufficient to offset the rise from $7,200 to $9,200 in the cost of fire protection, and the advance from $5,500 to $11,600 in poor relief. Stringent economy in the performance of the highway and educational functions made it possible for Milford to end this fourteen-year interval with a level of current expenditures lower than that with which it had begun.

The decline in expenditures between 1872 and 1877 had been accompanied by a drop from $1,500,000 to $1,200,000 in the value of personalty, but the advance in real-estate assessments had brought a rise from $4,800,000 to $5,100,000 in the town's total valuation. This was followed by a decline to 1881, a sharp rise to 1885, and a slight drop in the following year bringing the

[14] The school committee for the year ending February 1873 stated: "We have been as economical as possible. We have refrained from making some repairs, which good economy will not permit us to neglect longer and from purchasing some apparatus which some of the schools absolutely need. We are already violating the law in many schools by placing from 60 to 80 pupils under the charge of one teacher." (Report of the School Committee, 1873, pp. 44–45.)

[15] The same committee stated: "It has been plainly charged that the High School [which had only been erected because the town was under legal obligation to do so] was doing injury in place of good, and was costing the town too much" (*ibid.*, p. 44).

[16] The committee of 1876 stated that "the committee are all of the opinion that we really need more schools to suitably accommodate the scholars for whom we are legally bound to provide" (*ibid.*, 1876, p. 67). The response to this plea was a cut of $3,900 in the town's current expenditures on schools. The school report for 1880 contained the following statement: "Some of our citizens indeed think it is incurring a needless expense to hire a superintendent to do the work formerly done by the committee" (p. 4). The same committee expressed its regrets that the salary of this superintendent of schools had been lowered from $1,500 to $1,200.

town base to $5,200,000, which represented a net advance of about 8 per cent for the period as a whole.[17]

Milford had also been assisted to some extent by an increase in receipts from the state bank and corporation taxes from $2,160 in 1872 to $7,259 in 1886. Almost the whole of this advance had come after 1879.[18]

The net result of the rise in local valuations and the decline in expenditures was a drop in the town rate from $20.50 in 1872 to $15.00 in 1876. The increase in expenditures to 1885 more than offset the additional income received from state taxes and the town rate rose to $17.00 per thousand. It dropped back to $15.50 in the following year as a result of curtailed expenditures leaving a net reduction of 24 per cent for the period as a whole, and bringing the town rate down from 138 to 110 per cent of the current state average. Since the latter had changed little during the interval under consideration, the difference in the spread between the two rates reflects the unusual nature of the economy practiced by the Milford town meeting.[19] A further manifestation of this factor is furnished by the decline in the town's liabilities from $231,000 to $115,000.[20]

To justify this policy one can point to the growing burden of poor relief which accompanied the decline of the boot and shoe industry, and to the fact that the Milford rate, even under a system of rigid economy, was somewhat above the average for Massachusetts as a whole. Under these conditions economy would seem the logical policy to the majority of the property owners in the town, for with the exception of the Hopedale area Milford was not a wealthy community, and its citizens could not

[17] The statistics are presented below:

Year	Real Estate	Personalty	Total
		(In thousands of dollars.)	
1872	3,326.9	1,467.5	4,794.4
1877	3,852.2	1,218.2	5,070.4
1881	3,282.8	1,102.0	4,384.8
1885	3,874.6	1,362.8	5,237.4
1886	3,892.4	1,309.2	5,201.5

[18] The town received $2,959 in 1879.

[19] The state rate had been $14.84 in 1872 and $14.14 in 1886.

[20] This was in addition to a loss of $20,000 absorbed by the town in 1882 as a result of the sale of stock in a local railroad.

be expected to favor an expensive system of town government, no matter what benefits that government could offer.

But economy would be distasteful to the residents of the wealthy section. The owners and officials of the Draper organization were rich enough to afford and to desire a high type of local government. Particularly they would favor good educational facilities and well kept streets, and it was precisely at these points that the town meeting was accustomed to cut its appropriations.

Hopedale failed to receive the type of service its residents desired because the majority of the voters in Milford were unwilling to share in the burdens which increased expenditures entailed. Hopedale could expect no better service unless it was willing to pay for similar improvements for the whole town. It is not likely that Hopedale's residents would accept the latter alternative since they were already complaining that they were bearing too large a share of the burden of town expenditures, that they were paying taxes out of all proportion to the benefits which the town provided, and that they were in effect already "paying a subsidy to Milford." [21]

Whether this feeling was justified it would be difficult or impossible to determine but under these circumstances it is not surprising that the reduction in Milford's expenditures that took place during the year ending February 1886 and was directed mainly at the outlay on schools should precipitate a movement for separation in the wealthy section of town. To test this hypothesis it is necessary to examine the finances of the two new towns for the decades following division. Their expenditures are compared in the following table:

| | A. Milford | | | | B. Hopedale | | | |
Year	Total Expenditures Actual*	Per Cap.	Total Current Expenditures Actual*	Per Cap.	Total Expenditures Actual*	Per Cap.	Total Current Expenditures Actual*	Per Cap.
1886	73.1	$8.70	65.1	$7.73	10.0	$10.80	9.7	$10.48
1890	95.8	10.90	91.1	10.35	22.5	19.15	20.5	17.45
1896	109.2	11.58	95.9	10.15	39.3	25.85	39.3	25.85
1900	162.0	14.23	115.8	10.18	62.6	30.00	54.3	26.00
1906	194.4	15.80	132.7	10.80	47.3	22.80	47.3	22.80
1910	184.8	14.10	141.8	10.85	61.3	28.00	50.3	22.95

* In thousands of dollars.

[21] The attorney for the opponents of separation quotes this phrase and attributes it to George Draper (J. H. Benton, *The Draper Corporations against the People of Milford*, p. 20).

The current expenditures are the significant figures for the purpose at hand. A rise of 40 per cent in Milford during the four years following division was more than matched by a 110 per cent increase in the new town of Hopedale, and although Milford's expenditures continued to rise rapidly during the remainder of the period to a point 115 per cent above the 1886 level, this is dwarfed by a 420 per cent advance in the neighboring town. Reduction to a per capita basis not only fails to alter the conclusion that Hopedale was increasing its current expenditures far more rapidly than Milford, but also serves to emphasize the fact that this discrepancy was due to a sharp advance during the period immediately following division. It is clear that release from the restraint exercised by the old Milford meeting had produced distinctly more generous town expenditures in the Hopedale area.

The resulting changes in taxes levied are compared with the state total in the following table:

Year	Milford	Hopedale	State
		(In thousands of dollars.)	
1886	72.0	9.0	25,644
1890	82.8	16.5	30,295
1896	95.0	22.6	38,520
1900	107.1	41.9	46,371
1906	124.0	39.6	56,166
1910	158.6	37.0	66,718

The 120 per cent advance in Milford was substantially less than the 160 per cent increase in the state total, which in turn was far less rapid than the 311 per cent rise in the taxes levied in Hopedale.

A more detailed explanation of the differences in the spending policies behind these tax levies is furnished by the following statistics of current expenditures for 1886, 1896, and 1910. In the first year of its independent existence Hopedale paid out about two thousand dollars more than Milford had been spending on schools in that area.[22] This produced a per capita expenditure

[22] "The appropriation for schools in the annual meeting in March 1886, was $23,300. This was made before it was settled that the town was to be divided. At a subsequent town meeting the appropriation for schools was reduced to $20,000. This seemed a large reduction, as it could not be said that the annual cost of the education of all the school children within the limits of the new town would amount

more than twice that made by the other town. There was little change in this relationship down to 1896 and the rapid advance in Milford's school expenditure to 1910 was matched by the Hopedale total. It is clear that the latter town was decidedly more liberal in the provision of educational facilities.

A. Milford

	1886		1896		1910	
	Actual*	Per Cap.	Actual*	Per Cap.	Actual*	Per Cap.
Schools	20.4	$2.42	27.0	$2.86	45.6	$3.50
Highways ..	9.1	1.08	13.1	1.38	25.3	1.90
Poor	9.6	1.14	14.4	1.53	16.1	1.23
Fire	7.5	.89	14.0	1.49	19.2	1.47
Street Lights	3.2	.38	5.7	.60	9.0	.69

B. Hopedale

	1886		1896		1910	
	Actual*	Per Cap.	Actual*	Per Cap.	Actual*	Per Cap.
Schools	5.0	$5.40	8.2	$5.40	15.5	$7.07
Highways ..	2.7	2.92	20.7	13.60	9.5	4.34
Poor	.1	.12	.8	.53	.6	.27
Fire	.8	.86	3.1	2.04	9.8	4.47
Street Lights	.2	.21	1.5	.91	3.6	1.65

* In thousands of dollars.

Its highway accounts move more erratically, but here again the per capita expenditure is far in excess of that present in Milford. Although Hopedale was almost completely exempt from the burden of poor relief which weighed heavily upon its eastern neighbor, it was spending in 1896 and 1910 substantially more per capita for the provision of street lighting and fire protection. Nevertheless, it is the relatively large cost of its schools and highways which is mainly responsible for the more liberal nature of Hopedale's total current expenditures.

But the significance of these differences must be considered in the light of the ability possessed by the towns to bear the resulting burden of taxation, the chief determinant of this capacity being the local property valuation summarized below:

---

to $3,300 under a united administration. But the Committee made every reasonable endeavor to keep down to the limit of the appropriation as finally settled. . . . To do this it was necessary to confine the privileges of the High School strictly to those who were legally entitled to admission, and thus make a saving in the cost of teaching."
— Milford Town Report, "Report of the Committee on Schools," p. 3.

A. Milford

Year	Real Estate*	Personality*	Total*
1886...........	3,589.8	1,113.8	4,703.6
1890...........	3,856.2	1,015.5	4,871.7
1896...........	4,352.9	1,076.6	5,429.5
1900...........	4,589.9	1,106.2	5,696.1
1906...........	5,183.8	1,343.0	6,526.8
1910...........	7,060.4	2,271.0	9,331.4

B. Hopedale

Year	Real Estate*	Personality*	Total*
1886...........	501.6	189.1	690.7
1890...........	706.0	666.0	1,372.0
1896...........	897.8	1,366.9	2,264.7
1900...........	1,045.4	3,147.0	4,192.4
1906...........	1,456.7	3,818.1	5,274.8
1910...........	1,550.7	4,377.1	5,927.8

* In thousands of dollars.

At the time of division Milford was left with a per capita valuation of about $560; Hopedale with nearly $750 per capita was somewhat more favored, but neither could be considered particularly wealthy.

The Milford valuation rose slowly to 1900 and advanced decidedly more rapidly during the next decade, producing a net rise of 98 per cent and a per capita assessment of $714. The Hopedale total advanced 760 per cent, and in 1910 this town had a valuation of $2,710 per capita. Its real estate had tripled in value during the interval, but the bulk of the advance was the result of a violent rise in the personalty assessment, which now made up about 75 per cent of the town's total taxable valuation.

The chief items of taxable personalty in Hopedale were intangibles and machinery. The value of that portion of the machinery owned by corporations rose from $26,000 in 1886 to $129,536 in 1891, and then dropped to $75,000 during the next five years.[23] Since the net advance in personalty during this decade was $1,118,800, we may conclude that the value of machinery was insignificant in comparison with that of assessed in-

---

[23] This property was taxable locally under the corporation tax of 1864. The statistics quoted are taken from the reports of the Commissioner of Corporations. This document lists two corporations in 1886 and four in the other years quoted.

tangibles, and that it was the tremendous increase in the latter which made possible an advance in taxable valuations exceeding the rapid growth of town expenditures.

Further relief was accorded Hopedale by its receipts from the state tax on domestic corporations. The real estate and machinery owned by the latter were exempt from this levy, since they were assessed for taxation by the local officials at the place of situs. But the excess of the value of the corporation's assets over the locally assessed machinery and real estate was taxed by the state itself. The proceeds, so far as they represented shares owned by residents of Massachusetts, were redistributed to the several local governments. During the greater part of the period under review this was done according to the domicile of the owner of the corporation's capital stock.[24]

Milford had been receiving about seven thousand dollars from the tax before the town was divided, but the loss of Hopedale reduced Milford's income to $2,800 in 1886.[25] Although it rose somewhat during subsequent years, it never offset more than a negligible portion of this town's total current expenditures.[26] Hopedale, however, had received $6,600 in 1886, and by 1910 its income from this source had mounted to $21,100. Although current expenditures had advanced still more rapidly, and although revenue from the corporation tax could offset only 42 per cent of current expenditures in 1910 as against 66 per cent in 1886, it is nevertheless true that this revenue offered substantial relief to property in the town throughout the period under review.

The net result of these changes in expenditures, valuations, and receipts from state taxes finds expression in the record of the rates applied to property in these towns:

[24] In 1908 a law provided that taxes paid by manufacturing and mercantile corporations and distributed among the several cities and towns should be divided equally between the localities where the stockholders resided and those in which the business was carried on. Subsequent acts made further alterations in 1910 and 1914. See C. J. Bullock, "The Taxation of Property and Income in Massachusetts," *Quarterly Journal of Economics*, November 1916.

[25] The income quoted includes a small amount received from the bank tax which was collected at source and distributed on the same principle as the tax on corporate excess.

[26] In 1910 Milford received $3,400 or about 2.4 per cent of its total current expenditures.

Year	Hopedale	Milford	State
1885	.....	$15.50	$14.14
1886	$13.00	15.00	14.48
1896	10.00	17.50	15.10
1906	7.50	19.00	16.87
1910	6.25	17.00	17.60

Separation had brought a slight curtailment in the Milford rate, but the rise in expenditures soon cancelled this decline, and by 1906 the town was using a rate 13 per cent above the current state average. Reduced expenditures and rising valuations brought a sufficient decline during the next four years to bring the Milford rate below the state average for the first time during the period now under consideration.

Hopedale had financed itself in 1886 with a rate $2.50 less than that which residents of this area had paid in the preceding year, and the new town's rate had continued to decline in the face of rapidly rising expenditures until in 1910 property in Hopedale was subject to a rate only 28 per cent of the average for the state as a whole, and 73 per cent less than the rate being applied in the town of Milford.

The latter had reduced its total liabilities from $108,000 to $78,900 during the decade following the separation, but this reduction was more than offset by a subsequent increase which reached $265,000 in 1910, and produced a net rise of 145 per cent for the entire period under review. It is clear that taxes in Milford had not been raised sufficiently to offset the advance in its total expenditures. Hopedale, which had assumed 15 per cent of the net indebtedness of the old town of Milford,[27] had become free of debt before 1896, and had thereafter been subject to no liabilities beyond indebtedness to trust funds held by the town.[28]

This review of the finances of Hopedale and Milford during the period following their separation has demonstrated that the residents of the former town saw fit to provide themselves with a definitely higher scale of benefits than those accruing to the re-

[27] "An Act to Incorporate the Town of Hopedale," Senate Bill No. 70, *Documents Printed by Order of the Senate . . . 1886* (Boston, 1886).
[28] On this account Hopedale was indebted as follows: 1896, $1,764; 1906, $3,204; 1910, $4,779.

mainder of Milford. They had provided services which they desired and had been unable to obtain from the old town meeting, being aided in so doing by receipts from state taxes which, particularly in the early years of Hopedale's existence, paid a very large share of its total current expenditures. Further assistance had come in the shape of a tremendous increase in taxable valuation, making it possible to finance rapidly rising expenditures and to pay off the town's liabilities with the application of a steadily declining tax rate. It is clear that the people of Hopedale were able and willing to support a much more expensive local government than that which the town of Milford would have provided for them, a circumstance lending considerable support to the arguments used by the proponents of separation in 1886, and to the thesis that this division was largely the result of the impossibility of obtaining a satisfactory adjustment between taxation and the benefits received from the old town of Milford.

The effects of the division on the remainder of Milford were not so pleasant. Although this town's expenditures rose relatively slowly, the advance in the taxable valuation was also moderate; the town was receiving no great assistance from the bank and corporation taxes, and was being forced to bear a growing burden of poor relief, an evil from which its wealthy neighbor was almost entirely exempt. Hence the relatively moderate increase in Milford's expenditures meant a higher tax rate and a growing burden of indebtedness. It is clear that the financial structure of this town had been weakened appreciably by the loss of the Hopedale area, a circumstance which must be set off against the excessively easy financial position occupied by the new town of Hopedale when judgment is passed upon the results of this incorporation.

B. WELLESLEY

Needham was separated from its parent town, Dedham, in 1711.[1] This division was followed by growing restiveness among the inhabitants of the extreme western portion of the new town, a district known as Needham Leg, leading finally to the permanent

[1] Erastus Worthington, *The History of Dedham* (Boston, 1827), p. 9.

annexation of this area to Natick in 1797.[2] This act, as well as the incorporation of Needham, had followed persistent complaint on the part of the inhabitants of the regions in question about their inability to obtain a fair share of town services owing to the great distances separating them from the center of town.[3]

The dispute accompanying the annexation of the Leg to Natick is interesting because it brings to light for the first time the ambition of the western half of Needham to achieve the status of an independent town. Objections on the part of residents of this area towards contributing for a new church to be built in the eastern part of town had led to the organization of a west parish in 1778,[4] and in the following year the residents of this parish had proposed its incorporation as an alternative to the annexation of the Leg to Natick.[5] These events are important since they are based on the geographical separation of the two areas in which population tended to concentrate. To a considerable extent this condition has persisted down to the present day, and it is striking that when the western part of Needham was incorporated as Wellesley in 1881 the two new towns were separated by a line, which except for a slight deviation at either end, corresponded closely with the boundary separating the ancient parishes.[6]

The division of 1881 came quite suddenly.[7] The petitioners emphasized the geographic distinctness of the two parts of Needham, stressing the fact that they were really separate economic and social units.[8] But another factor seems to have entered the situa-

---

[2] The Leg petitioned for annexation to Natick in 1724, and succeeded temporarily in 1743. Eighteen years later the district was returned to Needham; but petitions for reannexation to Natick in 1763, 1765, 1767, and 1774 led up to the successful petition of 1797 (George Kuhn Clarke, *History of Needham*, Cambridge, 1912, pp. 141–153).

[3] *Ibid.*, pp. 69–70.   [4] *Ibid.*, pp. 210–212.

[5] *Ibid.*, p. 152.   [6] *Ibid.*, p. 154.

[7] The west parish had petitioned for town status in 1801 and had repeated its plea at frequent intervals down to 1859. There was no attempt at incorporation between this date and the successful movement of 1881.

[8] "No one crosses the line for his mail, or groceries, or his literature, or his amusement, and the only place of meeting is in the woods in the poor house [the town hall was in the poor house], a mile or more from the nearest village, where men succeed in misunderstanding each other, and through ignorance of the needs of each section, wasting the money of the town." — Joseph E. Fiske, *History of the Town of Wellesley* (Boston, 1917), p. 88.

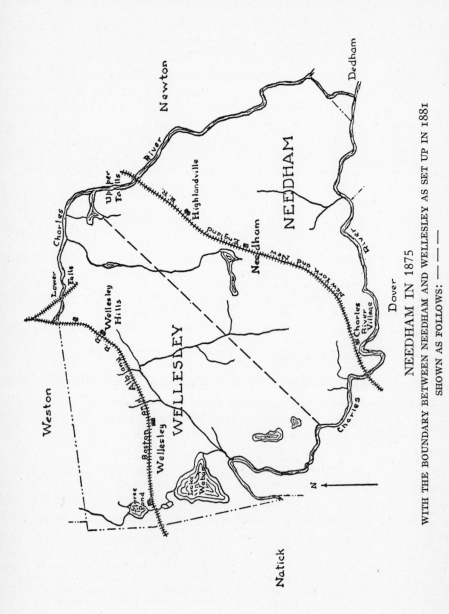

NEEDHAM IN 1875

WITH THE BOUNDARY BETWEEN NEEDHAM AND WELLESLEY AS SET UP IN 1881

SHOWN AS FOLLOWS: ———

tion at this time, a factor vital enough to revive the quiescent movement for independence, namely, the dissatisfaction with which the inhabitants of the western area regarded the services they were obtaining from Needham. These people felt that their village would advance more rapidly if freed from the control of the Needham town meeting. The basis for this contention is revealed by the finances of the old town during the decade preceding its division.

Needham's total and total current expenditures are summarized in the following table:

Year	Total Expenditures	Total Current Expenditures*
	(In thousands of dollars.)	
1869	24.5	23.8
1872	56.3	53.7
1873	48.9	40.7
1876	61.2	56.0
1878	47.7	35.6
1880	43.6	38.6

* No attempt has been made to deduct capital outlays on highways.

Current expenditures rose sharply to 1872, declined in the year of panic which followed, and then advanced to a maximum in 1876 which was 136 per cent above the level prevailing in 1869. Subsequent years brought a sharp reaction, and as a result Needham's current expenditures for 1880 were only 69 per cent of the maximum reached four years earlier.[9]

The advance in the town's expenditures had raised its tax levy from $39,500 in 1869 to a high point of $78,700 in 1874. This 100 per cent increase was far in excess of the 43 per cent advance in the total for the entire state.[10] A subsequent decline left a tax of $48,700 for Needham in 1880, and a net advance of 23 per cent for the period as a whole. The state total fell to $24,700,000 which was about 24 per cent above the level prevailing in 1869. It is clear that Needham's expenditures had been increasing with unusual rapidity during the early seventies, but that this increase

[9] Local expenditures were not seriously affected by the fluctuation of the national currency, the value of which in terms of gold had reached par with the resumption of specie payments in 1879. For the premium on specie, see D. R. Dewey, *Financial History of the United States* (11th ed., New York, 1931), p. 376.

[10] The latter rose from $20,000,000 to $28,700,000 between 1869 and 1874.

had been entirely offset by an abnormally severe contraction during the latter portion of the decade under review.

The rise in current expenditures to 1876 was largely the result of an advance from $8,000 to $17,100 in the cost of operating schools,[11] and an increase from $7,900 to $23,700 in the town's highway expenditures. School costs were cut to $15,100 in 1878, but almost the whole of this reduction was cancelled by an increase in the final year of the old town's existence.[12] Highway costs were reduced to $7,700 in 1878, and the expenditure for this purpose was almost as low in 1880. It is evident that the first effect of the movement for economy was felt by both the important town expenditures, but that it was found impracticable to enforce such rigid economy in the town schools, and that therefore the bulk of the contraction was the result of a violent decline in the highway account.[13]

The local assessments which financed most of these expenditures showed the following movement:

Year	Personalty	Real Estate	Total
		(In thousands of dollars.)	
1869	736	1,683	2,419
1872	1,064	3,180	4,244
1876	999	3,849	4,848
1879	960	3,349	4,309
1880	974	3,385	4,359

The total valuation followed the general course of current expenditures, rising steadily to 1876, declining in the next three years, and advancing slightly with expenditures in 1880. An abrupt rise in real-estate values was responsible for the bulk of the 100 per cent increase in assessments between 1869 and 1876; most of the subsequent decline and the slight revival which followed it were also due to changes in the real-estate assessment.

The town rate reached a high point of $17.30 in 1874, this being

[11] This is associated with the expenditure of a total of $38,000 between 1870 and 1873, and $39,800 between 1875 and 1877 on the construction of new school buildings.

[12] These years brought only one capital outlay, $4,813 spent in 1878 to replace a school building which had been destroyed by fire. The structure was located in the eastern part of town.

[13] Poor relief fell from $3,900 in 1872 to $2,400 in 1876, and then rose to $4,100 in 1880.

$1.70 above the rate applied in 1869 and 11 per cent in excess of the current state average. The subsequent sharp reduction in expenditures produced a rate of $9.40 in 1878, and the $10.20 rate applied two years later represented a net reduction of 34 per cent over the entire period. As a result property in the town was being subjected to a rate only two thirds of the current average for Massachusetts as a whole. The town's liabilities pursued a similar course. They rose from $31,900 in 1869 to $77,900 in 1875, and then dropped to $60,000 at the end of the period under review.

In short, Needham's finances for the decade preceding its division bear the record of two distinct reactions against the rising tide of expenditures characteristic of the early seventies. The first of these, coming with the panic of 1873, was separated by an advance in expenditures from the second and more violent retrenchment, which wiped out the major portion of the net increase appearing between 1869 and 1876. This second decline was considerably more violent than that prevalent in the state as a whole. It permitted a halving of the town rate at a time when the local assessment was declining and a reduction of over seventeen thousand dollars was being made in town liabilities. It is clear that Needham went to extremes in its desire for a low tax rate, and in so doing attempted to enforce a policy of stringent economy in the management of town schools,[14] and accepted a striking curtailment in highway expenditures.

However, it should be pointed out that the two portions of Needham seem to have differentiated sharply by the end of the seventies. The assessment of 1881, made in the year of division, shows that the total valuation in the Wellesley area was 65 per cent higher than in Needham. Wellesley, moreover, had four times as much personalty as was assessed in the remnant of the parent town. This item accounted for 37 per cent of its total

[14] "The reduction of the appropriation by the town for the support of the schools made it necessary for the school committee to devise means to do the school work upon some more economical plan. Three schools, in consequence, were discontinued, and the establishment of another, thought necessary, postponed; the spring vacation was lengthened two weeks and the salaries of the teachers were reduced by varying amounts. The expenditures have been brought within the appropriation." — Needham Town Report, 1878, "Report of the School Committee," p. 23.

valuation as compared with 15 per cent in the new town of Needham.[15] The explanation for this discrepancy is the beginning of the development of the western area as a wealthy suburb of Boston. This community, which was on the main line of a through railroad,[16] had become the legal residence of a group of wealthy families. Two of these alone had been listed for $361,000 in personal property in 1875 or approximately 35 per cent of the total personalty assessed in the entire town.

On the other hand, the eastern portion of Needham, which was not so easily reached by a suburban population,[17] had remained predominantly a farming community with most of its wealth tied up in real estate and with only a fraction of the taxable valuation of the western area. A community of this kind is not apt to grant the desirability of expenditures which seem indispensable to the inhabitants of a region developing into a wealthy suburb. The residents of eastern Needham naturally would be unwilling to consent to increased appropriations necessitating an advance in their own tax bills particularly when most of the money would be used to provide services desired by people living at the other end of town.

Yet the improvements involved would seem extremely important to the latter group which not only could afford the resulting taxes but also was interested directly in making the community a better place in which to live. But under the existing governmental structure the schools and roads these people wanted required an increase in the tax levy for the entire town. Since control of the

[15]

VALUATION OF 1881

	Wellesley	Per cent of Total	Needham	Per cent of Total
Real Estate	$1,925,000	63	$1,562,867	85
Personalty*	1,099,689	37	269,527	15
Total	$3,024,689	100	$1,832,394	100

* Includes bank stock and corporate shares assessed to residents.

[16] The main line of the Boston and Worcester reached Grantville (Wellesley Hills) in 1835 (Fiske, *Wellesley*, p. 26). This road was consolidated to form the Boston and Albany in 1867.

[17] Needham obtained a railroad connection with Boston in 1853, but this was not a through route and the service was poor. In 1906 the area was reached by another branch connecting with the Boston and Providence line at West Roxbury (Clarke, *Needham*, pp. 413–416).

town meeting did not lie in the west, the consent of the farming
element was indispensable, and that consent could not be expected so long as there seemed to be no prospect of accruing
benefits which would compensate the people in the east for a
higher tax levy. Instead, the element controlling the town meeting had seen fit to put into effect the economies which had
brought the town rate to $9.40 in 1878.

In the light of later developments it would seem that this condition, the divergent views held by the two communities concerning the benefits to be derived from services requiring increased
taxation, was the factor precipitating the division of Needham.
To test this hypothesis more completely it is necessary to examine the finances of the two new towns during the period following their incorporation. Their expenditures for 1882, the first
complete financial year after the separation, are shown in the
following table with those for 1892 and 1902:

A. Wellesley

	1882 Actual*	1882 Per Cap.	1892 Actual*	1892 Per Cap.	1902 Actual*	1902 Per Cap.
Total	33.3	$11.90	77.8	$18.85	134.4	$24.40
Total Current	22.1	7.90	50.6	12.25	134.4	24.40
Total Non-commercial Current†	22.1	7.90	46.6	11.30	130.4	23.70

B. Needham

	1882 Actual*	1882 Per Cap.	1892 Actual*	1892 Per Cap.	1902 Actual*	1902 Per Cap.
Total	37.2	$14.55	40.7	$12.60	107.9	$26.20
Total Current	22.2	8.65	40.7	12.60	77.8	18.90
Total Non-commercial Current†	22.2	8.65	36.8	11.40	72.8	17.65

* In thousands of dollars.
† Current expenditures minus the subsidy paid the water department.

Both total and total non-commercial current expenditures advanced considerably more rapidly in Wellesley than in the remainder of the old town, and this is particularly true during the
period immediately following the division. Correction for the
disturbing element of population growth reduces the discrepancy
to some extent. Nevertheless, Wellesley's per capita current non-
commercial expenditure advanced from a point about 8 per cent
below the corresponding expenditure in Needham in 1882 to a
level 34 per cent above in 1902.

The result was a rise from $34,000 to $121,300, or 257 per cent, in the taxes levied on property and polls in Wellesley. Although the corresponding advance in Needham from $22,200 to $62,200, or 180 per cent, was much smaller, it was nevertheless far in excess of the 94 per cent rise in the total for the entire state.[18] It is evident that the expenditures of both the new towns increased unusually rapidly during the period in question, but that the advance was particularly rapid in Wellesley, especially during the decade following 1882.

The most significant items among the current expenditures are shown below:

A. Wellesley

	1882		1892		1902	
	Actual*	Per Cap.	Actual*	Per Cap.	Actual*	Per Cap.
Schools	9.8	$3.50	14.8	$3.60	32.1	$5.85
Highways† ...	3.5	1.25	10.8	2.62	33.3	6.05
Poor	1.8	.64	5.4	1.31	7.8	1.42
Fire and Police	..	....	2.3	.56	8.1	1.47
Lighting	.6	.02	2.4	.58	9.5	.72

B. Needham

	1882		1892		1902	
	Actual*	Per Cap.	Actual*	Per Cap.	Actual*	Per Cap.
Schools	8.1	$3.16	12.5	$3.88	18.2	$4.40
Highways† ...	5.0	1.95	9.6	2.98	24.4	5.93
Poor	2.5	.98	3.7	1.15	4.6	1.11
Fire and Police	.3	.01	2.9	.90	5.9	1.43
Lighting	.3	.01	1.2	.37	3.9	.95

* In thousands of dollars.
† Includes capital outlays.

The distinct lag in Needham's expenditures is reduced somewhat by allowance for the rapid growth of Wellesley's population. Yet in 1902 the latter was spending more per capita for all the important town services, the discrepancy being greatest in the cost of town schools.

The relative ability of the new units to bear this rapidly advancing burden of expenditures is largely dependent upon the local assessments summarized below:

[18] The state total was $26,100,000 in 1882, and $50,800,000 in 1902.

A. *Wellesley*

	1882	1892	1902
		(In thousands of dollars.)	
Realty	1,980	3,657	6,012
Personalty	1,411	2,819	3,648
Total	3,391	6,476	9,660

B. *Needham*

	1882	1892	1902
		(In thousands of dollars.)	
Realty	1,583	2,300	3,432
Personalty	173	281	315
Total	1,756	2,581	3,747

The differences revealed by the valuation of 1881 become more pronounced in subsequent decades. In 1882 personalty in Wellesley made up 41 per cent of a local valuation 93 per cent higher than that listed for the town of Needham, where personalty accounted for less than 10 per cent of the property assessed. Although a striking advance in land values produced a 110 per cent rise in Needham's tax list during the next two decades, the advance in Wellesley was even more rapid. By 1902 the latter town possessed a total valuation 158 per cent above that existing in the remnant of Needham.

Personalty still made up 38 per cent of Wellesley's greatly increased local valuation, the slight decline in the importance of this item being the result of a violent advance in the real-estate assessment, an advance indicative of the town's suburban development. Moreover, the two families which had contributed so largely to the value of personalty in the old town, were now residents of Wellesley. In 1881 they were assessed for $469,000 or 51 per cent of the personalty taxed by the new town. In 1902 they were assessed for $2,380,000, which accounted for 65 per cent of the total personal property valuation. The possessions of these two families formed the backbone of the new town's wealth.

It will be recalled that during this period the proceeds of the state taxes on corporate excess and bank shares, so far as they were levied with respect to capital stock owned by residents of Massachusetts, were being distributed to the towns in which the shareholders resided.[19] In 1882 Wellesley received $2,500 from

[19] *Acts and Resolves*, 1865, c. 242, and 1873, c. 315.

these taxes, or enough to pay 13 per cent of its current expenditures. Needham's income of $1,700 offset less than 8 per cent of its current expenditures. Although Needham's revenue grew substantially during subsequent years until in 1902 the town obtained $7,300 or about 9 per cent of its greatly increased expenditures, this relief was slight in comparison with that afforded to property in the other town. By 1902 Wellesley's income had mounted to $22,900 or nearly 18 per cent of its comparatively large current expenditures.

The large quantity of personal property on Wellesley's local assessment rolls and the size of the revenues that the town received from state taxes reveal the wealthy character of this suburban community. Further evidence is afforded by the Tax Commissioner's estimated total valuation, which rises from $1,182 per capita in 1883 to $1,990 in 1901 [20] the latter being sufficient to place the town among the wealthiest communities in the state.[21]

The old town, it will be remembered, had used a rate of $10.20 in 1880. The loss of Wellesley had produced a rise to $11.50 in 1882 while the western area, which contained a relatively large proportion of the old town's wealth, was able to finance itself with a rate of only $9.50 per thousand.

The following decade brought a sharp advance in expenditures in both towns. Although increases in local assessments and in receipts from state taxes did not prevent an increase in the Needham rate to $16.60 in 1892, they more than canceled the rapid advance in Wellesley's expenditures and made it possible for this town to finance itself with a rate of only $9.00 per thousand. The subsequent decade brought a reduction to $14.50 in Needham,

[20] Needham's taxable wealth was estimated at $695 per capita in 1883, and $907 in 1901. The advance, while substantial, left the town with a per capita wealth less than half of that present in Wellesley.

[21] This measure of a community's wealth was used by Dr. Tsung Chen in an unpublished thesis written at Harvard University in 1926 and entitled, "The Relation between Local Governmental Expenditures and Density of Population in Massachusetts." The author stated (pp. 32–33) that "all towns, having a per capita value of property of $1,800 or more in the 1919 estimate" were to be considered as "exceptionally wealthy." Wellesley, it will be observed, had a per capita valuation in 1901 that was substantially above this estimate, which was intended for use on valuations that had felt the stimulus of the war-time boom.

and an advance to $12.00 per thousand in the other town. Both were now substantially below the current state average.

Wellesley's liabilities had risen from $50,000 to $124,000 in the twenty years following 1882. Needham had retired its outstanding indebtedness at the time of division, but by 1902 had acquired a total liability of $223,600 [22] which was 80 per cent in excess of the amount owed by its western neighbor.

This review of the finances of the two towns during the decades following the division has demonstrated that Wellesley persisted in spending on a substantially larger scale than the remnant of the parent town, and that this was true in spite of the fact that Needham itself was expanding considerably more rapidly than the state as a whole. On the other hand, Wellesley's original advantage in local valuations had increased during the period under review, owing particularly to a large advance in the personalty assessment, which was far more significant here than in the town of Needham.

The importance of personalty in Wellesley and the extremely large income received by this town from state taxes, together with the fact that Needham's wealth consisted mainly of real estate, point to a vital difference between the development of the two new towns. Needham did not acquire the wealthy suburban population so conspicuous in its western neighbor.

Although Wellesley had been able and willing to undertake a scale of expenditures higher than that to which the inhabitants of the less wealthy area had given their consent, the considerably less rapid advance in Needham's expenditures during the decade following division had entailed a substantial rise in the rate applied to property in this town. This was not entirely offset by the decline coming during the next decade, which was, moreover, accompanied by the appearance of a sizable town debt. It was not possible to finance Needham's expenditures out of an advancing taxable wealth to the extent that it was being done in the other town. Under these circumstances there would still be a divergence between the value which the residents of the two areas would place upon the benefits accruing from proposed improve-

[22] This figure is taken from the *Aggregates of Polls, Property, Taxes, etc.*

ments. This difference, however, would no longer be as violent as that which had precipitated the separation of 1881.

The independent suburban development of Needham made the results of the separation of Wellesley considerably better than those observed in the Hopedale-Milford case. It is possible that the division was beneficial to both Needham and Wellesley. Certainly, the greater freedom and easy financial position that its incorporation brought to the latter town must have been an important stimulus to its suburban development and to the further concentration of wealth within its borders.

CHAPTER II

THE FINANCES OF THE TOWN OF MAYNARD

THIS chapter and the next two following are concerned with the incorporation and subsequent financial development of three predominantly industrial towns. Maynard, Millville, and Adams are in no sense model communities of the Hopedale type, but ordinary mill towns, each dominated by a single large industrial enterprise. They are linked with the preceding cases by the fact that their incorporation bears upon the same theoretical problem encountered in the affairs of Milford and Needham, and the more or less common fate which they have met as independent towns lends unusual interest to their subsequent financial history.

A. THE INCORPORATION OF MAYNARD

I

The town of Maynard was incorporated in 1871; its area, previously known as Assabet village, comprehended parts of two agricultural towns, Stow and Sudbury. One of these, Stow, had grown rather slowly since its incorporation in 1683,[1] and in 1865 contained only 1,537 inhabitants. There were three villages in the town at this time: one at the center, where the town hall was located, Lower Village about a mile east of the center, and Rock Bottom at the south end near the town of Hudson.[2] The last named was the largest of the three, containing the only sizable

---

[1] This is in part the result of a reduction in area at the time of the incorporation of Harvard in 1766 and Boxborough in 1783. Another portion of Stow was annexed to Boxborough between 1860 and 1865. However, the chief cause of the slow increase in Stow's population was the fact that it continued to be largely an agricultural town. The state census of 1865 indicates that 191 men were employed in agriculture while the total number of individuals engaged in manufacturing was only 164. See also E. P. Conklin, *Middlesex County and Its People* (1927), II, 612.

[2] D. H. Hurd, *History of Middlesex County, Massachusetts* (1890), I, 637.

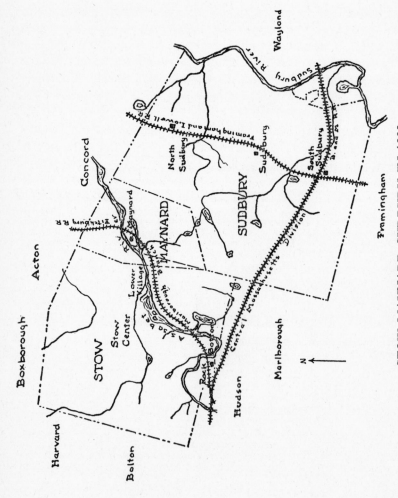

STOW–MAYNARD–SUDBURY IN 1889

SHOWING STOW–SUDBURY BOUNDARY BEFORE 1872 THUS: — · — · —

industrial enterprise, a woolen fabric mill founded in 1829.[3] The town's one railroad, the Fitchburg, also passed through Rock Bottom village.

Thus, in the sixties Stow remained a small, slowly developing community with a predominantly agricultural population. But there is reason to believe that a considerable number of the employees of the Assabet mills came to live in the town. These mills, located in Assabet village on the boundary between Stow and Sudbury, were situated in the latter town. Stow's valuation list shows that the corporation operating them was assessed for meadow and plowage land alone. Yet by 1870 the employees of the Assabet enterprise had given Stow a considerable industrial population and had placed upon it the burdens, in the form of school expenditures and poor-relief costs, which accompany a development of this nature.[4]

Stow had total expenditures of $2,662 or $1.62 per capita in 1860, which had grown to $12,445 by 1865. Although a large portion of the latter sum was spent for military purposes, and although town expenditures dropped sharply during the post-war years, by 1871 they had risen again to a total of $9,588 or $5.30 per capita, a net advance of 228 per cent over the per capita expenditure made in 1860. Current expenditures followed a similar movement, rising from $2,662 or $1.62 per capita in 1860 to $7,517 or $4.15 per capita in 1871.

The result was a 200 per cent increase in the Stow tax levy between the dates in question, this being slightly more than the 190 per cent increase shown by the state total.[5] Correction for the disturbing element of population growth does not alter the conclu-

[3] This mill employed seventy-six of the 164 persons engaged in manufacturing in Stow in 1865. Fifty persons were listed as employees of the town's one shoe factory, but this was a small plant with an invested capital of only $10,000 in 1876. At that date the woolen mill had a capital stock of $100,000 and turned out goods valued at $220,000.

[4] As a result of the incorporation of Assabet village as the town of Maynard in 1871, Stow's population dropped from 1,813 in 1870 to 1,002 in 1875. Sudbury's population fell from 2,091 to 1,177. This indicates that the towns lost about 800 and 900 inhabitants respectively, which in turn checks fairly well with a population of 1,965 in Maynard in 1875.

[5] The town levy was $4,312 in 1862, and $13,157 in 1871. The state total rose from $7,600,000 to $21,900,000 during this interval.

sion that Stow's taxes were rising at a rate about the average for this period in Massachusetts.[6] On the other hand the per capita tax levied on property in the town continued to be far less than the average for the state as a whole.

The increase in Stow's current expenditures came as the result of advances from $1,300 to $3,000 in the cost of schools, from $341 to $1,488 in the highway account, and from $225 to $575 in poor relief. No capital outlays were made for schools during these years, and only $1,401 was spent on highway construction.

The local assessment rose from $713,800 in 1860 to $1,009,000 in 1871, a net advance of 41 per cent, which was far less than the 260 per cent increase in the town's total expenditures. Real-estate and personalty valuations are not available until 1862. Between that date and 1871 real-estate assessments advance 25 per cent, personalty 80 per cent.[7]

Since the total valuation for the entire state rose nearly 65 per cent between 1862 and 1871,[8] while Stow's assessments were increasing only 37 per cent, and since the town's taxes were advancing at about the average pace, one would expect the rate applied to property in the town to rise even more rapidly than in the state as a whole. The $230 received by Stow in 1871 from the state tax on corporate excess, a tax which had not existed in 1860, paid only slightly more than 3 per cent of the town's current expenditures and did little to prevent the anticipated rise in the town rate.

This rate advanced from $4.93 in 1862 to $11.90 in 1871, a net increase of about 140 per cent as compared with an increase from $8.80 to $15.44 in Massachusetts as a whole. Nevertheless, property in the town was still subject to a rate only 77 per cent of the current state average.

Stow's debt rose from $4,415 in 1863 to $10,436 in 1866. By 1871 this had been reduced to $5,190 leaving an indebtedness of $2.90 per capita.

[6] The Stow levy increased from $2.57 to $7.27, a net advance of 182 per cent. The state total increased from $6.18 to $17.80, or 188 per cent.

[7] Real estate rose from $586,000 to $738,000; personalty from $148,000 to $272,000.

[8] The total for 1862 was $862,000,000, for 1871, $1,417,000,000.

To sum up, the sixties had brought a sharp rise in Stow's expenditures, an increase sufficient to cause the town's per capita tax to grow as rapidly as the average per capita tax in the state as a whole. Valuations had lagged far behind the rise in expenditures, and relief from the corporation tax had been slight. Although there was no sizable increase in the town's indebtedness, and although its per capita levy of $7.27 was still far below the average of $17.80 for the whole of Massachusetts, the taxable wealth of the town, as estimated by the Commissioner of Corporations and Taxation, was also quite small.[9] Hence, the fact that the town rate for 1871 was still 23 per cent below the state average must not be allowed to conceal the significance of the relatively rapid advance in Stow's tax levy and the fact that the latter was already quite high for a town of this character.

II

Stow's eastern neighbor, the town of Sudbury, was an equally old settlement. In 1870 it contained 2,091 persons most of them being concentrated in four distinct areas. A mile south of the center on the Boston and Worcester highway was the village of South Sudbury. At the center there was another settlement built around the town hall, and along the Boston and Fitchburg highway there was a group of about thirty houses known as North Sudbury. These portions of the old town were distinctly not industrial centers.[10]

But the Sudbury of the sixties also contained a part of Assabet village which was the site of a large woolen mill, and this had already become an industrial community. It contained the only railroad in Sudbury,[11] the rest of the town depending upon a stagecoach running to Weston, as well as the single outstanding valuation on the town list for 1861 — that placed on the mill

---

[9] It was only $496 per capita in 1865.

[10] A. S. Hudson, *History of Sudbury, Massachusetts* (1889), pp. 485 ff.

[11] A branch of the Fitchburg railroad reached Assabet village. In 1870 another railroad, the Framingham and Lowell, began construction in Sudbury. (*Ibid.*, p. 531.)

property in Assabet village operated by Amory Maynard.[12] The development of this village will be treated separately in a later section; it suffices to point out here that Sudbury during the sixties was divided into two distinct areas, a slowly developing agricultural community, and a rapidly advancing mill village.[13]

Town expenditures had risen from a total of $4,126 in 1860 to $6,495 in 1867, and then jumped to $12,822 in the year preceding the incorporation of Maynard. The per capita total had grown from $2.44 to $6.11, a 150 per cent increase over a period of eleven years. The record of current expenditures is incomplete and the total for 1871, which happens to be available, seems unduly small. However, the appropriations made for these years can be obtained from the town clerk's books, and total current appropriations have been found to rise from $2,995 in 1861 to $8,365 in 1870, producing a 127 per cent advance in the resulting per capita appropriation.[14]

There was a rise from $1,400 to $2,300 in the appropriation for schools, and from $900 to $1,500 in that made for the relief of town poor. However, these increases were considerably smaller than the advance from $390 to $2,000, and from $60 to $1,360 in the appropriations for highway maintenance and interest charges respectively. The available records show that at least $9,782 was spent during this interval on capital outlays for schools.

This increase in expenditures was accompanied by a rise in the town levy from $8,174 in 1862 to $16,837 in 1871, which meant an

[12] This property paid a tax of $418. The next highest assessment was for $106. Another Assabet property, a paper mill, paid a tax of $94.63.

[13] The census of occupations for 1865 shows 377 families resident in the town and 308 men employed in agriculture. It follows that a large portion of the actual residents were engaged in farming. However, there were also 401 persons employed in manufacturing enterprises, 367 of these in the woolen mill and eleven in a paper mill also located in Assabet village. Since the census offers no evidence that these mill hands resided as well as worked in Sudbury, it is reasonable to believe that a large portion lived in other towns, particularly in Stow.

The predominance of agriculture in the part of town outside Assabet village is also demonstrated by the census of 1875, the first to be published after the incorporation of that village as the town of Maynard. It appears that the remainder of Sudbury had an agricultural valuation of $810,764 while the buildings, stock on hand, and machinery of its industrial enterprises had a value of only $75,400.

[14] The latter increased from $1.77 to $4.00 over the interval under consideration.

advance from $4.85 to $8.05 in the per capita tax applied to property in the town. However, this 66 per cent increase was far less than the 188 per cent rise in the average levy for the state as a whole, and as a result Sudbury's tax dropped from 78 per cent of that average in 1862 to 45 per cent in 1871.

The total valuation rose from $1,043,000 to $1,484,000 between 1860 and 1871. This was not only far less than the corresponding growth of expenditures, but also considerably smaller than the accompanying advance in the total assessment for the entire state.[15] Sudbury's personalty valuation rose from $300,000 to $473,000 between the dates in question; real-estate values advanced from $781,000 to $1,010,000. Here, as in Stow, the relatively slow advance in valuations was due chiefly to a lag in the real-estate assessment.

Sudbury also received little assistance from the state corporation tax, the $411 obtained in 1871 paying only 3 per cent of its current expenditures. This fact, combined with the lag of valuations behind expenditures, explains the rise in the town rate from $6.80 in 1862 to $10.20 in 1871, which, however, was somewhat less rapid than the accompanying advance in the state average. As a consequence the town rate dropped from 77 per cent of the latter in 1862 to 66 per cent in 1871.

Although the Sudbury rate was advancing as a result of the lag in its assessments, and although the town's modest per capita wealth [16] had been subjected to a debt burden of $9.80 per capita by 1869, the rise in expenditures had been less sharp than in Massachusetts as a whole, and the advance in the town rate less rapid than the advance in the state average. This is about what one would expect of a predominantly agricultural community, yet it offers some justification for the claim that the industrial portion of town was not being developed as rapidly as circumstances seemed to permit.

---

[15] The Sudbury valuation rose 42 per cent between 1860 and 1871. The town's expenditures advanced 210 per cent. Sudbury's valuation rose 41 per cent between 1862 and 1871; the state total increased 64 per cent.

[16] The estimate used to apportion the state tax of 1865 showed a per capita total valuation of only $620 in Sudbury.

III

A part of Assabet had been a school district in Sudbury for about a hundred years before the incorporation of the village as the town of Maynard in 1871.[17] Although the water power furnished at this point by the Assabet River had been put to use by a paper mill as early as 1820,[18] the real development of the area had begun in 1847 when a carpet factory was constructed,[19] which turned out a product valued at $110,000 in the first year of its operation.[20] The Fitchburg railroad reached the village two years later,[21] and by 1852 the community was large enough to support a church of its own. The carpet mill failed in the crisis of 1857, was reorganized as the Assabet Manufacturing Company, and turned to the production of woolen goods under the direction of Amory Maynard, one of the founders of the enterprise, who had been retained as agent for the new corporation.[22] By 1861 this property constituted the only really large valuation on the Sudbury tax list, and by 1869 the village had a larger population and more business than the remainder of either of the parent towns.[23]

Two years later the residents of the village brought forward, apparently for the first time, the proposal to incorporate Assabet as an independent town. The petitioners pointed to the population of the village and to the distance separating it from the town houses in Sudbury and Stow. It was alleged that the loss of this territory would impoverish neither of the parent towns, and that nevertheless the proposed new unit would have ample resources of its own. But the most interesting argument raised was based upon the diversity of interests separating this industrial community from the agricultural portions of the two parent towns. The population of the latter areas was scattered, that of Assabet village concentrated within a small region the inhabitants of

[17] Hudson, *History of Sudbury*, p. 508.

[18] *Ibid.*, p. 508.

[19] W. H. Gutteridge, *A Brief History of the Town of Maynard, Massachusetts* (1921), p. 26.

[20] S. A. Drake, *History of Middlesex County, Massachusetts* (1880), II, 157.

[21] Gutteridge, *Maynard*, p. 36.

[22] *Ibid.*, p. 30.

[23] *Ibid.*, p. 7. See also Hurd, *Middlesex*, II, 456.

which "required street lighting and sidewalks, a local police, and special school privileges," and "needed town regulations adapted to their population and business." These things were not being supplied by the old towns, and it was implied that they could not be obtained from them. Hence it was deemed necessary to incorporate Assabet village as an independent town.[24]

Since the town halls in Stow and Sudbury were fairly accessible to the residents of this area, and since the wealth and population of Assabet village were not overly large, it is reasonable to attribute the separation movement to dissatisfaction based upon the diversity of economic interests. Census statistics have been quoted in preceding sections which tend to substantiate the claim that this was an isolated industrial center situated in two predominantly agricultural towns. When the population of such an area has grown sufficiently to require street lights, sidewalks, special schools, and a local police force, its residents are quite likely to have some difficulty obtaining those services from town meetings dominated by a farming element. The latter will be asked to increase its own tax bill to provide services for another section of town, services of such a nature as to promise only the most general sort of benefits to the farming population. Such taxation would seem to be inadequately adjusted to benefits received.

Yet the residents of the village will look upon these services as due them in return for taxes paid. Although they are willing to bear a heavier burden in order to obtain the desired improvements, they cannot do this without asking the farming population to contribute for services which will bring them no direct benefits. Such a situation is productive of trouble, and it is extremely likely that this was the precipitating factor in the movement for the incorporation of Assabet village.

Sudbury was opposed to the division, which would reduce its area about 1,900 acres. Although most of this was woodland, it also included the Assabet mill, the only large industrial enterprise in the town. Sudbury feared the financial results of the removal of so large a portion of its taxable wealth.

Although Stow was to lose 1,300 acres, including some good

[24] A. S. Hudson, *Annals of Sudbury, Wayland, and Maynard* (1891), pp. 80–81.

farming land, this town offered no objection to the proposed incorporation.[25] Its attitude is easily understood if considered in the light of a situation already described: while Stow taxed the Assabet corporation for meadow and plowage land alone, many of the employees of that enterprise apparently resided within the borders of the town. The taxes obtained from the corporation and the mill hands were probably far less than the expenditures necessitated by the presence of the latter group. Stow was pretty apt to benefit financially by the loss of this area, and hence offered no opposition to the incorporation of the proposed new town.

Before carrying their fight to the General Court, the petitioners asked the Sudbury meeting to arbitrate the separation. In the end the latter acceded to this request and appointed a committee which arranged a satisfactory settlement. "By mutual consent a bill was agreed upon and passed by the Legislature in 1871, by which the town of Maynard was incorporated." [26]

The new unit had a population of 1,910 and the third smallest area of all the towns in Massachusetts. It contained two industrial enterprises — one of these, a small paper mill, being absorbed by the other in 1882.[27] Agriculture was of small importance, the products of Maynard's farms being valued at less than $50,000 in 1875 when its single mill was turning out goods worth $1,500,-000. When the next state census was taken in 1885, the position of agriculture was still nominal.[28] The Assabet woolen mill was of such overwhelming importance to the economic life of this

---

[25] Drake, *Middlesex*, II, 153; Hurd, *Middlesex*, II, 655.

[26] Hudson, *History of Sudbury*, p. 530. The Act of Incorporation provided that Maynard was to pay $3,000 to Sudbury for the support of the poor. The latter town was to retain all its public property, and was to receive the equivalent of 38.5 per cent of its debts and liabilities at the date of the act's passage. Maynard was also required to take over at par 104 shares of Sudbury's subscription to the stock of the Framingham and Lowell railroad. Stow was to retain its poor farm, located in Maynard, and in addition was to receive $6,500 in return for which Maynard was to be relieved of all Stow's debts and liabilities. (See *Acts and Resolves*, 1871, c. 198.) It is striking that the money paid Stow on this account was larger than the town debt had been in March 1871.

[27] Conklin, *Middlesex*, II, 592.

[28] At this date 104 persons were engaged in agriculture, 965 in manufacturing. The cash capital of the single industrial enterprise was $1,420,225. The agricultural product was valued at only $65,171. The value of the industrial product is no longer quoted since there was now only one mill operating in the town.

town that it required no great stretching of the facts to say that the General Court of 1871 had incorporated this mill and its employees as the new town of Maynard.

The remnant of Sudbury was largely agricultural, the $170,000 worth of goods turned out by its industries in 1875 representing the output of seven small enterprises whose buildings, stock on hand, and machinery were valued at only $75,400. At the same time farm property was worth $811,000.

In spite of the appearance of a machine shop and two new railroads,[29] the value of industrial products turned out in Sudbury in 1885 was only $27,000; agricultural produce was now worth $268,000. Clearly agriculture was becoming more, rather than less, important in the economic life of the town of Sudbury.

The single shoe factory in Stow had burned in 1875, leaving only one significant industrial enterprise, the woolen mill in Rock Bottom village, which was turning out about $200,000 worth of flannels in 1880.[30] The industrial capital in the town totaled $102,590 in 1885, while farm property, which had been valued at $640,298 ten years before, must have been worth about the same amount in 1885.[31] Stow as well as Sudbury was becoming more completely agricultural during the years following the incorporation of Maynard.

IV

The total and total current expenditures which the three towns made during the period following this incorporation are summarized below:

Year	Stow		Sudbury		Maynard	
	Total	Total Current	Total	Total Current	Total	Total Current
			(In thousands of dollars.)			
1872	6.5	6.2	10.7*	9.6*	32.0	6.2
1877	6.9	5.9	11.7	9.7	27.5	8.1
1880	7.7	6.2	11.1	10.2	7.0	7.0
1883	4.6	4.6	13.0	9.3	12.4	9.4
1886	6.2	6.1	11.6	11.6	15.4	15.4

* These figures are for 1873, the first year for which the statistics are available.

[29] Hudson, *History of Sudbury*, pp. 531–532.
[30] Drake, *Middlesex*, II, 356.
[31] The value of agricultural products in Stow was $149,000 in 1875, and $144,000 in 1885.

The division brought a drop of $3,100 and $1,300 in Stow's total and current expenditures respectively, and both items showed a slight net decline during the fourteen years which followed.

Sudbury's total expenditure for 1872 was unusually large, owing to a purchase of railroad stock. Her current expenditures are not available, but appropriations for these purposes totaled $8,960, which was slightly in excess of the corresponding appropriations for 1870. The current expenditure for 1873 was still larger, but there was little additional advance until after 1883.

Maynard's total expenditures for 1872 were very large, owing to the cost of the incorporation, but by 1876 they had dropped to $8,700. A decline to 1880 was followed by a steady and rapid rise to a level 77 per cent above that of 1876. Although Maynard's current expenditures also changed little until after 1880, the rise during the next six years carried them to a level about 50 per cent above that prevailing when the town was set up. It is striking that this advance in the cost of operating Maynard did not set in until nine years after its incorporation.

Since the population of Stow and Sudbury declined in the decade following 1875 while the number of Maynard's inhabitants showed a considerable increase,[32] reduction of the expenditures to a per capita basis may be expected to yield somewhat different results. The following table contains the essential data:

Year	Stow		Sudbury		Maynard	
	Total	Total Current	Total	Total Current	Total	Total Current
1872	$6.37	$6.07	$9.15*	$8.13*	$16.75	$3.24
1877	6.90	5.72	9.95	8.23	13.15	3.87
1880	7.48	5.94	9.45	8.68	3.05	3.05
1883	4.60	4.60	11.14	7.95	4.90	3.69
1886	6.44	6.34	9.90	9.90	5.62	5.62

* Data for 1873 used here.

The immediate effect of the incorporation was to raise Stow's per capita current expenditure 47 per cent, and to produce a 15 per cent rise in Sudbury's per capita current appropriation. May-

[32] The census data follow:

Year	Sudbury	Stow	Maynard
1875	1,177	1,022	1,965
1885	1,165	976	2,703

nard, on the other hand, operated on a scale of expenditures only 53 and 40 per cent as large as the per capita totals in the remnants of Stow and Sudbury respectively.

Stow's current expenditures show a slight rise during the subsequent period owing to a sharp advance after 1883; Sudbury's current expenditures rise 21 per cent during these years. After dropping to a minimum of $3.05 per capita in 1880, Maynard's current expenditures advance to a level 73 per cent above that of 1872. Maynard was now spending 83 and 57 per cent as much per capita as Stow and Sudbury, and was not nearly as well off in this respect as it had been at the time of its incorporation.[33]

The more important items among these current expenditures are shown in the following table:

A. Stow

Year	Schools	Highways	Poor	Interest
1871	$2,969	$1,488	$575	$359
1872	1,761	1,456	325	401
1876	2,216	1,690	400	494
1880	2,134	1,067	1,200	300
1886	3,204	1,253	418	300

B. Sudbury

Year	Schools	Highways	Poor	Interest
1870*	$2,300	$2,000	$1,500	$1,360
1872*	2,800	1,600	1,683	1,360
1876*	3,000	2,000	500	2,405
1880	3,051	2,310*	923	1,993
1886	3,308	3,543	1,713	1,804

C. Maynard

Year	Schools	Highways	Poor	Interest	Light	Police
1872	$2,154	$1,050	$477	.....	....	....
1876	3,257	929	587	$1,390	....	....
1880	3,773	1,281	954	.....	$472	....
1886	7,022	1,716	2,079	.....	645	$597

* The figures quoted for these years are appropriations.

---

[33] The tax levies are compared in the following table with the total for the state:

Year	State	Maynard	Sudbury	Stow
		(In thousands of dollars.)		
1872..............	22,064	11.4	12.1	5.5
1875..............	28,701	13.8	10.5	5.6
1880..............	21,013	7.8	8.6	6.3
1886..............	25,850	13.0	13.5	4.0

These statistics move with total rather than total current expenditures and hence are distorted by the large outlays made in Maynard and Sudbury during the early

The Maynard incorporation took away 41 per cent of the cost of maintaining schools in Stow, and brought a similar reduction in poor relief. Highway charges, however, were not seriously affected. The slight rise in the cost of Stow's schools during the subsequent period was offset by declines in other current expenditures.

Sudbury's school appropriation was higher in 1871 than in the preceding year, and showed a substantial growth during the remainder of the period. This, however, was probably the result of the construction of new schools, the operation of which more than offset any reduction in costs resulting from the removal of Sudbury's portion of Assabet village.[34] Sudbury's highway appropriation was cut 20 per cent in the year of the incorporation of Maynard.

The latter town began its career by spending more than Stow but decidedly less than Sudbury for schools, roads, and poor relief. The sharp rise in the cost of Maynard's schools [35] and the relief of the poor together with the addition of street lighting and police services explain the relatively rapid advance in this town's current expenditures, an advance which would have been even more rapid had it not been for the absence of interest charges after 1879, and the relatively small amount required to maintain the highways in the small area which made up this town.

The relative wealth of the three units is indicated by the following estimate of their per capita taxable valuations:

Year	Sudbury	Stow	Maynard
1866	$618	$496	....
1873	974	762	$480
1877	884	604	610
1884	934	986	621

years of the period under review. However, they serve to emphasize the striking nature of the advance in Maynard's expenditures after 1880, and to bring out the fact that the Stow levy was actually being reduced during this period of generally increasing expenditures.

[34] Sudbury spent $10,301 for new schools between 1871 and 1873.

[35] Maynard found it necessary to build a new school immediately after its incorporation. This was found to be inadequate and additional outlays of $3,679 and $4,454 were made in 1878 and 1882 respectively. However, Maynard spent only $1,693 for highway construction between 1872 and 1886, as compared with $3,184 in Stow and $5,212 in Sudbury.

It is obvious that the per capita wealth in the parent towns had been raised substantially by the loss of the Maynard area. This was to be expected in Stow, which taxed little of the mill property, but in the case of Sudbury the result is rather surprising. At the end of the period Maynard still had a very much smaller per capita wealth than existed in either of the parent towns.

The local assessments appear below:

A. *Stow*

Year	Personalty	Real Estate (In thousands of dollars.)	Total
1871	271.6	737.7	1,009.3
1872	224.6	540.0	764.6
1880	264.8	512.2	777.0
1886	429.2	526.5	955.7

B. *Sudbury*

Year	Personalty	Real Estate (In thousands of dollars.)	Total
1871	473.2	1,010.3	1,483.5
1872	254.1	685.2	939.3
1880	194.0	774.9	969.0
1886	207.5	840.4	1,048.0

C. *Maynard*

Year	Personalty	Real Estate (In thousands of dollars.)	Total
1872	258.8	716.2	975.0
1880	416.1	954.2	1,370.3
1886	799.1	1,142.2	1,941.3

The incorporation cut the Stow valuation 24 per cent, most of the property lost being real estate. A far larger portion of the 37 per cent reduction in Sudbury was in the personalty valuation, because of the loss of the machinery in the Assabet mill.

The new town's valuation was considerably larger than the valuations in the remaining parts of Stow and Sudbury, and this difference had become even more pronounced by 1886. During the interval Maynard's total valuation had risen 99 per cent, real estate 59 per cent, personalty 210 per cent. The 12 per cent rise in the Sudbury total had come in spite of a 19 per cent drop in personalty; the 25 per cent rise in Stow, in the face of a 4 per cent decline in real estate values. Thus the more rapid increase in Maynard's expenditures was accompanied by a relatively large increase in taxable valuations, particularly in the amount of personal property assessed by the town.[36]

In 1872 Stow and Sudbury had obtained $347 and $800 respectively from the state taxes on bank shares and on corporate excess, income which had offset 7 and 8 per cent of their respective current expenditures. This was distinctly less than the 10 per cent which could have been paid with the $620 received by the town of Maynard.[37] By 1886 Sudbury's revenue had grown to $1,028 and Maynard's to $1,177, which was enough to pay 9 and 8 per cent of their respective current expenditures. Stow's income had increased much more rapidly, and in 1886 the town received $1,151, which paid 19 per cent of its reduced current expenditures. Stow alone obtained substantial relief from these state taxes during the period under review.

The net result of these changes can be seen in the tax rates given in the following table:

Year	Sudbury	Stow	Maynard
1871	$10.20	$11.90	.....
1872	12.20	7.20	$10.30
1880	8.20	7.50	5.00
1886	12.20	3.60	6.00

The Sudbury rate had risen abruptly at the time of the incorporation. Advancing valuations had brought a marked reduction to 1880, but six years later Sudbury's rate was again at its 1872 level. This, however, was a peak year, and if the figures for 1887 are used instead there is a net decline of $2.90 for the period following 1872.

There was a 40 per cent drop between 1871 and 1872 in the rate applied to property in the town of Stow and there was little additional change during the next eight years. Then the rise in valuations, the decline in expenditures, and the relatively large income received from the corporation and bank taxes brought the Stow rate to $3.60, which was half that applied in 1872, and only one third of the rate effective in the year preceding the incorporation.

---

[36] The census of 1885 indicates that there was $492,650 worth of machinery in Maynard, which would account for 60 per cent of the personalty assessed in that year.   [37] Average for 1872 and 1873.

Maynard itself had begun with a rate slightly higher than that applied to property in Sudbury in the preceding year, and very much less than the rate applied at that time by the town of Stow. The Maynard rate changed little until after 1877, when it began to drop, reaching a point in 1880 considerably below the rates formerly in effect in Stow. Although subsequent years brought a rapid increase, the 1886 rate was still only 58 per cent of that applied in the first year of Maynard's independent existence.

This town began its career with a debt of $19,600. There was a rise to $23,000 in the following year, but the bulk of this debt was retired by the use of an accumulated cash surplus in 1877, and the remainder was paid off during the next two years. In 1886 the town's only liability was a temporary loan of $1,200.

Stow had a debt of $5,190 in 1871, which had increased 70 per cent in the next year as a result of the establishment of a high school. The debt fell to $5,400 in 1879, rose in the following year, and then dropped to $5,000 in 1886.

Sudbury had liabilities, including indebtedness to trust funds held by the town, totaling $20,464 in 1869, and by 1876 this figure had increased to nearly $36,000. The next quotation is for 1887. At that date town liabilities totaled $34,453, which meant a per capita liability of $29.20 as compared with $9.80 in 1869. Sudbury alone had substantial liabilities at the end of the period studied.

Maynard began its career with a low level of current expenditures, but the fourteen years which followed its incorporation brought a rapid rise. The latter appeared in the face of a relatively small increase in highway costs, and the almost complete absence of interest charges after 1879. It was the result of a rapid increase in the cost of schools and poor relief, and the addition of expenditures for street lighting and for police protection. By 1886 the town had provided itself with an evening school, and had thus obtained all the services that it had wanted and had not been able to get from the parent towns. Since neither Stow nor Sudbury was making similar expenditures at this date, the evidence tends to substantiate the theory presented above, namely, that Maynard had desired separation because it had not been getting the services it considered its due in return for taxes paid. This theory is not invalidated by the fact that Maynard's per capita current expenditures for 1886 were still lower than those made by Stow and Sudbury. It is not reasonable to expect a mill town with a very low per capita wealth to set up an elaborate and expensive system of town government.

Maynard's taxable valuation had risen much more rapidly than its expenditures, and the result was a 42 per cent reduction in the rate applied to property in the town. Although it still had a low per capita assessment at the end of the period studied, it had no permanent debt and was operating with a relatively low tax rate. Maynard had obtained the type of services it desired, and seemed to be decidedly better off than it had been as a part of the parent towns.

Stow was even more favorably affected by the Maynard incorporation. Its expenditures were reduced more proportionately than the loss in taxable valuation, and its rate was cut 40 per cent at the time of the division. Subsequent years witnessed a decline in Stow's population, but expenditures were also reduced, and valuations mounted rapidly. In addition, Stow was receiving enough money from state taxes in 1886 to pay nearly a fifth of its total current expenditures. As a result, the town rate fell to $3.60 per thousand. In short, the incorporation had relieved Stow of burdens far in excess of the accompanying loss in taxable wealth, and the period which followed had only served to accentuate the advantages accruing to this town in 1872.

The only town that appeared to suffer from the incorporation was Sudbury. Although the latter had lost a large part of its taxable wealth, its expenditures had not been reduced. Hence there had been an immediate rise of 19 per cent in the rate applied to property in the remnant of this town. Expenditures showed little change during the period which followed, and the local assessment rose only 12 per cent. While the town rate was as high in 1886 as in 1872, it dropped sharply in the following year. Sudbury's liabilities increased rapidly, and it alone was burdened with a substantial per capita liability in 1886. Although its per capita wealth was much greater than Maynard's, its expenditures were also greater, and the tax rate more than twice as high. It is clear that Sudbury's finances had been weakened appreciably by the incorporation of Maynard, and had failed to recover from this blow during the period down to 1886.

B. THE FINANCIAL HISTORY OF MAYNARD, 1886–1933

Preceding sections of this chapter have dealt in some detail with the financial aspects of the incorporation of the town of Maynard in 1871. An attempt has been made to determine the causes of this action, and as a means of checking the theory presented, the finances of Maynard and its parent towns have been compared for a period of fourteen years subsequent to the incorporation. It is probable that this period was long enough to allow the financial results of the incorporation to work themselves out. Hence no attempt will be made to extend the comparison into the years following 1886.

Yet it has already been emphasized that Maynard possessed an unusual economic structure, that no great stretching of the facts was required in order to conclude that the General Court had really incorporated the Assabet mill and its adjacent mill village. Because of this peculiar situation the subsequent development of the town possesses enough interest to warrant the presentation of a sketch of its finances for the period between 1886 and 1933.

I

Between 1885 and 1890 Maynard's population decreased somewhat, but increased during the next decade to a figure 16 per cent greater than that for 1885. This lag behind the 44 per cent advance in the population of Massachusetts is in marked contrast with the unusually rapid development experienced by Maynard during the preceding period.[1]

The town's welfare was of course closely bound up with that of the Assabet mill, and although the latter had enjoyed great

[1] Maynard's population increased from 2,703 in 1885 to 3,142 in 1900. The state total increased from 1,900,000 to 2,800,000 during the same interval.

prosperity during the Civil War and immediately thereafter, it seems to have been declining during the period now being considered. The mill did not recover from the panic of 1893, and became insolvent five years later. Receivers operated it for four months, and in May 1899 it was taken over by the American Woolen Company. It was at that time the largest woolen mill in the country, having 66 sets of cards and 350 broad looms. The purchase price of $400,000 seems very low, particularly when compared with an estimated value of $1,500,000 placed upon the property in 1890.[2] The decline of this enterprise provides ample explanation for the distinct slowing up in Maynard's development.

The accompanying changes in town expenditures are summarized below:

Year	Total	Total Current* (In thousands of dollars.)	Total Non-commercial Current†
1886	15.4	15.4	15.4
1888	14.8	14.8	14.8
1890	94.2	19.1	16.2
1895	33.8	24.4	24.2
1898	41.7	24.2	23.9
1901	28.3	23.3	22.6

* Deficits on the construction account of the water works, so far as they are not covered by an operating surplus, have been deducted.

† The deficit of the water works on operating account has been removed from total current expenditures.

Both total and current expenditures drop to 1888 and begin to rise in the following year. Although the figure for total expenditures is very high in 1890, as a result of the construction of the town water works, it drops to $30,000 in 1896, and moves irregularly downward to 1901 leaving a net rise of 90 per cent for the period as a whole.

Current expenditures, exclusive of the operating deficit of the water works, rise to 1895, drop sharply in the following year, and show little change during the remainder of the period. There is a net rise of 68 per cent, which is cut to 26 per cent if allowance is made for the accompanying growth of population.

[2] Gutteridge, *Maynard*, pp. 32 ff.

The town levy increases from \$13,000 to \$30,500 between 1886 and 1901, and this 135 per cent advance is considerably in excess of the 80 per cent advance from \$25,900,000 to \$47,900,000 in the total for Massachusetts. The statistics indicate that the town's expenditures were increasing at an unusually rapid pace.

The bulk of the increase in current expenditures was the result of a rise from \$7,000 to \$9,500 in the cost of schools, from \$1,200 to \$2,600 in highway charges, from \$2,100 to \$4,300 in poor relief, and the addition of expenditures of \$813 and \$522 for fire protection and interest charges respectively. Between 1886 and 1901 the town also made non-commercial outlays totaling \$39,617 as compared with \$13,893 during the fourteen years preceding 1886.[3]

How much of this added burden was offset by an increase in the town's wealth? The best index of the latter, the Tax Commissioner's estimate, rises from \$621 per capita in 1884 to \$780 in 1890, and then drops to \$687 in 1902. This leaves an increase of 10 per cent for the entire period, which was, of course, far less than the increase in per capita current expenditures.

The local assessments appear below:

Year	Personalty	Real Estate (In thousands of dollars.)	Total
1886	799.1	1,142.2	1,941.3
1890	618.7	1,331.7	1,950.4
1895	661.0	1,454.3	2,115.3
1901	631.8	1,493.7	2,125.5

A sharp drop in personalty to 1890, very probably the result of declining assessments placed upon the machinery in the Assabet mill, was more than offset by a rise in the value of real estate. A continued advance in the later item produced a net increase of 9 per cent in the town's local assessment for the entire period under review.[4]

[3] Between 1886 and 1901 a total of \$36,290 was spent for school construction, \$7,018 for the construction of highways, and \$6,309 on outlays for the fire department.

[4] It is interesting to note that a large portion of the increase in real estate was the result of an advance in the building assessment from \$823,000 in 1886 to \$1,128,000 in 1901. Buildings made up 71 per cent of the real-estate assessment in 1887, and 78 per cent in 1901. The importance of this item is indicative of the predominantly industrial nature of this town.

Revenue from the state bank and corporation taxes dropped with the declining profitableness of the Assabet mill from $1,177 in 1886 to $673 in 1890, rose somewhat to 1895, and then fell to $488 in 1901. At the latter date this income paid only 2 per cent of Maynard's non-commercial current expenditures.

The contraction in this income served to aggravate the condition produced by the relatively rapid increase in town expenditures. The result was a rise in the tax rate from $6.00 in 1886 to $15.00 in 1895. Although the $13.50 rate applied in 1901 was decidedly lower, it represented a net increase of 125 per cent for the period as a whole. As a result, property in the town, which had been subject to a rate only 42 per cent of the current state average in 1886, was now burdened by a rate equal to 84 per cent of a distinctly higher state average.[5]

Maynard had had no non-commercial debt until 1892, when it borrowed $27,000 to build a new school. A sinking fund had wiped out all but two thousand dollars by 1901. Hence the town was not much worse off in this respect than in 1886.

Maynard had constructed a water works, however, and had borrowed heavily for this purpose. The original plant, begun in 1889, was completed three years later at a cost of $105,000 and financed entirely with borrowed money. Between 1891 and the end of this period another $32,000 was spent for construction, raising the total cost to $137,700. Since the town had received $1,966 in service installation fees, its own investment totaled $135,800.

The operating record of the enterprise is summarized in the following table:

Year	Current Receipts*	Current Expenditures†	Net Receipts
1890	.....	$2,938	− $2,938
1891	$1,049	3,960	− 2,911
1895	6,427	6,597	− 170
1897	5,443	19,870	− 14,427
1901	6,165	6,857	− 692

* Receipts include water rates and miscellaneous income; they do not include the yearly grant appropriated by the town ostensibly in payment for the water it used. The logic of this omission will be discussed in the Hopkinton chapter.

† Expenditures include maintenance costs, interest charges, and miscellaneous expenses. The third group of items includes the cost of law suits brought against the water board.

---

[5] The state average rose from $14.14 to $14.80 in 1895, and to $16.14 in 1901.

The large deficit in 1897 reflects the cost of settling a sizable legal judgment. The deficit for the entire interval totaled $33,300, of which $17,400 represented the cost of legal proceedings brought against the town by aggrieved property owners.[6]

The water board debt was $110,000 in 1901, or $5,400 more than at the time the original plant was completed, the increase coming in spite of a town contribution of $22,000 to the water-board sinking fund. But the investment in the enterprise had risen to $137,700, and it may be concluded that 20 per cent of the equity had become the property of the town. It must be pointed out, however, that this apparent improvement in the financial status of the enterprise was accomplished entirely at the expense of the town itself, the payments which the water board made on its debt being less than the additional amount borrowed during these years. When this is considered, together with the fact that a yearly grant from the town had not prevented a sizable operating deficit for the period under review, it becomes clear that the enterprise constituted a serious financial burden to the town, and that its presence accounted for a considerable portion of the increase in the Maynard tax levy.

Yet the water works were approaching the point where they would become self-supporting, and this circumstance, together with the fact that Maynard had acquired 20 per cent of the equity during the period, indicates that the financing of the enterprise had been fairly sound. It does not alter the conclusion, however, that the construction and maintenance of the town water works was a substantial burden during the years prior to 1902.

This period had witnessed a decline in the rate of Maynard's development associated with the diminishing prosperity of the Assabet mill. A sharp drop in personalty and a small rise in the value of real estate had produced a 9 per cent advance in the local assessment, which was far less than the 68 per cent increase in the town's current expenditures. Receipts from state taxes

---

[6] The town made a yearly appropriation to the water board beginning in 1892, and these grants, made ostensibly in return for water consumed by the town itself, totaled $21,400 during the subsequent period. They more than covered that portion of the operating deficit which was over and above the cost of the law suits into which the water board had been drawn.

had decreased and added burdens had been assumed in an attempt to finance a water system. Although there had been no significant addition to the non-commercial debt, the rate applied to property in the town had risen 125 per cent. It is clear that Maynard's financial position was much weaker in 1901 than in 1886.

A large part of this decline was undoubtedly the result of the collapse of the Assabet Manufacturing Company. Particularly, this accounts for the slow growth of the town's local assessment, for the decline in receipts from the corporation tax, and for the rapid rise in the burden of poor relief. Yet it must not be forgotten that in the face of the decay of the only significant industry, the town meeting continued to increase its current expenditures and undertook the construction of a water supply which, for this period at least, placed a real burden upon the town's finances. Maynard had clearly made little attempt to adjust its expenditures to its declining financial strength, and in the light of this conclusion the position of the poll-tax payer in the Maynard town meeting assumes peculiar significance.

This type of voter pays a fixed tax of nominal amount. Larger appropriations add nothing to his burden of taxation, while he benefits heavily from most of the services resulting from increased town expenditures. It is clearly to his interest to favor generous expenditures, especially those providing better schools, good drinking water, and generous poor relief. A town meeting dominated by this element can hardly be expected to pursue conservative financial policies. Persons paying only the nominal tax on polls made up 67 per cent of Maynard's taxpayers in 1887, 65 per cent in 1895, and 51 per cent in 1901.

On the other hand, the Maynard family had attempted to exercise a rigid control over the actions of their employees. They are reputed to have dictated to a large extent the moral and social habits of their workers and to have attempted a similar regulation of the town meeting. This circumstance would tend to offset the pressure which so large a group of poll-tax payers would exert in the direction of increased expenditures, but the influence of the Maynards was either insufficiently strong or not exercised harshly enough to force upon the town meeting a policy of adjusting expenditures to the relatively slow growth of the town's taxable valuation. Consequently, Maynard's finances show a definite decay during the period between 1886 and 1901.

II

When the American Woolen Company took over the Assabet mill, it installed new machinery, and in 1901 it constructed an additional unit called mill number five. Since the resulting increase in the number of operatives exceeded the housing capacity of the village, the company was also forced to construct a total of 160 new tenements.[7] This explains the greater portion of the 87 per cent increase in the town's population between 1900 and 1905. Maynard grew more slowly during the next decade, but by 1915 had 6,770 inhabitants, which was 116 per cent more than it had at the turn of the century. The population of Massachusetts had risen only 31 per cent during this same interval.

The state census no longer gives data relating to the economic condition of the town, but as there had been no change in the direction of its development, it is safe to conclude that in 1915 Maynard was still an industrial community dominated by a single large enterprise. However, it now contained a much larger population, and since many of the new residents seem to have been foreign-born floating labor, the importance of this element in the community had increased greatly.[8]

The change in the number and character of Maynard's inhabitants necessarily had its effect upon the town's finances. Its expenditures appear below:

---

[7] Gutteridge, p. 34.

[8] Evidence of this fact is present in the Tax Collector's Report for 1904. This official complained that the collection of the poll tax was made extremely difficult by the presence of a large floating population, and that this was particularly true among the foreign groups, especially the Poles. The collector proposed that a deputy accompany the assessors on their annual round among the "foreign element" and "floating help" who occupied the boarding houses. By this means a tax list might be compiled more rapidly and collections made immediately under a special warrant, thus "avoiding great delay and the possible loss of hundreds of dollars."

Year	Total	Total Current	Total Non-commercial Current
		(In thousands of dollars.)	
1901	28.3	23.3	22.6
1902	31.1	24.9	24.4
1903	43.3	39.0	39.0
1910	70.4	52.2	52.2
1916	114.0	85.1	85.1

Total expenditures rise sharply in the year following the construction of the new mill. They range between $50,000 and $75,000 during the period prior to 1910, and then begin an almost steady ascent to a level which in 1916 was more than 300 per cent above that for 1901. Current non-commercial expenditures follow a similar movement and show a net increase of 275 per cent for the period as a whole.

Naturally, a considerable portion of these changes is offset by the accompanying growth of population. Yet the per capita total expenditure rises from $9.00 in 1901 to $11.00 in 1910, and then to $16.85 during the next six years. Current expenditures increase from $7.20 per capita to $12.50 between 1901 and 1916.

Rising expenditures raised the town tax from $30,500 in 1901 to $66,700 in 1907, an increase of 119 per cent, while the state total was rising from $47,900,000 to $57,900,000, or about 21 per cent.

After 1907 it is possible to obtain a direct comparison between the movement of Maynard's expenditures and that of the total for all the towns and cities in the state by means of data contained in the *Statistics of Municipal Finances.* Total expenditures [9] in Maynard rose from $76,500 to $129,400 between 1907 and 1916, a net advance of about 70 per cent. The state total rose from $91,000,000 to $134,000,000 or about 48 per cent.[10] It is clear that the relatively rapid advance in town expenditures persisted throughout the period now under consideration.

[9] Maintenance and interest charges, capital outlays for all purposes, payments on the town debt from the sinking fund and from revenue, net payments on temporary loans, and payments to sinking funds.

[10] The rise in the state total is overstated somewhat as the result of the absence of the expenditures of fifty-six small towns from the report for 1908. However, these towns had a population of only 100,525 according to the census of 1905, when the state total was 3,003,680.

The chief items among current expenditures are summarized in the following table:

Year	Schools	Highways	Poor Relief	Fire and Police	Interest Charges
			(In thousands of dollars.)		
1901	9.5	2.6	4.3	1.3	.5
1903	14.5	4.3	4.9	3.8	.2
1910	24.0	5.2	4.3	5.4	1.2
1916	41.6	9.5	7.1	7.2	3.1

Substantial increases in the cost of schools, highways, and fire and police protection in the year following the construction of the new mill continued during subsequent years and by 1916 the changes in all the items listed above had become quite revolutionary.

Although most of the expansion appearing between 1901 and 1903 can be accounted for by the construction of the new unit at the woolen mill and the resulting expansion of the town's population, the subsequent and much larger increases cannot be explained away in this fashion. They seem to be the result of a deliberate spending policy proposed by the selectmen in 1903,[11] and put into effect apparently without either the encouragement or the intervention of the American Woolen Company, which of course bore the major portion of the increased burden of taxation.[12]

The personal control which the Maynards had exerted in town meeting had been removed and no similar restraint had taken its place. In addition, the influx of floating labor, which followed the opening of the new mill, had so increased the number of the poll-tax payers that this group made up three fourths of the persons taxed in 1905. In 1914 they constituted 69 per cent of that total,

[11] "It is the opinion of the Board of Selectmen that the time is ripe in the Town of Maynard for some systematic expenditure of the people's money, that the greatest possible good may be brought to the greatest possible number of the citizens of our town." — Maynard Town Report, 1903, p. 8. More specifically this board pointed to the need for better roads. In addition they reported that the police force of the town had been expanded in accordance with a vote of the town, and that a contract had been made with the American Woolen Company which provided that the latter was to supply the town with electricity for lighting the streets. The same plant also supplied the town of Acton.

[12] The present cashier at the mill asserts that until recently the company has pursued a hands-off policy in regard to town affairs, and in the main the statements of a town assessor were in agreement with this assertion.

and although their majority was declining they still represented 65 per cent of the town's taxpayers in 1916.[13] Domination of the town's voting population by taxpayers of this character, combined with the removal of all control on the part of the officials of the woolen mill, offers an adequate explanation for the rapidity of the increase in Maynard's current expenditures.

Naturally, there was also a striking increase in the town's non-commercial capital outlays. Between 1902 and 1916 these totaled $140,000 as compared with $40,000 between 1886 and 1901. As in the earlier period, most of this money was used for the construction of town schools.[14]

Meanwhile, the influx of population during the first years of the twentieth century had more than offset the expansion in the town's wealth. The Tax Commissioner's estimate dropped from $687 per capita in 1902 to $550 in 1905. The subsequent advance to $648 in 1916 did not prevent a net decline of about 6 per cent for the period as a whole.

Local assessments moved as follows:

Year	Personalty	Real Estate (In thousands of dollars.)	Total
1901	632	1,494	2,126
1905	1,308	2,217	3,525
1910	1,322	2,549	3,871
1916	1,309	3,016	4,325

The total valuation rose slightly more than 100 per cent because of a sharp increase in personalty during the early years of the period and a steady advance of 110 per cent in the value of real estate. While this was substantially in excess of the 65 per cent increase in the total assessment for the entire state,[15] it was far less

---

[13] The statistics follow:

Year	Number paying Poll Tax only	Total Taxpayers
1901	569	1,107
1903	947	1,352
1905	1,430	1,908
1914	1,641	2,376
1916	1,687	2,573

[14] The outlay for schools totaled $119,773; for highways, $17,016; and for miscellaneous objects, $2,800.

[15] This rose from $2,961,000,000 in 1901 to $4,926,000,000 in 1916.

than the accompanying 300 per cent advance in Maynard's total expenditures.

Income from the bank and corporation taxes continued to decline. In 1908, however, the General Court altered the method of distributing the proceeds of the tax on corporate excess. Taxes paid with respect to shares held by residents of Massachusetts had previously been distributed to the town of the shareholder's domicile. They were now divided equally between the towns where the shareholders resided and those in which the business was carried on.[16] Although this change increased Maynard's share of the receipts, the $607 received in 1908 paid less than 2 per cent of the town's current expenditures. Beginning in 1910 all the taxes on the stock of domestic business corporations owned by residents of the state was allotted to the town where the business was carried on. This brought Maynard's receipts to $1,002 in the following year; but it was not until 1916, when a similar change was made in the distribution of taxes on public utilities, that the town obtained any really substantial income.[17] The $11,000 which these taxes brought to Maynard in that year paid 13 per cent of its greatly increased current expenditures. Nevertheless, it was only at the very end of the period under review that receipts from this source furnished appreciable relief from the burden being put upon property in Maynard as the result of the rapid rise in her local expenditures.[18]

The consequence was an advance in the rate from $13.50 to $16.60 in 1910, and to $20.00 in 1916. This 48 per cent increase was considerably in excess of the average rise in Massachusetts. As a result the Maynard rate rose from 16 per cent below to 4 per cent above the current state average.

The town's non-commercial debt was wiped out in 1902. In the following year, however, a school loan of $22,500 was floated and by 1906 the school debt had reached $35,500. It dropped until 1914, only to be raised to $63,000 in the following year, and

[16] *Acts and Resolves*, 1908, c. 614.

[17] For a discussion of this legislation see C. J. Bullock, "The Taxation of Property and Income in Massachusetts," *Quarterly Journal of Economics*, XXXI, 41.

[18] Maynard obtained no significant revenue from taxes on the street railway which had reached the town in 1901. The largest income was $190 in 1906.

to decline to $57,000 in 1916. With the exception of temporary
loans from the water-board surplus in 1914 and 1915, in each instance repaid in the following year, Maynard in 1916 had acquired only this school debt and a small highway debt of $2,000.
Yet the town's non-commercial debt was very large in comparison
with the negligible liabilities existing in 1901.

The accounts of the water board show outlays for construction
amounting to $57,000 between 1902 and 1916, raising the cost of
the enterprise to $195,000 and the town's investment to $191,-
000.[19] The operating record is summarized below:

Year	Current Receipts	Current Expenditures	Net Receipts
1901	$6,165	$6,857	− $692
1903	9,408	8,866	542
1907	12,891	8,870	4,021
1912	13,137	9,288	3,849
1916	16,377	9,956	6,421

The first real operating surplus appeared in 1903, and by 1907
this had risen to $4,000. The next large increase, coming in 1915,
raised the net receipts to more than $7,000, and the operating
surplus for the following year was almost as large. The excess of
receipts over expenditures for the period as a whole totaled
$51,061.

It ought to be emphasized that this figure does not represent a
profit. It neglects interest charges on the equity held by the
town, makes no allowance for the tax exemption received, and
includes no charge for depreciation or obsolesence. Yet the appearance of these net receipts made it possible for the town to dis-
continue its yearly grant in 1909, causing the water board to
operate on a self-supporting basis.

Moreover, the net debt on this enterprise had dropped from
$110,000 to $12,000. Since the cost of construction had risen to
$195,000, the equity owned by the town had grown from 20 to 94
per cent of the total. This situation, however, had been brought
about entirely at the expense of the town itself.

The water system was clearly a much smaller burden than it

[19] So far as can be ascertained from published reports only $2,162 had been re-
ceived in service installation fees.

had been in the years prior to 1901. It had now become self-supporting, and the reduction in its debt had been carried to a point which made possible operation on a self-sustaining basis during the years following 1916. The record of the water board is a good one; it contrasts strikingly with that of the town itself.

To sum up, the increase in Maynard's expenditures had exceeded the growth of its population and was far in excess of the increase in local expenditures for the state as a whole. Although Maynard's assessment was also advancing rapidly, the increase was far less than that shown by town expenditures. Little assistance was received from the bank and corporation taxes until the final year of the period under review, and the per capita taxable wealth showed a distinct decline. Maynard benefited by the improvement in the finances of the water works, but this benefit was of slight importance when compared with the rapid advance in non-commercial expenditures. As a consequence the rate applied to property in the town rose much more rapidly than in the state as a whole.

In spite of the revival of the only significant industry in the town, Maynard's financial position, which had weakened noticeably during the years preceding 1901, weakened much more rapidly during the subsequent period. This took place under a town meeting which was now in the hands of voters paying only the nominal tax on polls — a further illustration of the fact that a town so governed is apt to spend considerably more freely than one in which the people who vote appropriations will also share in the increased burden of taxation.

III

In response to the war-time demand for textiles the American Woolen Company added another unit to its Maynard plant in 1918. As a result this property included, in 1920, twelve buildings containing 128 sets of 60-inch cards and 760 broad looms. It employed about 2,500 operatives.[20] The mill continued to function at nearly full capacity down to 1929, and at the beginning of the

[20] Gutteridge, *Maynard*, pp. 34 ff.

latter year was employing 2,800 persons. The reversal of business conditions during the latter half of the year brought a curtailment of production which continued during the subsequent depression until in 1933 the number of employees had fallen to 1,000,[21] and most of these were no longer full-time workers.

The expansion in 1918 is reflected in the 5 per cent growth of Maynard's population between 1915 and 1920. There was little change during the next decade; in 1930 Maynard had 7,165 inhabitants.

The town's expenditures showed the following movement:

Year	Total	Total Current	Total Non-commercial Current
		(In thousands of dollars.)	
1916	114.0	85.1	85.1
1923	227.7	187.5	187.5
1929	389.0	243.1	243.1
1932	304.4	281.6	281.6
1933	251.3	243.5	243.5

There was a sharp rise in both total and current expenditures between 1916 and 1923. The former item continued to advance to a maximum in 1929 about 275 per cent above the total expenditure for 1916. This increase gave place to a sharp reduction during subsequent years. Current expenditures, after a decline in 1924, rose to their maximum in 1932, when they were 230 per cent higher than at the beginning of the period. Although these expenditures were cut vigorously in 1933, it was still costing as much to operate the town as it had in 1929.

The *Statistics of Municipal Finances* show a rise in Maynard's expenditures from $129,000 to $326,000 between 1916 and 1932, a net advance of 152 per cent. The total for the entire state rose from $134,000,000 to $344,000,000, or 156 per cent. It is apparent that the relatively slow growth of Maynard's population had failed to prevent an advance in town expenditures approximating the average.

The following table contains the chief items among current expenditures:

---

[21] Estimate by company official.

Year	Schools	Highways	Poor Relief	Fire and Police	Interest Charges
			(In thousands of dollars.)		
1916	41.6	9.5	7.1	7.2	3.1
1920	67.5	20.5	15.1	13.1	5.8
1930	116.3	38.7	22.8	23.0	14.4
1932	102.8	18.9	55.0	18.1	15.7
1933	100.0	14.2	60.9*	15.6	13.9

* Includes old age assistance.

Poor relief, which had shared the striking advance in the other items down to 1930, assumed a dominant role during the years which followed. The tremendous increase in this burden offset most of the economies practiced in other departments, and explains the failure of current expenditures to drop below the level prevailing in 1929.

Maynard had incurred capital outlays totaling $707,000 for the period between 1917 and 1932. Of this, $212,000 was used for school construction, $265,000 for sewers, and $192,000 for new streets and highways. Nearly 65 per cent of the last amount was offset by grants from the state and county highway authorities, and if this income is deducted, a total non-commercial outlay of $580,000 remains. If a similar correction is made for the preceding period, total outlays are reduced to $130,000. Thus the burden put upon the town was four and one half times as great as that borne during the period ending in 1916.[22]

It will be recalled that total expenditures had reached their peak in 1929, and that the subsequent advance in current expenditures was largely the result of an increase in the presumably unavoidable burden of poor relief. Now it is significant that the period ending in 1929 was one in which the mill was booming and the company not interfering very much in town affairs. Moreover, while the percentage of Maynard's taxpayers who were being assessed for the nominal levy on polls alone had dropped from 65 to 46 per cent between 1916 and 1928 (the last year in which these statistics are available), the political dominance of this group had remained unchallenged.[23]

[22] There were no outlays in 1933.
[23] A town assessor and a company official agreed on this point. The company official stated that the property-tax payers usually did not attend town meeting.

Up to 1929 there had been no great resistance to the rapidly expanding town services favored by these voters, but when the company felt the pinch of depression, it began to exert pressure on town officials in an effort to reduce expenditures and cut its own tax bill. This pressure was strong enough to check the extravagant spending policies favored by the poll-tax payers, and to produce the subsequent decline in total expenditures as well as the reductions in the cost of maintaining highways and schools and furnishing fire and police protection.

Meanwhile, the Tax Commissioner's estimated valuation had risen from $648 per capita in 1916 to $1,488 in 1925. This was a net advance of 227 per cent, but the whole of this gain has not been retained. By 1928 Maynard's per capita wealth had been reduced by a fifth, and in 1932 its valuation had fallen to $945 per capita. Although this figure still represented a 45 per cent gain for the period as a whole, it was dwarfed by the accompanying advance in per capita current expenditures.[24]

Local assessments moved as follows:

Year	Personalty	Real Estate (In thousands of dollars.)	Total
1916	1,309	3,016	4,325
1917	1,350	3,334	4,684
1925	1,621	4,613	6,234
1930	1,581	5,347	6,928
1933	1,268	4,980	6,248

The enactment of the state income tax in 1916 removed all intangibles from the local lists. Although this measure produced a 62 per cent drop in the personalty valuation for the entire state, it failed to prevent an increase in Maynard's personalty assessment. The negligible role played by intangibles in this town's finances is indicative of its industrial character. Tangible personalty rose to 1925, and then began to decline. By 1933 it had fallen well below the level existing at the beginning of this period.[25]

[24] These rose from about $12.60 in 1916 to about $34.00 in 1932.

[25] Part of this decline was a result of the motor vehicle excise tax passed in 1929 (*General Laws*, c. 60, A., sec. 1). Although this law had removed such vehicles from the local lists, the property remained taxable by the town at the state average rate, the identity of the vehicles being certified to the town by the state registration officials. The tax was simply an administrative device intended to facilitate collection. If the value of this property is added to Maynard's personalty the latter rises to $2,128,000 in 1930.

Real estate continued to rise until 1930, and the decline during the next three years left a net rise of about 65 per cent. Building values, which made up 81 per cent of this total in 1933, were far and away the most important part of Maynard's local valuation.

The latter rose steadily till 1930, and throughout these years the assessment placed upon the American Woolen Company's property was large enough to cause this enterprise to bear about 50 per cent of the taxes levied in the town.[26] In 1929, when the company began to press for lower expenditures, it also asked for a revaluation of its property. It obtained a considerable reduction, so that in 1933 it paid only 40 per cent of the town's taxes. This circumstance is responsible for a large part of the subsequent decline in Maynard's assessed valuation. The latter, however, was still nearly 45 per cent larger in 1933 than at the beginning of the period.

Receipts from the state bank and corporation taxes, after dropping from $11,000 to $2,000 between 1916 and 1918, rose to $38,793 in 1924. At this date these taxes were paying 22 per cent of Maynard's total current expenditures. Although they still yielded $35,000 in 1930, the next three years brought a sharp drop to $11,000, which paid only 4.5 per cent of the total current expenditures.

The Massachusetts income tax which went into effect in 1917[27] was levied in lieu of the property tax on intangibles, the latter being exempt from local taxation. The state collected the income tax and distributed the proceeds, so far as they exceeded the cost of administration, among the several cities and towns. At first this was done by paying each town an amount equal to the difference between the revenue it had derived from the taxation of personalty in 1915 and the amount the Tax Commissioner estimated that the same rate would yield if applied to the remaining taxable personalty in the current year. The excess was distributed in proportion to the state tax paid by the several towns.

In 1919, however, legislation was enacted providing a gradual transition to a system under which all proceeds in excess of the

[26] Estimate furnished by the company cashier.
[27] *Acts and Resolves*, 1916, c. 269.

cost of administration were distributed in accordance with the amount of state taxes paid by the respective towns.[28] This in turn was amended by an act passed in the following year segregating a portion of the receipts for use as grants in aid for educational purposes.[29] These changes were meant to favor the less wealthy towns which had been taxing only a small amount of intangible property, the latter having become concentrated in a few wealthy communities.[30]

Maynard of course benefited greatly by the new system. Its receipts rose from $3,000 to $20,600 during the three years following 1917, and then to $49,000 in 1930 when income from this source was paying 19 per cent of total current expenditures. The depression cut deeply into the productivity of this tax, and by 1933 Maynard's receipts had dropped to $24,000 or less than 10 per cent of its somewhat reduced current expenditures. It is clear, however, that the town obtained substantial relief from both the corporation and the income tax during the better part of the period under review.

Yet the advance in expenditures so far outstripped the growth of the local tax base and the addition to income received from these state taxes that it was necessary to raise the rate applied to property in the town from $20.00 in 1916 to $31.50 in 1924. A decline in expenditures combined with a rising local assessment and an increase in revenue from the income tax to produce a rate of $24.50 in 1928, which was again well below the current state average.[31] The town rate for 1931 was still $25.00 per thousand, but a continued rise in current expenditures, falling valuations, and a rapid decline in receipts from the income and corporation taxes forced the Maynard rate up to $36.00 in 1932. The rate of $35.75 applied in the following year was nearly 20 per cent above the current state average, and 78 per cent in excess of that applied to property in the town in 1916.

[28] *Ibid.*, 1919, c. 314.

[29] *Ibid.*, c. 363, part 1.

[30] This concentration was pointed out in the *Report of the Commission on Taxation*, January 1908, pp. 38–52, in which the tendency of this property to accumulate in so-called "favored" towns where the rates were low was made the basis for the recommendation of the application of a three-mill tax by state authorities.

[31] This was $29.07 in 1928.

Increased borrowing for schools and highways had raised the town debt from $59,000 to $145,000 by 1925. Although the highway debt had been repaid by 1928, and the school loans considerably reduced, the town had begun to borrow to finance the construction of sewers. As a result, its debt rose to $336,000 in the following year. The decline to $260,000 in 1933 left a non-commercial debt 340 per cent in excess of that outstanding in 1916.[32]

Meanwhile the water board had spent a total of $78,000 for construction purposes, thus raising the cost of the enterprise to $274,000 and the town's investment to $265,000.[33] The operating record follows:

Year	Operating Receipts	Operating Expenditures	Net Receipts
1916	$16,377	$9,956	$6,421
1922	21,646	8,900	12,746
1929	20,976	11,673	9,303
1933	18,269	14,634	3,635

Although receipts exceeded expenditures throughout the period, the difference was being seriously reduced during the last years by the relatively rapid advance in operating costs. Between 1917 and 1933 the water works showed an operating surplus of approximately $140,000; this was done without assistance from the town itself.

The debt on the enterprise had amounted to just under $12,000 in 1916. Accumulating interest in the sinking fund and a grant of $8,241 from the water board itself wiped out this debt two years later. There was no borrowing during subsequent years, all extensions being financed by means of an accumulated cash surplus. The latter amounted to more than $22,000 in 1930, the last

[32] The statistics on which this paragraph is based appear below:

Year	Schools	Highways	Sewers	Miscellaneous	Total
		(In thousands of dollars.)			
1916	57.0	2.0	....	...	59.0
1922	69.0	30.0	....	10.0	109.0
1925	129.0	12.0	....	4.0	145.0
1928	102.0	...	150.0	...	252.0
1929	93.0	...	243.0	...	336.0
1933	57.0	...	203.0	...	260.6

[33] A total of $4,126 was received in service installation fees between 1916 and 1933.

year in which this information is provided by the water-board report.

Thus the enterprise had more than met all maintenance and capital charges out of its current income. It was clearly self-sustaining and no longer a burden to the town except in so far as the loss of taxes resulting from the exemption of the enterprise and the loss of interest on invested capital are taken into account. Since these things are usually neglected, it is possible to conclude that the Maynard water board presents an exceptionally good record for the period under consideration.

This record again stands in sharp contrast with that of the town itself, and it is for this reason that so much attention has been paid to the water board's finances. The enterprise serves practically the entire town and its rates are considered exceptionally low. Yet the compactness of the village and the efficiency of the management have allowed the water works to become clearly self-sustaining. Under these circumstances, and in a town controlled by the poll-tax payer, it is surprising that rates have not been cut to a still lower level. Upon inquiry it was found that such proposals appeared frequently in town meeting, but that they had always been defeated by the water board. The board has been controlled by the members of a single family whose successful management has given them sufficient political influence to make possible a successful resistance to any attempt to tamper with their policies in town meeting. This situation has enabled the water department to go along independently of the town, and to produce an exceptionally good record during a period when town finances were undergoing a serious decline.

Up to 1929 the rapid advance in Maynard's expenditures, fostered by the dominance of the poll-tax payer in town meeting, had been accompanied by a growing local assessment, and by rising income from state taxes. The town had also seen fit to finance most of its non-commercial outlays with borrowed money, and was no longer required to assist its water works. Hence, it was possible for Maynard to operate in 1929 with a rate very much less than the current state average, and this situation was not greatly altered during the next two years.

But by that time the decline in receipts from the corporation tax, which had begun in 1925, had been joined by a decline in revenue from the state tax on incomes, and the effect of these changes was accentuated by a substantial drop in the local assessment. Total expenditures were reduced, but the rising cost of maintaining the town poor offset most of the economies applied to other current expenditures. Hence, in 1933 property in Maynard was subjected to a rate 20 per cent above the current state average and 78 per cent in excess of that applied in 1916. Since there has also been a large increase in the burden of indebtedness, it is quite clear that the deterioration characteristic of the town's finances during the two preceding periods was also present during the years following 1916.

The prominence of the poll-tax payers in town meeting again accompanied the rapid development of Maynard's expenditures, furnishing added evidence that this type of voter will, if given control of a town meeting, force upon that town a relatively burdensome system of governmental expenditures.

Hence, it has finally become obvious that the incorporation of Maynard was not the innocuous performance which the statistics for the years prior to 1886 seemed to indicate. The new town had an overspecialized economic structure. It was not in a position to attract residents with great personal wealth, and was forced to rely upon a single large industrial enterprise for the major portion of its tax revenue. The rapid development of that enterprise during the years following 1900 brought burdens which considerably exceeded the financial benefits accruing to the town, and the latter's experience during recent years has made all too clear the financial hazards which confront a single-industry town during a period of declining business activity.[34] Further evidence along these same lines will be furnished in the next two chapters.

---

[34] There is only one period for which evidence exists that might lead one to think that the pressure on Maynard's finances was being relieved. Between 1925 and 1929 there was a sharp reduction in the rate applied to property in the town. This, however, was accompanied by the acquisition of a substantial debt resulting from the financing of capital outlays with borrowed money, raising the level of operating costs, and increasing the difficulties encountered when depression set in. Yet, even if this is left out of consideration, it appears that the seeming improvement is to a large extent the result of a more favorable method of distributing state taxes rather than to the increasing strength of the financial structure of the town itself.

CHAPTER III

THE INCORPORATION OF MILLVILLE

THIS chapter is concerned with the division of Blackstone in 1916, and with the subsequent financial history of the two new towns. But since Blackstone itself was part of the old town of Mendon until 1845, and was separated from the latter as the result of a situation which in fact and principle resembled that existing in 1916, an account of the events leading up to this earlier incorporation is appropriate.

I

The Millville-Blackstone area was organized as the south precinct of Mendon in 1766. At that date Mendon was a purely agricultural town, but the streams flowing through its southern precinct endowed that region with a considerable amount of water power, a circumstance foreshadowing its subsequent industrial development.[1] There was some power available on the Mill River, a small stream in the eastern portion of the south precinct, and it was here that the first cotton mill in the town was erected in 1801.[2] By 1817 two more cotton mills and a machine shop had been built in this area; a woolen mill had been constructed on the much larger Blackstone River at what is now the town of Millville; and the first unit of the Blackstone Manufacturing Company had been put into operation in Blackstone village.[3]

Although the industrial development of the south precinct continued into the period following 1820, it was now concentrated entirely in the Blackstone valley. By 1845 this region contained twelve cotton mills employing 653 persons and producing goods

---

[1] The south precinct contained only two mills at this date, a grist mill on the Mill River and a corn mill on the Blackstone at what is now Millville. — E. B. Crane, *History of Worcester County* (1924), II, 763; and *A History of Worcester County* (1879), I, 281.

[2] Crane, *op. cit.*, II, 764.

[3] *History* (1879), p. 286.

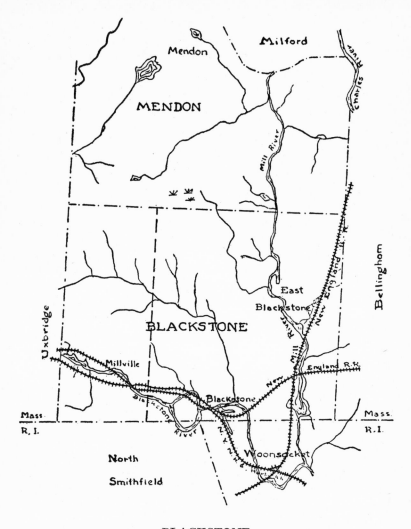

BLACKSTONE

AND VICINITY ABOUT 1895, SHOWING THE LINE OF DIVISION
SET UP IN 1916 THUS: — — —

valued at $387,000, in addition to seven woolen mills with 514 employees and a product valued at $685,000. The northern precinct remained primarily agricultural; its only significant industry, the manufacture of boots and shoes, employed 226 persons and turned out a yearly product of $59,000.

The population of Mendon increased about 117 per cent between 1800 and 1840,[4] and the statistics for the years following the division of the town indicate that this growth was associated with the industrial development of the south precinct.[5] The appearance of the new center of population quite naturally had its effect on the town's finances. New demands were made for highway and school expenditures,[6] and these were distasteful to the people of the north precinct who saw themselves taxed to provide services benefiting the residents of another section, the residents of an area with a very different economic structure, which must have seemed rather remote to the people living in the north end of town. Naturally, the demands for larger appropriations met with severe resistance,[7] and under these circumstances the appearance of a movement to divide the town is not surprising.

One historian mentions a "feeble movement for division" in 1779,[8] but no serious threat had been made until 1816. Seven years later the proposition to set off the south precinct again appeared in town meeting, and in 1825 an appeal for separation reached the General Court. After 1827 the controversy lapsed but in 1843, with the appearance of a new issue, namely, the location of a proposed town meeting house, the separation movement revived. A bitterly contested dispute followed which culminated, in 1848, in the incorporation of the south precinct as the town of Blackstone.

[4] The population of Mendon in 1800 was 1,628; in 1820, 2,254; and in 1840, 3,524.

[5] Between 1850 and 1860 the population of the remainder of Mendon increased from 1,300 to 1,351. That of the new town of Blackstone grew from 4,391 to 5,453.

[6] The road appropriation averaged $580 between 1800 and 1810. In the latter year it reached $700; in 1812, $1,000; and by 1816 an appropriation of $1,200 had been found necessary. Although an average of $460 was voted for town schools during the decade following 1800, $620 was deemed necessary after 1810, and $1,000 after 1828. — D. H. Hurd, *History of Worcester County* (1889), I, 612.

[7] Hurd, *Worcester County*, p. 612.

[8] *Ibid.*, p. 377.

It should be noted that the bulk of the support for this separation seems to have come from voters in the north precinct, a circumstance indicating that taxpayers in that area had become tired of contributing for the provision of services affording them no direct benefits.[9]

By 1850 Blackstone contained 4,391 persons, but its local assessment was small, and its per capita valuation only $389. Mendon had lost three fifths of its population but only one half of its assessment, and hence its per capita valuation was $513 in 1850 as compared with $369 ten years earlier.[10] This town had been relieved of responsibility for a relatively poor industrial area. It is clear that Mendon benefited financially by the incorporation of the town of Blackstone.

II

The decade following 1850 brought a further increase in Blackstone's population, but sharp reductions during the Civil War and between 1870 and 1875 left the town with only 230 more inhabitants in the latter year than it had had in 1850. There were now only three cotton mills with a joint capital of $520,000. Yet this industry was employing 853 persons as against 653 in 1845, while the value of its products was 65 per cent more than it had been at the earlier date. There were six instead of seven woolen mills and the number of their employees had fallen from 514 to 454, but here again the value of the product had risen; it was now 135 per cent higher than it had been thirty years before. Although a good deal of farming was still going on in the northern part of town, the production of textiles continued to dominate Blackstone's economic life.

[9] The *History* published in 1879 contains the following: "By a majority of the former [the residents of the south precinct], the proposition was strenuously opposed; and so did the opposition hold over after the incorporation, that in the first election of town officers the issue was 'Who favored incorporation?' and the officers elected were all men who had opposed it" (I, 280). And this statement appears in the chapter on Mendon in Hurd's *History of Worcester County*: "It appears that very probably a large majority living in what is now Mendon desired division, while divisionists were so unpopular in Blackstone as to be excluded from town office at the first town election" (I, 377).

[10] *History of Worcester County* (1879), I, 280.

The next twenty years brought a further increase of 30 per cent in population and a concentration of the textile industry into two enterprises, one turning out woolens, the other cotton goods. Together these mills were employing a total of 550 persons, which was 757 less than the number engaged in the textile industry in 1875. Most of this discrepancy was offset by the erection of a rubber goods factory employing 641 persons.

The remaining cotton mill, that of the Blackstone Manufacturing Corporation, was situated in Blackstone village. The woolen mill was operated by the Lawrence Felting Company, which in 1877 had absorbed the several woolen mills in Millville.[11] The rubber-goods factory had been built at the latter village in 1882 by the Woonsocket Rubber Company, and had been absorbed subsequently by the newly organized United States Rubber Company. The woolen mills in Blackstone village had been closed as a result of the emigration of this industry into Rhode Island.

Blackstone's population dropped sharply between 1895 and 1900, and showed a further small decline over the period down to 1915, the year preceding the division of the town. About 1904 the Blackstone Manufacturing Company, having become involved in a dispute with the town over a tax abatement, transferred its activities to a new mill just over the Rhode Island line. Sometime after 1900 the United States Rubber Company had absorbed the other Millville enterprise, the Lawrence Felting Company, using the latter's plant to make a lining for the hip boots which were the major product of the rubber-goods mill. As a result of these changes the economic structure of the two precincts of Blackstone became sharply differentiated. The western precinct contained the only substantial industrial enterprise left on the town's tax list. Since there was very little agriculture in this area the precinct was dominated by its single mill and the attendant mill village. The other precinct had lost its industries as a result of the decay of the East Blackstone area, and the removal of the Blackstone river mills to Rhode Island. The northern portion contained some farms, but most of the population was concentrated in Blackstone village, a residential community the ma-

[11] *History of Worcester County* (1879), I, 286.

jority of the inhabitants of which were employed in Woonsocket and in the textile mills just over the Rhode Island line. This working-class population brought a relatively large number of children to be educated, and inflicted upon the town a potentially heavy burden of poor relief. At the same time the industrial property which would normally bear a large portion of the burden had passed from the town's tax roll.[12] Hence the eastern section of Blackstone was in a bad financial position. It was, from this point of view, much worse off than the mill village which dominated the western precinct.

III

This, in short, is the economic background against which the movement for the division of the town must be observed. The first attempt to encroach on the boundaries of Blackstone occurred in 1904 when it was proposed to annex a strip of land on the eastern border of the town to Bellingham.[13] There seems to have been little connection between this and the proposal made in 1906 to separate the two precincts of Blackstone and to incorporate the town of Millville. The latter petition met defeat in the Senate of the General Court;[14] an identical proposal advanced ten years later succeeded after a stormy career,[15] and as a result the Millville district became an independent town.[16]

It is quite evident that local politics played an important part in engineering this separation. The petitioners alleged that their section was not getting its fair share of town offices, and advanced

[12] The Blackstone Manufacturing Company continued to be taxed by the town on its water rights and on certain non-industrial property which remained in the town.

[13] Blackstone Town Report, 1904, p. 3. This proposal was referred to the selectmen. It was brought before the rules committee of the General Court in the following year but was referred to the next session (*Journal of the House*, 1904, p. 161). This seems to have ended the movement.

[14] *Journal of the Senate*, 1906, p. 32.

[15] After having passed both House and Senate the bill was recalled from the Governor for reconsideration. It was passed again only to be vetoed by the Governor on the ground that it did not give the new town the right to collect taxes for the current year. The bill was passed over the veto by a vote of 28 to 4 in the Senate but came near being defeated in the House, where the record vote was 145 to 69. See the *Journal of the House* and the *Journal of the Senate* for 1916.

[16] *Acts and Resolves*, 1916, Special Acts, c. 282.

the claim that they were a submerged minority in town meeting, an argument supported by the fact that in the year after division there were 1,059 male polls in Blackstone, and only 625 in Millville. The liquor policy pursued by the Blackstone town meeting was also questioned, and this of course dragged the churches of the town into the controversy. But behind these issues was a diversity of economic interest which formed the basis for the lack of unity displayed. An understanding of this condition requires a consideration of the finances of Blackstone during the period preceding the separation.

The town's expenditures are summarized in the following table:

Year	Total Expenditures	Total Current Expenditures
	(In thousands of dollars.)	
1890	50.0	38.2
1895	47.6	46.4
1901	54.3	54.3
1907	49.0	41.8
1910	50.0	48.5
1912	44.0	44.0
1916	61.4	58.9

Current expenditures rose rapidly between 1890 and 1895, and continued to move irregularly upwards until 1901. They dropped sharply to 1907, rose slowly during the next three years, dropped again, and then rose to a maximum in the year preceding division. At this time they were 41 per cent in excess of the 1907 level, and 54 per cent above that of 1890. Total expenditures also rose to a maximum in 1916, but were at that time only 23 per cent above the 1890 figure. Reduction to a per capita basis does not alter the movement of either current or total expenditures.[17]

During the early part of the interval it is necessary to rely on tax levy data in order to compare the movement of Blackstone's expenditures with those of all the towns and cities in the state.

[17] The per capita expenditures were as follows:

Year	Total	Total Current
1890	$8.13	$6.22
1895	7.89	7.65
1901	9.48	9.48
1907	8.57	7.18
1910	8.85	8.58
1912	7.92	7.92
1916	10.82	10.35

The town levy rose from $47,300 in 1890 to $53,600 in 1901, an increase of 16 per cent as compared with a 57 per cent increase in the state total. Between 1901 and 1907 Blackstone's tax levy dropped 13 per cent to $46,600, the state total rising more than 20 per cent. It is clear that the town's taxes had increased much less rapidly than was generally the case during the years down to 1901, and that the decline in its expenditures during the following period did not reflect forces common to the state as a whole.

The *Statistics of Municipal Finances* show that the increase in Blackstone's expenditures after 1910 produced a net advance of 21 per cent during the period 1907 to 1915.[18] This was far less than the 46 per cent advance in the state total. Although most of the discrepancy is explained by the relatively slow growth of the town's population,[19] it is striking that Blackstone was spending only $10.90 per capita in 1915 as against an average of $36.10 for the entire state.

The cost of maintaining fire protection, highways, and street lighting, together with the burden of poor relief, had risen sharply between 1890 and 1895; but the remainder of the period under review had brought a significant advance in only one current expenditure. The cost of operating town schools had risen from $13,300 in 1895 to $25,100 in 1916. At the latter date the town's highway expenditure was no larger than it had been in 1901, and although poor relief was on the upgrade after 1910, it was still far below the peak of $11,652 reached in 1897.[20]

[18] Statistics follow:

Year	Blackstone*	Massachusetts†
1907	55.9	90.7
1910	59.0	103.0
1915	67.7	132.1

* In thousands of dollars.　　　　† In millions of dollars.

[19] Blackstone's per capita expenditures advance 14 per cent; the state average 16 per cent.

[20] Current expenditures appear below:

Year	Schools	Highways	Poor	Interest	Lighting	Fire
			(In thousands of dollars.)			
1890......	13.5	3.3	8.4	3.6	.7	.7
1895......	13.3	6.8	11.0	1.2	5.3	1.3
1901......	16.4	7.3	7.4	2.3	5.9	2.2
1907......	19.5	3.7	4.3	2.4	5.0	1.6
1916......	25.1	7.3	6.0	2.6	5.3	1.2

The relatively small change in Blackstone's current expenditures assumes added significance when compared with the movement of the town's estimated total valuation. The latter rose with expenditures from $410 per capita in 1889 to $460 in 1901, declined to $392 in 1907, and then rose with expenditures to $457 in 1916. Since this last figure was only 14 per cent above the extremely low figure given for 1889, it is obvious that Blackstone was still a relatively poor industrial town, a fact which goes far to explain the low level attained by its expenditures during the period now under consideration.

The local valuation on which these expenditures were actually based is given in the following table:

Year	Personalty	Real Estate (In thousands of dollars.)	Total
1890	734.8	1,820.7	2,555.5
1901	683.5	1,981.7	2,665.2
1904	538.7	2,081.6	2,620.3
1905	386.3	1,921.5	2,307.8
1908	340.6	1,903.0	2,243.6
1916	440.3	2,026.8	2,467.1

The period of rising expenditures ending in 1901 brought a steady decline in the value of personalty which, however, was offset by the increase in the real-estate assessment. The latter also began to shrink in the years which followed, the major portion of the decline appearing between 1904 and 1905, apparently as a result of the removal of the Blackstone Manufacturing Company. Although valuations had risen to a level in 1916 about 10 per cent above the low point of 1908, they were still somewhat below the level of 1890, the discrepancy being due almost entirely to the decline in the value of personal property.

It is to be expected that buildings will dominate the real-estate assessment in an industrial town, and it is also to be anticipated that the departure of industries will reduce the relative importance of this type of property. Hence it is quite natural to find the Blackstone building valuation dropping from 67 per cent of the real-estate assessment in 1895 to 61 per cent in 1916.[21]

---

[21] The presence of an industrial establishment adds little to the value of the land on which it is built. It may enhance the value of some business sites in the immedi-

An increase in receipts from the bank and corporation taxes, from $413 in 1890 to $1,224 in 1916, and the addition of revenue from the street-railway tax, which brought in $1,532 in 1916, brought some relief. But these changes were slight in comparison with the rapid increase in expenditures. The latter combined with a net decline in valuations to produce a rise in the town rate from $16.00 in 1895[22] to $24.10 in 1916. This was a net advance of about 50 per cent as compared with one of 28 per cent in the state average, and by 1916 property in Blackstone was being subjected to a rate 25 per cent above the average for the state as a whole.

Town liabilities, which had fallen from $33,800 to $28,800 between 1890 and 1895, had risen to $50,700 in 1899 as a result of the construction of the Millville water supply. There was little change during the next ten years, then a drop to $39,900 in 1912, and a rise to $70,400 in 1916. Since Blackstone now had per capita liabilities of $12.40 as compared with $5.50 in 1890, it is apparent that the advance in the tax rate had not prevented a substantial increase in the burden of debt resting upon property in the town.

Blackstone's financial record for the period prior to its division reflects a striving for economy which is particularly marked during the years immediately preceding the first attempt to incorporate Millville. Nevertheless, a shrinking tax base and the relatively slight relief provided by receipts from state taxes produced a substantial increase in the burden of taxation placed upon property in the town. Per capita liabilities had more than doubled, and the very low per capita valuation in 1916 indicated that the town was by no means well off financially. Under these circumstances it is easy to understand the town's reluctance to increase the scale of its expenditures.[23]

---

ate vicinity, but its effect on good residential property will be unfavorable. Buildings constructed to house a laboring population are themselves of no great value, and add little to the worth of the land on which they are constructed. Hence the chief addition to the town's assessed valuation will be the value of the industrial plant itself and the machinery which it contains.

[22] It had declined from $17.20 in 1890.

[23] The people paying only a poll tax were a very substantial element throughout this period. They constituted half of the total number assessed in 1896, 63 per cent of that total in 1901, 53 per cent in 1909, and 51 per cent in 1915. This element, which would normally be expected to induce a liberal spending policy, does not seem to have controlled the Blackstone town meeting.

It is not to be expected, however, that the residents of the Millville area would entirely favor such stringent economy. This district was in a somewhat more favorable financial position than the eastern section, which was burdened with a large residential population and at the same time could tax no substantial amount of mill property.[24] The larger per capita wealth in the Millville area,[25] and the presence of a large, and at the time flourishing, industrial enterprise, combined with the fact that people paying only a poll tax made up a good majority of the voters in this portion of the town[26] to make the Millville residents take a less pessimistic attitude than that common to the inhabitants of the eastern precinct. Millville would be more anxious to expand, but its wishes could be fulfilled only with the consent of the residents of the eastern area who apparently controlled the town meeting.[27] Since the latter group would necessarily share in the resulting burden of taxation, and since these people could expect to receive no direct benefits in return for the taxes they paid, it is not to be anticipated that their consent would be freely given. In fact it would not be surprising if under these conditions Millville should have difficulty in obtaining services equivalent to those provided for the residents of other parts of Blackstone.

It is quite likely that Millville was not receiving the scale of services which the taxes raised in this area fairly entitled it to receive, and this probability is increased by a consideration of certain peculiarities inherent in Blackstone's expenditures which are not revealed by the statistics presented above.

It is clear that the quality of the Blackstone schools must have been rather low in 1900; the town report for that year called particular attention to the crowded condition of one of the Millville

---

[24] It is interesting to note that Millville, which had in 1916 (Blackstone Report, p. 153) 465 pupils, or 35 per cent of a school population of 1,330, in 1917 had a valuation equal to 45 per cent of the combined valuation of Blackstone and Millville.

[25] The first state assessment after separation came in 1919. At that time Millville had a per capita wealth of $570; Blackstone's was only $475.

[26] In 1917 no less than 448 out of 750 persons assessed by Millville paid only the poll tax.

[27] In 1917 there were 625 male polls assessed in Millville and 1,059 in Blackstone. The total number of persons assessed for taxation in that year was 750 in Millville and 1,059 in Blackstone.

schools, pointing out that the school committee had found it necessary to hold one class in a basement store room.[28] By 1903 the school committee was forced to take action.[29] It added a two-story wing to one of the schools at a cost of $5,605. Although this addition brought an increase of $1,800 in the cost of operating town schools, it proved to be an inadequate remedy for the problem at hand.[30] It is extremely significant that these events took place immediately preceding the first attempt to incorporate Millville as a separate town.

Only one new school was constructed between 1905 and 1916 and that was in the far eastern portion of Blackstone. Moreover, it is quite apparent that the increase in expenditures which took place during the interval had not produced a high quality of school accommodations, for the committee of 1914 was able to point out that Blackstone was spending only $19.18 per pupil as compared with a state average of $38.60. Although these relatively low expenditures constituted a heavy burden,[31] the schools which they supported could not have been very strong.

Direct evidence of the neglect of the Millville schools, present prior to 1906, is absent in the town reports for succeeding years. Nevertheless, the changes noted in the school equipment are such as to make it highly probable that this neglect persisted during the period immediately preceding the division of the town.

A second source of dissension was the question of a water supply. In 1889 the town had installed apparatus in Millville which provided water for the fire department. Since the water

[28] Blackstone Town Report, 1900, p. 103. This committee also pointed out that the schools were operated during a forty-week term, that they had added a business and college preparatory course in the town high school, and at the same time were expected to operate on an appropriation formerly used for a thirty-six-week term and for a high school which lacked the courses mentioned (p. 104).

[29] "In none of the rooms in the buildings referred to was there an enrollment of less than fifty pupils, while in the primary grades the registration at times reached one hundred. The seating capacity was about one half the number enrolled." — *Ibid.*, 1903, p. 122.

[30] In 1905 the school superintendent pointed out that the lower grades were still overcrowded and must remain so. He stated that a new four-room building should have been erected in place of a wing. — *Ibid.*, 1905, Report of the School Committee, pp. 3–6.

[31] The expenditure per thousand dollars assessed valuation was $8.03 in Blackstone as compared with $4.54 in the state at large. — *Ibid.*, 1915, pp. 123–124.

was unfit for drinking purposes, this remedy did not satisfy the residents of the district, and the resulting ill feeling was one of the reasons for the petition of 1906. Blackstone village obtained drinking water from a Woonsocket company in 1912 and this led the people in Millville to insist upon the provision of drinking water in their part of town. In 1914 the Woonsocket company was approached but refused to lay pipes to Millville or to supply this area through pipes rented from the town. The town meeting then voted to establish a municipal water system for Millville and authorized a loan of $20,000 for this purpose.[32] A similar vote was passed in the following year, the loan authorized being increased to $30,000, but up to the time the town was divided no steps had been taken to put the plan into effect.

A third cause of ill feeling between the residents of the two precincts was the expenditure of $10,000 in 1915 and 1916 for the construction of a sidewalk in Blackstone village, the entire expense being borne by the town.

At the time of the separation Millville claimed that it had great difficulty obtaining a fair share of the services provided by the town, and it is clear that a basis for this argument existed. Its schools had been neglected in the years prior to the petition of 1906 and there is reason to believe that they were not up to the quality desired during the period which followed. The Millville area had just been forced to contribute towards the construction of an improvement directly benefiting Blackstone village, while at the same time it had failed to obtain the drinking water it desired. The residents of this area were subject to a town meeting pursuing a policy of persistent economy but nevertheless requiring a tax rate considerably in excess of the average for the state as a whole. In short, Millville paid relatively high taxes and received what it considered to be an unduly small proportion of the services provided by the town. It seems clear that the impossibility of adjusting taxation to benefits received was one of the major causes of the movement which attempted to divide Blackstone in 1906 and ten years later succeeded in incorporating the town of Millville.

[32] *Ibid.*, 1914, pp. 23–24.

IV

There has been no substantial alteration in the economic structure of the two new towns. Blackstone has retained the farming
population living in its northern portions, but continues to be
chiefly a suburb of the neighboring city of Woonsocket. A considerable number of farmers have settled in the northern part of
Millville, but the village surrounding the rubber-goods plant still
dominates the economic life of this area.

As a result the fate of Millville has been vitally dependent on
the fortunes of its single industrial enterprise.[33] This concern was
extremely active during the World War, but its chief product was
manufactured largely for sale in foreign markets and these began
to contract after 1921. In 1929 they were cut off entirely, and at
this time the United States Rubber Company began to shut down
its Massachusetts factories, among them the one in Millville.
Since the subsidiary factory turning out felt products had already
been closed, the town was thrown into an extremely bad financial
position. For this reason it is best to consider separately the
periods before and after 1929 in order that the effects of the
economic depression may not be allowed to confuse the analysis
of the immediate results of the incorporation.

The expenditures of the two new towns during the years
through 1928 are summarized below:

| | Blackstone | | | | Millville | | | |
Year	Total Expenditures Actual*	Per Cap.	Total Current Expenditures Actual*	Per Cap.	Total Expenditures Actual*	Per Cap.	Total Current Expenditures Actual*	Per Cap.
1918..	44.2	$10.50	39.1	$9.35	24.9	$11.20	24.9	$11.20
1921..	69.9	16.20	68.6	15.90	54.5	24.55	40.1	18.20
1925..	134.9	30.05	81.5	18.15	79.3	36.50	51.3	23.60
1926..	105.3	23.35	90.6	20.05	79.3	36.90	65.8	30.60
1928..	152.9	32.90	93.4†	20.30	101.6	47.70	57.1	26.80

* In thousands of dollars.
† After deduction of $6,000 expended for flood relief.

---

[33] During the twenties this mill's property accounted for 50 per cent of the town's
total valuation. For this estimate, as well as for the general story of the events
following the incorporation of the town, I am indebted to Mr. McLaughlin, collector
of taxes during a large part of the period under consideration, and at the present time
the agent of the state board administering the town.

Owing to a delay in completing the financial adjustments incidental to the division of the old town, the Millville and Blackstone
accounts did not become completely independent until 1918.
Hence it was necessary to use this as the base year in the preceding table.[34]

The more accurate comparison is furnished by the per capita
statistics, which show that the smaller town (Millville) had
larger expenditures throughout the period under consideration.
Reduction to a per capita basis also serves to emphasize the relatively rapid rise of Millville's total expenditures, and to demon-
strate that the slightly more rapid advance of current expenditures in Blackstone was more than offset by the relatively large
growth of this town's population. It may be concluded that Millville's spending policy was somewhat more liberal than that pursued by the remainder of the old town.

The total expenditures listed in the *Statistics of Municipal
Finances* show increases of 240 and 250 per cent between 1918
and 1928 in Blackstone and Millville respectively. Since the state
total rose only 118 per cent, it is clear that both towns were increasing their expenditures at an unusually rapid pace.[35]

Before drawing any further conclusions it is necessary to consider the current expenditures in somewhat greater detail. This
can be done with the statistics appearing on the opposite page.
It is apparent at a glance that the bulk of the increase in total
current expenditures was due in both instances to a rapid rise in
the cost of operating schools. Moreover, even though Millville
made no attempt to organize a high school of its own, it was, in

---

[34] No Millville report is available for 1917. The *Statistics of Municipal Finances*
quotes data showing current and total expenditures of $8,400 and $10,200 respectively. These totals are unduly low as compared with those for 1918, and in the light
of a 1917 levy of $19,400. The Blackstone total for 1917, which amounted to
$40,400, included $6,305 spent on joint account.

[35] Statistics follow:

Year	Blackstone*	Millville*	State†
1918	49.9	25.4	143.4
1925	140.1	90.9	280.3
1928	171.1	89.4	312.5

* In thousands.
† In millions.

1918, financing a per capita school expenditure about 30 per cent above that made in the town of Blackstone. In spite of a substantial increase in the per capita cost of operating the Blackstone schools, Millville's expenditures showed a considerably larger increase over the period under consideration. In 1928 the per capita cost of operating its schools was nearly half again as large as in the other town.

A. *Millville*

	1918		1926		1928	
	Actual*	Per Capita	Actual*	Per Capita	Actual*	Per Capita
Schools ...	11.9	$5.70	31.7	$14.75	31.6	$14.85
Highways	3.0	1.35	9.9	4.60	5.1	2.39
Poor	2.9	1.30	3.1	1.44	3.9	1.82
Interest ..	.4	.18	3.2	1.49	2.8	1.31
Lighting ..	1.9	.86	3.1	1.44	3.4	1.60
Fire	.8	.36	2.5	1.16	2.7	1.27

B. *Blackstone*

	1918		1926		1928	
	Actual*	Per Capita	Actual*	Per Capita	Actual*	Per Capita
Schools ...	18.8	$4.37	46.8	$10.30	46.5	$10.00
Highways	4.8	1.12	11.3	2.50	8.0	1.74
Poor	2.6	.61	4.9	1.08	6.9	1.50
Interest ..	2.2	.51	6.8	1.50	6.7	1.45
Lighting ..	3.2	.74	3.6	.80	4.4	.96
Fire	.4	.09	.8	.18	.9	.20
Police	...	....	3.5	.78	3.4	.74

* In thousands of dollars.

Between 1918 and 1928 Millville spent slightly more than $17,000 for the construction of a portable school building and an addition to the overcrowded Longfellow school. In spite of the fact that the equipment in Blackstone was admittedly inadequate,[36] this town made no capital outlays during the decade in question. This fact, together with the record of current expenditures, seems to offer rather definite substantiation for the argument that Millville had been unable to obtain from the Blackstone town meeting a system of schools considered adequate by the residents of this area.

[36] See Blackstone Report, 1918, pp. 46–47; 1919, p. 113; 1921, p. 50; 1922, p. 58; and 1924, p. 25.

Millville's per capita highway maintenance charges were also larger throughout the period, and they too advanced at a more rapid rate than in the parent town. Outlays for highway construction financed with town funds were also slightly higher in Millville than in its more populous eastern neighbor.[37]

It is striking that the new town had not seen fit to provide itself with drinking water in spite of the fact that the failure to supply this service had been one of the charges brought against the Blackstone town meeting.[38] This does not mean that the argument advanced in 1916 was insincere. At that time the residents of the area were paying a part of the cost of bringing water to Blackstone village. Moreover, it is not unlikely that there was some connection between the vote of the sidewalk for Blackstone village and the authorization of a water system for Millville, and under these circumstances it would be natural for the residents of the latter area to feel themselves unjustly treated if their share in the proposed improvements was never received. The fact that Millville rejected the project in later years because of the cost involved does not invalidate the argument that the benefits of town expenditures were not being allocated properly during the years preceding 1916.

In short it is quite clear that Millville provided itself with more expensive services than it would have obtained as a part of the town of Blackstone. It was aided in so doing by its relatively high per capita wealth. The Tax Commissioner's estimate for 1919 was $570 per capita in Millville as compared with $475 in the

---

[37] Highway construction costs for the period 1918 to 1928 were as follows:

	Blackstone	Millville
Total Outlay	$105,129	$88,317
Received from State and County	25,322	8,357
Net Outlay	$79,807	$79,960

[38] In 1918 a committee had been appointed to investigate the feasibility of a municipal water system (Millville Town Report, 1918, p. 13). It had made tests and obtained permission to borrow but had concluded that it would be necessary to pipe water from Uxbridge. This plan failed to receive the approval of the town meeting. The proposal was revived in 1923 (*ibid.*, 1923, p. 16), but again nothing came of it. The water system used by the fire department was extended between 1923 and 1926 at a cost of $6,933.

remainder of the old town; and in 1928 Millville's valuation had
risen to $955 per capita as against $695 in Blackstone. Although
neither could be classed as anything but a poor industrial town, it
is nevertheless true that Millville was considerably better off in
this respect, a fact which tends to alleviate the burden of its relatively high per capita expenditures.

The locally assessed valuations are summarized in the following
table:

A. *Blackstone*

Year	Personalty	Real Estate (In thousands of dollars.)	Total
1917	148.9	1,339.8	1,488.7
1925	354.0	2,093.9	2,447.9
1928	278.7	2,222.2	2,500.9

B. *Millville*

Year	Personalty	Real Estate (In thousands of dollars.)	Total
1917	347.8	859.8	1,207.6
1925	473.3	963.6	1,436.9
1928	443.3	990.0	1,433.3

Although the enactment of the state income tax in 1916 had taken
intangibles from the local tax lists,[39] the personalty remaining on
the rolls of these two towns in 1917 was actually larger than the
amount assessed by the old town in the previous year, a situation
reflecting the small personal wealth of the people residing in this
area. Millville, with a tax base 20 per cent smaller than Blackstone, had 133 per cent more tangible personalty in 1918 than was
listed for the other town. This was due to the absence of industry
in Blackstone and to the importance of the industrial valuation in
Millville. The presence of the rubber goods plant and its attendant
mill village also accounts for the fact that buildings made up 72
per cent of the value of real estate in Millville and only 63 per cent
of the corresponding total in Blackstone.

There was little change in the relative position of the personalty
and building valuations during the next decade, but a substantial
difference appeared between the growth of the two total assessments. The Blackstone total advanced 68 per cent between 1917
and 1928 as a result of this town's suburban development. Mill-

[39] *Acts and Resolves*, 1916, c. 269.

ville, which was less influenced by this factor, experienced an advance of only 19 per cent, which combined with the rapid growth of Millville's expenditures may be expected to produce a considerable advance in the relative burden of taxation borne by property in that area.

Large increases in revenue from the state income tax accrued to both towns. Blackstone obtained $1,795 in 1917 and $17,200 in 1928, the latter sum being sufficient to offset 18 per cent of total current expenditures. Millville's revenue rose from $1,200 to $11,000, the latter figure being equal to 19 per cent of its greatly increased current expenditures. However, since these changes were about of the same magnitude, they have little effect on the probability of a relatively rapid rise in the Millville tax rate.

But receipts from the state corporation taxes were of much more assistance to this town than to Blackstone. In 1918 the latter obtained $328 from this source; in 1927, $1,320; and in 1928, $2,744. Although Millville's income was only $285 in 1918, it jumped to more than $13,000 in 1921.[40] A subsequent decline to $6,493 in 1928 left a net advance far in excess of that accruing to its eastern neighbor.

The results of these various changes are reflected by the tax rates shown below together with the average for the entire state:

Year	Blackstone	Millville	State
1916	$24.10	.....	$19.30
1918	17.60	$14.50	21.50
1919	24.00	24.50	23.75
1924	36.00	24.00	27.71
1926	37.00	50.00	30.34
1928	39.00	43.75	29.07

Both Blackstone and Millville used much lower rates in 1918 than the old town had applied two years before. This, however, was a temporary condition giving place to a rapid advance in both places. By 1928 the Blackstone rate was 62 per cent higher than the one it had used in 1919, and 34 per cent in excess of the

---

[40] This was the result of a change in the tax law removing stock in trade belonging to foreign corporations from the local tax lists and making it taxable as part of the corporate excess. Since the increased revenue from the latter source would be offset by a decline in the personalty assessment, the change was of no real benefit to the town.

current state average. The rate applied to property in Millville had risen even more rapidly and had reached a level half again as large as the average for the state as a whole. It is clear that any advantage in the form of a lower rate which Millville may have gained as a result of its independence was a purely temporary phenomenon. Ten years later property in this area was subject to a burden considerably in excess of the heavy load which increasing expenditures had placed upon the remainder of the town of Blackstone.[41]

The incorporation had set up two towns with small per capita wealth, but in this respect Millville had had a distinct advantage due to the fact that it alone was able to tax a substantial amount of industrial property. Millville was favored by increasingly large receipts from the state income tax, derived substantial revenue from the corporation taxes, and was assisted by a considerable expansion in the local valuation. However, these factors were more than offset by increasing expenditures for highways, fire protection, street lighting, and schools. As a result, the extremely low tax rate used by Millville during the first two years of its separate existence had given place to a rate so high as to put an absolute ban on any further expansion in the services provided by the town. By 1928 Millville's finances had become definitely strained; the town was in no condition to meet the stress of the coming depression, to the effects of which its overly specialized economic structure rendered it unusually susceptible.

Blackstone had been left with less per capita wealth than Millville. Although this town, too, was favored by increasing receipts from the income tax, it received very little assistance from the

[41] The liabilities of the two towns showed the following movement:

Year	Blackstone	Millville
	(In thousands of dollars.)	
1916	70.4	. . .
1918	56.0	*
1920	96.0	35.7
1926	150.0	52.2
1928	85.0	37.1

* Undetermined.

It is striking that their combined liabilities in 1928 were 75 per cent greater than Blackstone's liabilities in the year of the division.

state taxes on corporations. However, Blackstone's expenditures had risen less rapidly and its tax base had grown at a somewhat more rapid pace. Hence, it used, in 1928, an appreciably lower rate than that applied by its western neighbor. Although Blackstone was also in a precarious position, and although its economic structure was not an enviable one, this town was less specialized than Millville and consequently less exposed to the evils of the impending industrial depression.

But before turning to the record of the depression years one further point should be mentioned. The separation had left Blackstone with but 250 persons paying only the poll tax out of a total of 1,059 assessed for taxation. This low percentage had not been maintained, for by 1921 the poll-tax payers constituted a majority of the persons assessed, a condition which continued down to 1928, the last date for which these statistics are available. Although this group does not seem to have dominated the Blackstone town meeting, it possessed considerable political importance.

Millville, on the other hand, had begun its career with a very high percentage of its taxpayers paying only the poll tax. While this element became a minority after 1920 it continued to run the town, owing to the fact that no appreciable percentage of the property-tax payers attended town meeting. This is the same situation which was present in the town of Maynard. It is significant that there as well as in Millville an extremely high portion of the local property tax was borne by a "foreign" corporation. Under these circumstances it is not surprising to find the remaining property-tax payers failing to check the liberal spending policies pursued.

The dominant position occupied by the poll-tax payers in Millville, and the increasing importance of this group in Blackstone during the years following 1921, created a condition peculiarly conducive to extravagant financial policies. The poll-tax payer is in a position to benefit by most of the services resulting from larger town expenditures but bears no portion of the accompanying increased burden of taxation which those expenditures necessitate. It is more than probable that this is the explanation for the excessive expenditures which drove the Blackstone and Millville tax rates up to the precariously high level reached in 1928.[42]

V

Blackstone's total current expenditures rose 24 per cent between 1928 and 1931.[43] Although its school and highway maintenance costs had increased, the bulk of this advance was due to a rapid rise in the burden of poor relief.[44] The highway construction costs (over and above the outlays covered by grants from the state and county) were only $7,612 for the years 1929 to 1931 inclusive, as against $18,627 between 1926 and 1928. The town

[42] The position of the poll-tax payer is shown by the following statistics:

A. *Blackstone*

Year	Number Paying Only Poll Tax (1)	Total Number Assessed (2)	Percentage Column (1) To Column (2)
1917	250	1,059	24
1921	1,144	2,025	55
1925	1,528	2,607	59
1928	1,164	2,280	51

B. *Millville*

Year	Number Paying Only Poll Tax (1)	Total Number Assessed (2)	Percentage Column (1) To Column (2)
1917	448	750	60
1921	331	698	47
1925	331	784	42
1928	294	755	39

[43] The town's expenditures for these years were as follows:

Year	Total	Total Current
	(In thousands of dollars.)	
1928	152.9	93.4
1929	130.8	97.5
1930	126.9	101.0
1931	142.7	115.4

[44] The more important current expenditures are itemized in the following table:

Year	Schools	Poor	Highways	Interest	Lighting	Police
			(In thousands of dollars.)			
1928	46.5	6.9	8.0	6.7	4.4	3.4
1929	46.0	8.2	11.2	5.5	4.7	4.5
1930	45.5	14.1	12.9	4.3	4.4	3.7
1931	49.2	25.3	13.0	3.3	4.5	3.6

made no outlays on its schools, and its total expenditure for 1931 was considerably less than that in the year preceding the collapse of 1929.

Blackstone's wealth was considerably reduced by the depression, the tax commissioner's valuation for 1932 being about 20 per cent less than the estimate for 1928. However, up to 1931 no equivalent reduction had been made in the local tax base. Motor vehicles had been removed from the local lists in 1928, and this measure was responsible for the greater part of a 35 per cent reduction in the personalty assessment.[45] But real-estate values were not seriously lower, and as a result Blackstone's total valuation dropped only 4 per cent between 1928 and 1931. Receipts from the various state taxes were greater at the latter date but paid no larger portion of the town's current expenditures.[46] Hence the town received no relief from this source.

Although Blackstone's declining tax base was accompanied by a rising level of current expenditures, the total expenditures did not experience a similar advance, and it is their movement which seems to determine the course of the town tax rate, as well as the changes in its total liabilities. The latter were sharply reduced in 1928, and since total expenditures were correspondingly high a tax rate of $39 per thousand was required. Liabilities remained

[45] The local valuation moved as follows:

Year	Personalty	Realty	Total
		(In thousands of dollars.)	
1928	278.6	2,222.3	2,500.9
1929	182.3	2,217.2	2,399.4
1930	178.3	2,202.6	2,380.9
1931	182.2	2,221.8	2,404.0
1932	165.7	2,260.1	2,425.8
1933	174.8	2,137.1	2,311.9

[46] The income from this source was as follows:

	1928	1931
Income	$17,205	$19,031
Corporation	2,744	964
Motor Vehicles	......	3,605
Gas	......	1,229
Total	$19,949	$24,829
Per Cent of Current Expenditures	21.4%	21.6%

about the same in 1929, expenditures fell, and the tax rate was reduced. Further debt repayment in the two following years produced tax rates of $54.60 and $44.00 respectively, but by this time the town's debts had fallen to $47,000 from a peak of $150,000 in 1926.

At the time of writing, the only data available for the next two years were contained in the *Aggregates of Polls, Property, Taxes, etc.* These showed a slight increase in total valuation in 1932 and a substantial decline in the following year. This decline was accompanied by a sharp drop in the tax levy from $108,000 in 1931 to $87,600 in 1933. As a consequence the rate fell to $37, which was the lowest achieved since 1926. In spite of a heavy burden of poor relief, and mainly as the result of the retirement of a large portion of its debt, Blackstone was able to survive the worst years of depression. It was extremely hard pressed and forced to bear the burden of a very high tax rate, but managed to emerge with a fairly creditable financial record.

The same cannot be said of Millville. Its current expenditures rose nearly 20 per cent between 1928 and 1931,[47] the bulk of the increase being the result of a rapid advance in the cost of poor relief.[48] Total expenditures, after falling well below their unusually high 1928 figure, rose with current expenditures to 1931. Since the town's income from state taxes had changed but little,[49] the

[47] The town's expenditures were as follows:

Year	Total	Total Current
	(In thousands of dollars.)	
1928	101.6	57.1
1929	75.6	57.5
1930	84.8	68.2
1931	91.8	66.6
1932	64.4	52.9

[48] The more important current expenditures moved as follows:

Year	Schools	Poor	Highways	Interest	Lighting	Fire
			(In thousands of dollars.)			
1928	31.6	3.9	5.1	2.8	3.4	2.7
1929	29.5	4.7	7.2	3.2	3.5	1.9
1930	35.7	8.1	6.7	2.8	3.5	1.8
1931	33.2	15.1	3.0	2.6	3.5	1.7
1932	20.1	14.0	3.2	1.5	2.2	1.5

[49] In 1928 Millville received $11,040 from the income tax and $6,493 from the corporation taxes; in 1931 its income from these sources was $10,556 and $6,491 respectively. It received only $732 from the gas tax in 1931.

effect of these expenditures was almost entirely dependent on the movement of Millville's tax base.

The tax commissioner's estimate indicates that there was 41 per cent less taxable wealth in the town in 1932 than there had been the year before the depression began,[50] but the local valuation shows that this decline was almost entirely due to the collapse of assessed values in 1932. There had been a considerable drop in both personalty and real estate in 1929, but an increase in the valuation placed on machinery and buildings had raised the 1931 total to a level only slightly below that of 1928.[51]

For two years this procedure warded off an increase in the tax rate, but the inevitable advance in expenditures drove the rate up to $49 in 1931, and only a process of raising the assessment on mill property, which was obviously declining in value, kept the rate from rising still higher. In 1932 the United States Rubber Company appealed to the State Board of Tax Appeals and received a substantial abatement. The town officials allowed a proportionate reduction in the value of other property in the town, thus cancelling the effect of the smaller mill valuation but at the same time wiping out 45 per cent of the town's tax base.

Total expenditures were considerably reduced and substantial economies were realized in most of the important current expenditures, but these changes were insignificant when compared with the drop in valuations and as a result the town rate shot up to $75 per thousand.

Millville's indebtedness at the beginning of 1932 was $41,500. By the end of the year its bonded and temporary debt had been reduced to $30,000, but an additional $17,000 was due the rubber

---

[50] The total valuation dropped from $2,034,000 in 1928 to $1,393,900 in 1932.

[51] The statistics are given below:

Year	Personalty	Real Estate (In thousands of dollars.)	Total
1928	443.3	990.0	1,433.3
1929	377.8	961.6	1,339.4
1930	340.9	1,042.7	1,383.6
1931	348.9	1,055.4	1,404.3
1932	228.4	543.5	771.9
1933	68.2	1,106.0	1,174.2

The assessed value of machinery rose from 213.4 thousand in 1929 to 320.7 thousand in 1931.

company as a result of the abatement granted by the Board of Tax Appeals. Against these liabilities the town held claims amounting to well over $57,000, but as the greater part of these became uncollectable in the following year, Millville found itself unable to raise money by taxation, and was soon denied further credit by the banks. It did not seem possible to reduce operating costs any further,[52] and the burden of poor relief continued to mount.

The town soon ran out of cash. It met the needs of its welfare recipients by allowing them to open charge accounts with local merchants and by accepting the resulting bills, but it was not able to provide funds to retire the $14,000 worth of notes which came due in 1933. As a consequence Millville became bankrupt. The General Court put a state board, headed by Tax Commissioner Long, in charge of the town;[53] the regular government was suspended; and an attempt was made to push through a financial reorganization.

A total of $70,000 was borrowed from the Commonwealth, $14,000 of this being used to retire the accruing notes. The accumulated welfare bills were paid and a balance of about $10,000 was devoted to road work. The town's tax levy was cut from $59,000 to $46,900, and real-estate values were raised to within 17 per cent of their 1931 level.[54] As a result the rate dropped back to $39, but tax collections have continued to be extremely difficult and it seems unlikely that Millville will be able to pull out of its present predicament. None of the surrounding towns is in a position to assume the burdens incidental to the annexation of any part of Millville and it seems probable that the latter will remain a state ward for some time to come.[55]

[52] The selectmen pointed out that 70 per cent of the existing expenditures were mandatory (Millville Report, 1932).

[53] *Acts and Resolves*, 1933, c. 341.

[54] The remaining discrepancy is due to the decreased assessment on the mill property. Mr. McLaughlin states that the rubber company was assessed for only $6,000 in taxes in 1934 as against $28,000 in 1932.

[55] In spite of the economic collapse of the town and in spite of the improbability of any industry setting up in the town under present conditions, the population of Millville actually increased during 1934. This is a striking demonstration of the immobility of labor under modern conditions of welfare relief.

Thus ends the story of the most recent of the Massachusetts town separations. It is true that the closing of the rubber-goods plant would have placed a great strain on Blackstone if the Millville area had remained a part of that town. But it is probable that Blackstone's finances would never have become as strained as Millville's were in the years preceding the depression, and it is also true that the shock produced by the economic collapse of Millville village would have been considerably lessened had it been spread over a wider area. On the other hand there was a certain amount of inevitability in the separation under the conditions present prior to 1916. It is not probable that a sizable, compact community possessing a large share of the taxable wealth in a town will remain complacent and inactive when its residents have become convinced that a town meeting which they do not control is imposing high taxes upon them and at the same time is failing to provide them with services even roughly commensurate with the proportion of town taxes paid by residents of this area.[56]

[56] The state commission operating Millville recommended its annexation by the neighboring town of Uxbridge, a proposal which was rejected with great vigor by the inhabitants of the latter town.

CHAPTER IV

THE FINANCES OF THE TOWN OF ADAMS

I

THE territory along the south branch of the Hoosac River, which had been surveyed as early as 1735,[1] was incorporated as the town of Adams in 1778. An additional tract was added to the new town a few years later, only to be taken away again in 1793 at the incorporation of Cheshire. With this single exception Adams retained its original boundaries until 1878, when it was divided by the incorporation of its northern section as the town of North Adams.

The population of the town increased at a fairly even rate until 1820, when a more rapid development began. This resulted in an increase of more than 300 per cent during the first sixty years of the nineteenth century, which was substantially in excess of both the 190 per cent increase in the population of the state as a whole, and the 64 per cent increase shown by Berkshire County.

Adams' rapid growth after 1820 was due to its industrial development, which in turn was based on the water power available along the north and south branches of the Hoosac River. By 1829 there were sixteen textile mills operating in the town.[2] All had been built since 1810, all but six after 1815, and the greatest number during the years following the enactment of the tariff of 1824. These establishments were small spinning mills, the weaving process at this time being carried out with hand looms operated on neighboring farms. The number of spindles in the cotton-goods mills ranged from 144 to 1,092, the number of persons employed from seven to forty. Taken together they were employing a total of 346 persons in 1829. In 1845 a state census enumerated

---

[1] For this and other information regarding the history of Adams I am indebted to Mr. W. B. Browne of North Adams.

[2] John W. Yeomans, "A History of the Town of Adams," in *A History of the County of Berkshire, Massachusetts* (1829).

nineteen textile mills employing 841 persons and having a total capital stock of $153,500. In 1860 there were only seventeen mills, but their combined valuation was in excess of $330,000 and by 1865 sixteen of these mills were employing 1,593 persons.

Adams' population continued to grow. The town contained 6,924 inhabitants in 1860 and 15,760 in 1875, a net gain of 128 per cent as compared with an increase of only 33 per cent in the total for the entire state. This was the period during which the Hoosac tunnel was under construction. A project of such size naturally provided a substantial stimulus to industrial activity in the town containing its western portal while the completion of the tunnel in 1878 made the Boston market much more accessible to the enterprises in Adams, a circumstance that helps to explain the development of the town's industrial life, which in turn was chiefly responsible for the growth shown by its population.[3] In 1875, its eighteen textile mills were producing a product valued at more than $5,900,000. They had at that time an invested capital of $3,600,000 as compared with $153,000 in 1845, and as against an assessed valuation of around $334,000 in 1860. The town also contained at this time a boot and shoe industry producing goods valued at more than $1,000,000, and two paper mills whose product was worth nearly $530,000.[4] However, the textile mills which accounted for nearly 77 per cent of the capital stock invested in the town's industries, and nearly 70 per cent of the value of the goods produced continued to dominate the economic life of Adams.

While the southern part of town contained a rich limestone valley, the northern portion was for the most part rugged and infertile. Hence the early agricultural population had tended to concentrate in the southern area. The subsequent industrial development had produced two distinct villages at opposite ends of

---

[3] The value of agricultural products advanced from $66,939 in 1845 to $179,230 in 1875. However, the total assessed value of all agricultural land, buildings, implements, etc., was less than $1,000,000 in 1874, while capital stock employed in manufacturing totaled $4,768,000.

[4] The boot and shoe industry had produced goods worth $13,850 in 1845. The paper mills appeared for the first time in the census of 1860. They were then awarded a valuation of $40,200. The capital stock of these two enterprises was $290,000 in 1875.

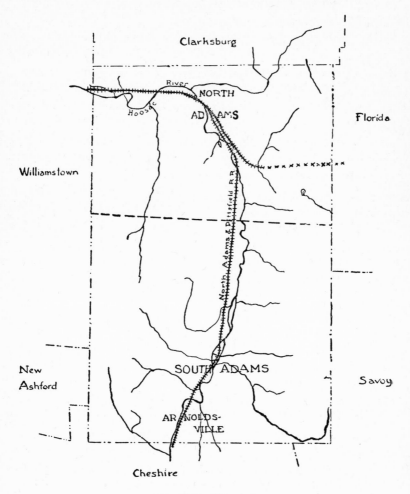

ADAMS IN 1858

SHOWING THE LINE OF DIVISION SET UP IN 1879. THE UNCOMPLETED
HOOSAC TUNNEL IS INDICATED THUS: ✕ ✕ ✕ ✕ ✕ ✕

the town, but the fact that the streams in the north were larger, the facilities for water power more extensive, and the stimulus of the construction of the Hoosac tunnel more direct, brought a relatively rapid growth to the north village. The census of 1880, the first following the division, showed a population of 10,191 in North Adams as compared with 5,591 in the southern portion of the old town.

The relative industrial importance of these two villages is revealed by the state census of 1885. At that date manufacturing enterprises in the southern area were producing goods worth $3,700,000; those in North Adams, nearly $6,500,000. The rather confused material contained in this census indicates that the southern village was dominated by four cotton mills, which accounted for 48 per cent of the value of goods produced, nearly 70 per cent of invested capital, and about 68 per cent of the total number of persons employed in the industrial establishments in the town.[5] North Adams was also dominated by textile mills which accounted for nearly 70 per cent of the value of goods produced in this area. It is worthy of note, however, that the boot and shoe industry, which seems to have been concentrated entirely in the north village, added more than a million dollars to the value of manufactured goods produced in this area in 1885.

A clear picture of this situation — a rapid industrial development concentrated in two distinct and rather widely separated villages, one of which had grown to a considerably greater size than the other — is an indispensable prerequisite to a study of the finances of this somewhat unusual town.

II

Since we are interested in Adams' financial history chiefly because of the light it may throw on the causes for the subsequent division, we may very well begin by considering as a unit the entire period between 1855, the date of the earliest available printed town report, and 1878, when North Adams broke away. A

[5] There was one woolen mill and a paper mill in this area but the census contains no information as to their size.

summary record of Adams' expenditures during this interval
appears below:

	Total Expenditures		Current Expenditures	
	Actual*	Per Capita	Actual*	Per Capita
1855	13.8	$1.98	13.8	$1.98
1868	114.0	10.80	53.4	5.05
1871	108.4	8.45	108.4	8.45
1874	116.1	7.70	90.9	6.05
1877	71.6	4.43	71.6	4.43
1878	104.2	6.38	84.2	5.14

* In thousands of dollars.

Total expenditures mounted very rapidly after 1864, reaching a
maximum of $120,700 in 1869, a year in which the town voted to
purchase a poor farm and spent a very large amount for the construction of new schools.[6] The disappearance of these capital outlays was accompanied by a drop in the total to $97,900 in 1872.
The resumption of school construction and the addition of a large
expenditure for sidewalks brought a rise during the next two
years, which, however, was followed by a downward movement to
1877 and a sharp upswing in the final year of the old town's
existence.

When capital outlays and net payments on debt are removed,
expenditures show a much more comprehensible movement. The
upward swing to a maximum in 1871 was far in excess of the
growth of population, and as a result per capita current expenditures at this date were 325 per cent above the level of 1855. There
was a decided drop between 1871 and 1877 which was only partially offset by a sharp rise in the following year. Hence the per
capita current expenditures for 1878 were 39 per cent less than
they had been in 1871.

The bulk of the increase in current expenditures between 1855
and 1871 is explained by the advance in highway costs from
$3,700 to $22,900, in school maintenance from $2,300 to $36,200,
and by the rise in interest charges from $1,000 to $21,600. The
1871 total also includes $13,000 spent for sidewalks, the first ex-
penditure of this type during the period in question. The decline
to 1877 was mainly the result of reductions of 25 and 40 per cent

[6] The poor farm cost $13,995. A total of $47,853 was spent on school construction.

in the cost of schools and highways; the upswing in 1878 reflects a rise in poor relief, a sizable advance in highway expenditures, and a small increase in the cost of town schools.[7]

The town reports for this period separate the two most significant of these items, namely school and highway expenditures, into those made for the south and those for the north end of town. Highway costs in the latter area dropped from $10,700 to $3,400 between 1872 and 1877, a net decline of 68 per cent, as compared with a drop from $4,900 to $2,000, or 59 per cent, in the southern area. But expenditures for the latter district continued to fall in 1878, while those for the north increased by nearly $2,000 in this final year of the old town's existence.[8]

The cost of repairing and operating schools plus the salaries paid to teachers in the north end dropped from $17,500 in 1873 to about $17,000 in 1878, a decline of about 3 per cent, during a period when the total for the southern area was rising from $9,700 to $11,700, an advance of 20 per cent. In the year of division Adams was spending $1.66 per capita for the operation of schools in the north as against $2.08 per capita in the southern end of town.

These statistics indicate that the curtailment of highway expenditures was not as sharp in the south end until 1878, and that this area had been obtaining an increasingly large portion of the money spent for operating the town schools.[9]

Although the change in Adams' current expenditures cannot be checked directly against that shown by the total for the state

---

[7] Detailed statistics follow:

	Highways*	Schools	Interest	Poor	Sidewalks†
			(In thousands of dollars.)		
1855	3.7	3.3	1.0	1.2	...
1871	22.9	36.2	21.6	5.3	13.0
1877	9.2	27.1	23.3	4.5	.2
1878	11.9	28.7	20.6	7.2	.6

* No attempt has been made to remove capital outlays.
† No information is available as to the location of the sidewalks constructed.

[8] Per capita highway expenditures for 1878 were 53 cents in the north as against 33 cents in the south. This cannot be used as evidence that roads in the latter area were being neglected. Mileage statistics are missing, and it is probable that the maintenance of roads was a more serious problem in the rougher country at the north end of town.

[9] Two new schools were constructed in 1874 and 1875. One was in the north. Its cost was $17,747. The other, in the south end, cost $10,694.

as a whole, it is possible to compare the taxes levied on general property, which during this period supplied the bulk of the revenue expended by the various local governments. The following table supplies the necessary data:

	Adams	Massachusetts
	(In thousands of dollars.)	
1862	20	7,601
1871	140	22,064
1877	104	24,773
1878	113	23,917

It is clear that for the period 1862–1871 Adams' taxes were rising far more rapidly than those for the entire state. It is also obvious that the reduction of Adams' expenditures during the period which followed was not typical of the state as a whole, and that the increase in 1878 came at a time when taxes levied in the state at large were going down.

In 1850 a committee of the General Court estimated that the total taxable valuation in the town amounted to about $1,700,000 or $280 per capita. In 1872 the Commissioner of Corporations and Taxation produced an estimated total of about $6,700,000 or $495 per capita. It is quite evident that the rapidly rising expenditures which characterized this period were accompanied by a very substantial increase in taxable wealth. But the latter rose only slightly between 1872 and 1876 while population continued to grow and as a consequence Adams' per capita wealth dropped from $495 to $420 during these years of declining expenditures. Although the per capita total valuation for 1876 was still 50 per cent in excess of the 1850 total, it nevertheless fell far below the level which would have placed Adams among the wealthy communities in Massachusetts.

The record of the locally assessed valuation which formed the bulk of the town's taxable wealth is summarized in the following table:

	Personality	Real Estate	Total
		(In thousands of dollars.)	
1862	885	1,687	2,572
1872	1,874	3,995	5,869
1874	2,030	4,280	6,310
1877	1,791	4,556	6,347
1878	1,534	4,411	5,945

Although the growth of the tax base was checked after 1874, the subsequent decline in the personal property item was not sufficiently large to prevent a rebound in the total to a new maximum in 1877, and the 6 per cent drop in the total during the year in which the town was divided was not sufficient to produce a net decline over the entire period 1872–1878.

These years saw a sharp reduction in the assessed value of personal property in Adams;[10] they witnessed a decided slowing down in the growth of the town's total valuation; but it is not possible to conclude from this evidence that the period of economy which followed 1872 was one in which the town tax base was being seriously impaired. The combination of a falling tax levy plus a slowly rising total assessment was one which would be expected to produce a substantial reduction in the tax rate adopted by the town meeting.

Moreover, Adams benefited substantially by the receipt of income from the state corporation tax enacted in 1864. The town received $1,588 in 1865. This dropped to $204 in 1870, rose during the next five years, dropped somewhat to 1877, and then increased to a maximum of $4,715 in the last year of the old town's existence.[11] This also is a circumstance which would indicate a reduction in the rate applied to property in the town.

As a result of the great increase in expenditures between 1862 and 1872, the town rate rose from $6.90 in the former year to $23.00 in the latter, advancing from a point more than 20 per cent below to one 55 per cent above the average for the state as a whole. The subsequent moderate growth in the tax base combined with a substantial reduction in current expenditures to reduce the rate to $15.50 in 1877, which was one third less than the rate in effect five years earlier and 17 per cent below the current state average. A sharp drop in valuations and an upward spurt in expenditures brought the Adams rate back to $18.00 in the follow-

[10] This item made up 32 per cent of the total valuation in 1872 and only 26 per cent of the corresponding total in 1878.

[11] Income from the bank tax was of negligible importance. The town began to receive money in 1874, but obtained no substantial amount until 1878, when it received $362. A more significant income was that received in 1878 as a result of the granting of the first liquor licenses. These brought in $7,723, of which $1,903 was turned over to the Commonwealth.

ing year, but this was still 22 per cent less than the rate in force in 1872 when current expenditures had been at their maximum.

In spite of the very substantial increase shown by the town rate between 1855 and 1872, net liabilities, after deduction of cash on hand, rose from $13,900 to $366,800. In part this substantial increase was the result of a subsidy to a local railroad;[12] a somewhat larger share is to be accounted for by military expenditures in 1865 and 1866.[13] About $120,000 was probably the result of school construction between 1868 and 1870, and about $14,000 may be explained by the purchase of a town farm in 1869. The remainder must be accounted for by a simple failure to make current revenues cover current expenditures.[14]

Dissatisfaction with this state of affairs caused the town meeting to embark on a policy of debt repayment which brought a reduction of about 13 per cent in the net liabilities of the town between 1872 and 1878.[15] This policy of debt retirement explains the decline in interest charges during the period in question, and partially accounts for the failure of total to follow the downward movement of total current expenditures.

Thus the period between 1871 and 1873 marks a definite transition in the financial affairs of the town of Adams. In previous years expenditures had been mounting at a pace that far outstripped the rapid growth of the town's total valuation. The tax

[12] Of the 1872 total, $60,000 represented scrip used to purchase bonds issued by the Boston and Troy railroad between 1858 and 1860. Between 1860 and 1876 these bonds paid $1,800 a year, which was sufficient to offset one half of the interest on the town scrip. No interest was received in 1877. The railroad paid $900 in the following year but this was the last interest received. In 1889 the state took over these securities for $3,200, Adams' share being $1,000.

[13] Expenditures for this purpose totaled $41,169 in 1865 and $67,765 in the following year.

[14] It seems highly likely that the affairs of the town were not well managed during this period of rapidly rising expenditures. In 1871 it became necessary to appoint a special committee to investigate the town's finances. The resulting report (Adams Town Report, 1872) charged that selectmen for previous years had drawn orders without receiving vouchers from the party to whom the money was paid, that orders had been paid where no money was due, and that at least one sum had been expended in defiance of the express wishes of the town. In addition this committee charged that the town had received no rent from occupants of the town building, and that the school moneys had been too lavishly handled.

[15] At the latter date total liabilities were $319,600. There was no cash on hand at this time.

rate had risen sharply and net liabilities had reached a maximum in 1872 which was 480 per cent above the level of 1865.

This expansion apparently had brought with it a certain laxness in the administration of the town's affairs.[16] Irritation due to this condition was intensified by the fact that town government was becoming more difficult as a result of the continued concentration of population in two distinct and rather widely separated areas.

The first attempt to alleviate this situation was the lumping together, in 1872, of the selectmen, assessors, highway surveyors, and overseers of the poor in a single board having general supervision over the affairs of the town. Hope was expressed that this measure would subject town business to a more careful scrutiny, and hence check the growth of expenditures.[17] It is obvious also that the device of a large board made possible more adequate representation of the several factions in town meeting and thus seemed to offer remedy for an increasingly difficult problem.[18]

That this was immediately recognized to be an inadequate solution is indicated by the following excerpt from the selectmen's report for 1873:

"We doubt whether any town in this Commonwealth is discommoded more than ours in respect to the transaction of its business affairs. The North and South villages are situated six miles apart, each important in population, in manufacturing, mercantile, and other important pursuits. These villages seemingly represent distinct interests, and in the management of the business matters of the town represent two towns in many respects."

As a possible solution to the problem of conflicting interests it was suggested that the town meeting consider the possibilities of incorporating as a city, but nothing came of this proposal. Adams continued to operate under a single large board of town officers acting on the orders of town meetings which were held alternately in each of the two villages. The retrenchment policy

---

[16] See Note 14 above.

[17] Adams Town Report, 1872.

[18] The board was reduced in size from nine to five in the next year, owing to the establishment of a school committee.

pursued during this period was quite apt to increase the tension in relations that were already strained, and this is particularly to be expected in the light of the fact that there were grounds for believing that the northern area was bearing somewhat more than its share of the inconveniences involved.

By 1876 dissatisfaction with the existing situation prompted an appeal to the General Court for division of the town.[19] The failure of this proposal did not prevent another unsuccessful appeal in the following year. In 1878 the state senate sanctioned division in the event that a proposed act should be acceptable to two thirds of the legal voters in Adams. The latter restriction was removed upon the remonstrance of the majority of the business men in both villages, and North Adams was then incorporated as a separate town.

III

Some conception of the forces which brought about this separation may be derived from the subsequent behavior of the two new towns. The population of the southern area increased 48 per cent between 1880 and 1885, while that of North Adams increased only 23 per cent. The former continued to grow until 1890, but the subsequent decline was sufficient to produce a net loss of about 6 per cent for the decade ending 1895.

Adams' rapid growth during the early eighties was apparently due to an influx of laborers attracted by its industrial development.[20] The decline after 1890 was just as clearly associated with difficulties encountered by the cotton mills in the town, the invested capital represented by these enterprises totaling $2,600,000 in 1895 as against $5,000,000 ten years earlier. The value of the goods produced had fallen from $1,798,000 to $1,653,000; the number of persons employed had dropped from 2,021 to 1,746.

[19] *Facts Concerning Town Divisions*, p. 3. This was the second of these proposals, the first having been made in 1861.

[20] The selectmen pointed out in 1883 that the increased burden of poor relief was to be "accounted for in a great measure by the great influx of population, most of whom are workmen and by far too often in destitute circumstances" (Adams Town Report, 1883, p. 20).

The population of North Adams increased throughout the period, reaching in 1895 a level about 87 per cent above that prevailing when this town was incorporated.[21] The value of the products of its manufacturing establishments increased from $6,500,000 to $14,200,000 between 1885 and 1895, the bulk of the total again being accounted for by the textile and the boot and shoe industries.

Because of the abrupt change in Adams' development during the nineties this comparison of the financial history of the two new towns has been restricted to the decade immediately following their incorporation. Total and total current expenditures are presented for selected years in the following table:

A.   Adams

Year	Total Expenditures		Total Current Expenditures	
	Actual*	Per Capita	Actual*	Per Capita
1879	20.9	$3.72	20.9	$3.72
1880	25.5	4.55	20.5	3.67
1884	62.7	8.10	34.2	4.40
1889	65.3	7.25	45.3	5.00

B.   North Adams

Year	Total Expenditures		Total Current Expenditures	
	Actual*	Per Capita	Actual*	Per Capita
1879	63.5	$6.22	63.5	$6.22
1880	59.5	5.85	51.1	5.00
1884	97.8	8.10	67.7	5.60
1889	129.4	8.40	92.7	6.05

* In thousands of dollars.

Since the unusually large amount paid for interest charges distorts the 1879 total in North Adams, the statistics for 1880 furnish a somewhat fairer indication of the relative amounts being spent in the two villages at the time the town was divided. It is quite clear that expenditures were substantially higher in the northern area, and that this discrepancy is not to be explained away by differences in population. It is also clear, however, that expenditures rose considerably more rapidly in the southern area during the subsequent decade, and this too is not to be accounted for entirely by the relatively rapid growth of population in this district.[22]

[21] In 1895 Adams contained 7,837, North Adams, 19,135 inhabitants.
[22] Between 1880 and 1889 total expenditures in Adams rose 155 per cent as against

The resulting changes in the tax levies of the two new towns are compared with the movement for the state as a whole in the following table:

Year	Adams*	North Adams*	Massachusetts†
1879	36.5	77.2	21.2
1885	61.5	105.4	28.7
1889	61.1	104.3	29.4

* In thousands.
† In millions.

In all three instances the tax levy rose rapidly to a peak around 1885, declined in the years which followed, and recovered sharply in the final year of the period under review. It is clear, however, that both the new towns raised their taxes a great deal more rapidly than did Massachusetts as a whole. It is also obvious that this increase was concentrated in the period immediately following the division of the old town.

The more important items among the current expenditures which these taxes financed are summarized in the following table:

A. Adams

Year	Highways	Schools	Interest	Poor	Police
		(In thousands of dollars.)			
1879	3.1	10.0	5.1	1.4*	...
1884	4.3	14.3	7.3	3.7	.05
1889	5.9	24.2	3.8	3.4	.05

B. North Adams

Year	Highways	Schools	Interest	Poor	Police
		(In thousands of dollars.)			
1879	8.4	16.1	26.8	4.3	...
1884	10.4	24.3	9.6	6.6	4.9
1889	21.5	33.7	7.0	6.6	6.8

* Includes expenditures of $883 due for this year but not paid until 1880.

School expenditures and poor-relief costs expanded more rapidly in Adams. North Adams spent a great deal more for highways and police protection. In addition it paid out a total of $27,477 between 1880 and 1889 for the purpose of constructing and main-

---

113 per cent in North Adams. Per capita total expenditures rose 59 per cent in the former, and 43 per cent in the latter. Total current expenditures rose 120 per cent in Adams, 80 per cent in North Adams. Per capita current expenditures rose 36 per cent in Adams and 21 per cent in North Adams.

taining sewers, a service which the remainder of the town of Adams did not begin to provide until 1890.

These statistics must be reduced to a per capita basis before an adequate notion of the relative level of expenditures in the two towns can be obtained. This has been done in the following table:

A. Adams

Year	Highways	Schools	Interest	Poor	Police
1879	$.56	$1.78	$.91	$.25	...
1884	.55	1.85	.94	.48	$.01
1889	.65	2.68	.42	.37	.06

B. North Adams

Year	Highways	Schools	Interest	Poor	Police
1879	$.82	$1.62	$2.62	$.42	...
1884	.82	2.00	.80	.54	$.41
1889	1.40	2.20	.46	.43	.44

In 1879 Adams had been spending more generously in only one item, the cost of operating town schools. Its highway and poor-relief expenditures were only 46 and 68 per cent of those incurred by its northern neighbor. The general advance in current expenditures during the following decade did not seriously alter these relationships, and in 1889 the smaller town was still spending more per capita for its schools, while North Adams was spending more than twice as much per capita on its highways, and 16 per cent more for poor relief. North Adams alone was paying out substantial sums to provide its inhabitants with police protection.

Over the period 1879 to 1889 Adams spent $59,500 for school buildings as compared with $65,000 in the more populous town. North Adams spent a great deal more on the construction of highways, but the cost of a new town hall brought Adams' total outlays to $136,000 as compared with $132,900 in North Adams. Taken together, the two new towns spent $268,985 as compared with an outlay of $169,507 made by the old town during the eleven years preceding the division.

There is, thus, a striking contrast between the open-handed spending policies pursued by the new towns in the period following 1879 and the striving for economy which had been so marked during the last years of the old town's existence. It was obviously easier to obtain appropriations from meetings dominated by citizens who benefited directly by increased expenditures for schools, highways, sewers, and police protection than to obtain similar grants from a town meeting which was the battleground of two distinct factions neither of which would benefit to any considerable extent as the result of concessions made to the desires of the other.

The new towns which had pursued these spending policies had begun their careers with approximately the same per capita wealth. That of North Adams had declined during the next six years while the Adams total was rising. As a result the latter possessed in 1889 a valuation of $440 per person which was 17 per cent higher than the per capita total of $375 in North Adams. It is obvious, however, that neither town remotely approached the valuation necessary to give it the status of a wealthy community.[23]

The local tax base upon which property taxes were levied showed the following movement:

Year	Personality		Real Estate		Total	
	Adams	North Adams	Adams	North Adams	Adams	North Adams
			(In thousands of dollars.)			
1879	596	1,040	1,425	3,036	2,021	4,076
1884	1,030	1,391	1,847	3,548	2,877	4,939
1889	1,161	1,341	2,297	4,270	3,458	5,611

The total valuation rose steadily in both towns, but the net advance in Adams was 72 per cent as compared with 38 per cent in North Adams. A similar lag appears in the taxable value of both real estate and personal property. Thus the town in which expenditures were advancing more rapidly was also benefiting by a relatively rapid growth in the base upon which the resulting taxes were assessed.[24]

[23] The following statistics make this clear:

Year	Adams		North Adams	
	Actual*	Per Capita	Actual*	Per Capita
1883	3,078	$427	4,769	$410
1886	3,641	430	5,260	398
1889	3,961	440	5,772	375

* In thousands of dollars.

[24] It is of course to be expected that buildings will make up a relatively large portion of the real-estate assessment in an industrial community. Hence it is not surprising to find that in 1889 buildings constituted 69 per cent of the North Adams real-estate valuation and 67 per cent of the corresponding total in Adams.

Receipts from the state bank and corporation taxes must also be taken into account:

| | Adams | | North Adams | |
Year	Receipts	Per Cent of Current Expenditures	Receipts	Per Cent of Current Expenditures
1879	$1,211	5.8	$2,322	3.7
1884	5,407	15.8	2,955	4.4
1888	10,542	23.9	3,298	3.5
1889	7,287*	16.0	3,208	3.5

* Includes $3,101 due for this year but received in 1890.

It should be pointed out that during this period the proceeds of these two taxes, in so far as they were paid on the basis of corporate shares owned by residents of Massachusetts, were distributed to the towns and cities in which the shareholders resided. Adams' income from this source soon exceeded that of its northern neighbor, reaching a total in 1888 sufficient to pay nearly one fourth of the town's current expenditures. A sharp decline in this revenue during the following year left an income which was still capable of paying 16 per cent of current expenditures. It is a striking fact that no comparable income was received by North Adams.

Further relief for the property-tax payer was provided by what is normally a minor source of revenue, namely, liquor licenses. Adams received $2,498 on this account in 1880, and by 1889 these receipts had grown to $12,128, a sum that was in the neighborhood of 27 per cent of the town's total current expenditures. North Adams' receipts rose from $8,700 in 1881 to $21,300 in 1889, and at the latter date this income was sufficient to pay 23 per cent of the total current expenditures.

Thus, the liberal spending policies pursued by the two towns during the period following their separation must be set off against the growth of the local tax bases, against increased receipts from liquor licenses, and in the case of Adams against a very substantial increase in income from the state corporation taxes. The net result of these changes is to be found in the movement of the tax rates. North Adams began its career with the same $18.00 rate used by the old town in 1878. The Adams rate was one dollar per thousand less. The subsequent movement is very irregular, but in

1889 Adams was using a rate of $16.50 while property in North Adams was subject to a levy of $17.00 per thousand. This downward tendency conflicts sharply with the rise in the state average from $12.54 in 1879 to $14.68 in 1889.

The net liabilities of both the new towns dropped sharply to 1882, rose in the following year, and declined to the end of the period under review. The Adams total for 1889 was $56,900 as compared with $101,700 in 1879. The North Adams total had dropped from $203,700 to $124,500. This reduced the per capita liabilities in the former town from $18.20 to $6.30 and brought the total for North Adams from $20.00 to $8.10 per capita.

Thus, the rise in expenditures during the period following the division of Adams was not sufficiently rapid to prevent a downward movement in the tax rate and a very substantial reduction in the burden of indebtedness resting upon property in the two new towns.

There is no indication in all this that the separation of 1879 was put through in the particular interest of either the north or the south village. The new towns had about the same per capita wealth. They both benefited during the subsequent decade by a substantial growth in the base upon which local property taxes were levied. Liquor licenses brought substantial relief to taxpayers in both instances. Both towns found it possible to expand their corporate standard of living and at the same time bring about a substantial reduction in their current liabilities without raising the rates applied to property within their borders.

Of the two, Adams seems to have been somewhat more favored. It alone received substantial revenues from the state corporation taxes, and its rate was consistently lower than that effective in North Adams in spite of the fact that its current expenditures were advancing at a relatively 'rapid pace. But it is the uniformity of experience of the two new towns which is most striking. In both there were spending campaigns of sizable proportions contrasting sharply with the record of the old town during the years immediately preceding division. The evidence goes far towards substantiating the theory that one of the underlying causes of this division was the impossibility of obtaining desired appropriations from a town meeting that always contained a sizable faction which would derive no substantial benefits from the proposed expenditures, and at the same time would be forced to assume a sizable portion of the resulting tax burden. It is evident that we have again been dealing with a situation in which trouble has arisen out of the impossibility, under the existing organization, of bringing about a reasonable adjustment between local taxation and benefits received.

IV

A projection of this comparison between the financial experiences of the new towns into subsequent decades would add little to the results obtained in the preceding section. However, the town of Adams soon developed peculiarities which lend more than the usual amount of interest to its financial affairs, a circumstance which warrants a sketch of this town's subsequent financial history. As in previous cases it will be found convenient to subdivide the interval between 1890 and the present day into two parts at the year 1916, which is at the same time the end of the pre-war era and the year in which the state income tax was established.

It has already been pointed out that the growth of Adams' population had slackened after 1885, and that its population had shown a net decline of 15 per cent during the five years following 1890. This, it will be recalled, was associated with a sharp reduction in the invested capital, employment, and the value of goods produced by the four cotton mills in the town. The textile industry expanded considerably during the next decade. Its invested capital rose from $2,600,000 to nearly $6,200,000 between 1895 and 1905; the value of goods produced increased from $1,200,000 to $4,600,000; the number of employees was raised from 1,746 to 3,502.

This revival was undoubtedly associated with the rapid development of the enterprises operated by C. T. and W. B. Plunkett. These men were members of one of the oldest families of mill owners in Adams, but it was not until the period now under consideration that the Plunkett enterprises began to dominate the economic life of the town. Thus in 1889 the bulk of this family's property was incorporated as the Berkshire Cotton Manufacturing Company, and it was the growth of this enterprise, together with the smaller Greylock Shirt Company,[25] also managed by Mr. C. T. Plunkett, which accounts for the rapid development of the textile industry in Adams after 1895. Although there were two sizable paper mills operating in the town at the end of this period, the textile industry was definitely the most important factor in Adams' economic life, and the industry in turn was dominated by the enterprises operated by the Plunkett family. The response to this development was a rapid increase in population to a number which in 1915 was 60 per cent in excess of the population of 1895.[26]

Town expenditures reacted as follows:

Year	Actual*	Total Per Capita	Actual*	Total Current Per Capita
1889	65.3	$7.25	45.3	$5.00
1895	57.6	7.35	57.6	7.35
1899	111.1	10.60	86.8	8.30
1910	160.1	12.30	115.7	8.90
1916	186.5	14.15	147.8	11.20

* In thousands of dollars.

Current expenditures continued to rise during the years when population was declining, and total expenditures, which had not participated in this advance, joined the upward movement after 1895, reaching a maximum four years later at the time of the Spanish American war. The decade as a whole produced a net advance of 46 per cent in per capita total expenditures, and one of 66 per cent in per capita current expenditures.

There was a sharp reduction in 1900, followed by a resumption of the upward movement, which, in the case of current expendi-

[25] Organized in 1872 as the Greylock Manufacturing Company by General William Plunkett.
[26] Census data follow:

Year	Adams	Year	Adams
1890	9,213	1905......	12,486
1895	7,837	1910......	13,026
1900	11,134	1915......	13,218

tures, did not greatly outstrip the growth of population until after 1910. As a result, per capita total and total current expenditures reached levels in 1915 which were 35 and 33 per cent respectively higher than those prevailing in 1899.

The years of declining population witnessed a substantial increase in only one item among current expenditures, namely, poor relief, which rose from $3,000 to $9,000 between 1889 and 1895. The rapid growth of population during the next four years brought sizable increases in the cost of providing schools, highways, and police protection.[27] The subsequent period of slow growth which ended around 1910 was marked by a continued rise in all the important current expenditures, but the sharp upswing during the next six years was concentrated in the school and highway accounts.[28]

The only important capital outlays made prior to 1908 were those for the construction of a school building in 1891, and a town hall paid for mainly in 1898 and 1899. The year 1908 marked the opening of a sizable program of school and highway construction, the school outlays being completed by 1911, the road construction continuing throughout the remainder of the period under review.[29]

Thus the record of Adams' expenditures divides itself into four rather distinct periods. There was an interval of slow growth between 1889 and 1895, followed by a much more rapid expansion during the next four years. The result was an advance in the town tax levy considerably greater than that shown by the total for the entire state.[30] A period of more leisurely expansion followed, during which the town tax failed to advance at a rate equivalent to that shown by the state total.[31] A more rapid up-

[27] Between 1895 and 1899 school expenditures rose from $27,200 to $37,400, highway costs from $6,400 to $11,200, and police protection from $1,300 to $5,900.

[28] Between 1910 and 1916 highway costs rose from $19,000 to $25,800 and school expenditures from $47,400 to $56,000.

[29] The school construction of 1891 cost about $25,000, the town hall in the neighborhood of $42,000. Between 1908 and 1911 Adams spent $102,000 for school construction. A total of $171,000 was spent building roads between 1908 and 1916.

[30] The town tax levy rose from $61,100 to $94,500 between 1889 and 1899; the state total rose from $29,400,000 to $43,800,000 during this same interval.

[31] Between 1899 and 1908 the town levy rose from $94,500 to $111,900, an in-

ward movement set in after 1908, bringing the town's total expenditures to a level about 188 per cent above that prevailing in 1889. Nevertheless, it remains true that the town was spending a great deal less per capita in 1916 than the state at large.[32]

The local tax base which supported the bulk of these expenditures moved as follows:

Year	Personalty	Real Estate		Total
		Buildings	Land	
		(In thousands of dollars.)		
1889	1,161	1,541	757	3,459
1891	1,263	1,622	765	3,650
1893	1,080	1,609	771	3,460
1899	1,788	1,976	848	4,612
1916	2,852	3,149	1,089	7,090

The upward movement of local assessments continued until 1891. There was a sharp drop in the personalty and building valuations during the next two years[33] which gave place to an upward movement that continued at an approximately uniform pace throughout the remainder of the period studied.

The town tax base approximately doubled between 1889 and 1916. The building assessment kept pace with this increase and personal property advanced even more rapidly, but the land valuation displayed a very noticeable lag. As a result, the latter made up only 15 per cent of the total in 1916. The relatively large value of personal property and of buildings is indicative of the increasingly industrial character of this community, the bulk of its tax base being accounted for by the assessments placed upon mill buildings and the machinery which they contained.[34]

---

crease of 18 per cent. The state total rose from $43,800,000 to $59,900,000, an advance of 36 per cent.

[32] *The Statistics of Municipal Finances* indicate that the town was spending only $15.90 per capita in 1916 as compared with a state average of $38.10.

[33] This was due to the closing down of one mill and the burning of another. The latter, the Renfrew mill, was subsequently rebuilt.

[34] Between 1916 and 1917 intangible personal property was removed from the local tax lists, the income from this property being henceforth subject to the state income tax. This change brought a drop of only $25,000 in the personal property assessment. It is clear that the bulk of the personalty in this town was of a tangible nature. No data as to valuation of machinery are available until 1929, but in that year this item constituted $3,871,970 out of a total personalty assessment of $4,288,745. Of the remainder, $269,050 was accounted for by stock in trade.

Income from the state bank and corporation taxes dropped from $7,287 in 1889 to $2,403 in 1896. Receipts from this source increased almost steadily throughout the remainder of the period under review. A substantial advance appeared in 1902, and further sharp increases came in 1907 and 1910 as a result of changes in the method of distributing the receipts of the corporation tax.[35] By 1916 income from these taxes was sufficient to pay 23.7 per cent of Adams' total current expenditures.[36]

Liquor licenses provided a substantial income throughout the period,[37] and in 1910 the street railway tax began to yield some revenue,[38] but it is mainly to the substantial growth of the town's tax base and to the rapid increase in receipts from the state corporation tax that we must attribute the considerable increase shown by the Tax Commissioner's estimate of total taxable wealth. The latter had dropped from $3,961,000 in 1889 to $3,894,000 in 1895 and the increase during the next six years had been more than matched by the accompanying growth of population.[39] But an increasingly rapid rise during the years which followed brought the 1916 estimate up to $9,000,000, or $685 per capita, which was 128 per cent above the estimate for 1889.

The result of the substantial net increase in expenditures, the growth of the local tax base, and the rising receipts from the state corporation taxes may be seen in the movement of the rate levied on property in the town. This is given in the following table together with the average for the state as a whole:

Year	Adams	Massachusetts
1889	$16.50	$14.68
1895	14.50	14.80
1899	19.50	15.69
1910	20.00	17.60
1916	20.00	19.14

[35] *Acts and Resolves*, 1908, c. 614; *ibid.*, 1910, c. 456.

[36] The bank tax was of negligible importance. The town's income from this source in 1916 was $343.

[37] Liquor licenses yielded $12,000 in 1889, and $19,000 in 1916.

[38] The largest amount received from this tax was less than three thousand dollars in 1915. We must conclude that this type of revenue was of small importance to the town of Adams.

[39] The per capita estimate for 1895 was $495; for 1901, $460.

The reduction of expenditures between 1889 and 1895 brought a substantial drop in the town rate, causing it to fall from a point 12 per cent above to one slightly below the average for the entire state. The period of rapid development which ended in 1899 brought the town rate to a point 24 per cent above the current state average, and the slight reduction during the years which followed was wiped out by the increase after 1907. It is clear that the substantial growth of the town tax base and the rapid increase in income from state taxes did not prevent a rise of 20 per cent in the rate applied to property over the period as a whole. The state average, however, had advanced even more rapidly, and as a result the town rate, which had been a full 12 per cent above that average in 1889, was only slightly higher than the current average at the end of the period under review.

The town's net liabilities dropped from $56,900 in 1889 to $47,300 in 1907, in spite of a large loan floated in 1898 to finance the construction of the new town hall. The subsequent program of school and highway construction brought Adams' net liabilities to a maximum of $152,000 in 1912, which was followed by a reduction to $101,600 in 1916. There was a net advance of 78 per cent for the period as a whole. Reduced to a per capita basis it meant a rise from $5.45 to $7.73, an increase of 42 per cent, substantially less than the 72 per cent increase in estimated per capita taxable wealth.

It is clear that the latter portion of the period under consideration was marked by a definite expansion in the town's corporate standard of life. Per capita current expenditures for 1916 were more than twice as large as those made in 1889. The 56 per cent increase in the local tax base and the rapid rise in income from state taxes were not sufficient to prevent a net advance of about 20 per cent in the town rate and a 78 per cent increase in the town's total net liabilities. Yet we find that in 1916 Adams was spending only half as much per capita as was customary in Massachusetts as a whole, and that the town was using a rate which was only 4 per cent in excess of the state average as compared with a town rate 12 per cent above the current average in 1889. The town's liabilities were not advancing as rapidly as its taxable wealth, and we may be fairly certain that no charge of undue extravagance could be brought against the Adams town meeting for the financial policies pursued during the period now under review.

This conclusion is particularly significant when considered in the light of the following statistics:

Year	Poll-tax Payers (1)	Total Taxpayers (2)	Per cent Column (1) to Column (2)
1889	1,459	2,298	64
1895	1,151	2,056	56
1899	1,658	2,620	63
1910	2,032	3,328	61
1916	1,935	3,848	50

It is apparent that the poll-tax payers must have constituted a substantial majority of the town's voting population throughout the period in question. As a result, we should expect on *a priori* grounds that the Adams meeting would pursue relatively extravagant spending policies. The failure of such extravagance to appear in this instance is to be attributed to the personal influence of Mr. C. T. Plunkett, who had built up the industrial enterprise that had become the backbone of the town's economic life. The interest which this man took in the affairs of the town and the high esteem in which his opinions seem to have been held is quite clearly the explanation for the relative slowness of the rise in town expenditures. It is highly unlikely that in the absence of such a restraining influence an electorate of this type would have resisted the temptation to spend freely, particularly during a period when increased receipts from state taxes and a substantial growth in the local tax base were creating a condition of financial ease favorable to liberal spending policies.

V

There was a net decline of 4 per cent in Adams' population between 1915 and 1930,[40] a fact which reflects a definite decline in the economic health of the community. Two textile mills were

[40] Census data follow:

1915	13,218		1925	13,525
1920	12,967		1930	12,697

closed during the twenties and an iron foundry became practically inoperative. The Berkshire Cotton Manufacturing Company continued to show a favorable dividend record during the first half of this decade,[41] but the death, in 1928, of its president, Mr. C. T. Plunkett,[42] was followed by the absorption of this enterprise by the newly formed combination known as the Berkshire Fine Spinning Associates.[43] The latter organization has not been particularly successful; its Adams mills have grown increasingly inactive.

At the present writing, the narrowing economic life of the town centers around the mills owned by the Berkshire combination, the one remaining warp mill operated by the Plunkett family (W. C. Plunkett and Sons), and two rather moderate-sized paper mills. Adams now approaches the status of a single-industry town, a circumstance which makes its financial welfare depend upon the success of its dominant enterprise, and exposes the town to very serious hardships during periods of acute industrial distress. The truth of this proposition is apparent in the town's recent financial experiences.

Adams' expenditures during the period following 1916 are summarized below:

Year	Total Expenditures	Total Current Expenditures
	(In thousands of dollars.)	
1916	186.5	147.8
1922	434.1	368.1
1923	674.7	335.2
1928	453.4	414.5
1932	718.1	572.5
1933	395.2	379.9

Current expenditures rose nearly 150 per cent between 1916 and 1922. A sharp cut in the following year was followed by a rather slow increase which continued down to 1928, the year of Mr. Plunkett's death. A much more rapid rise began in 1929 and carried total current expenditures to a maximum in 1932 nearly four times as high as the figure for 1916. This increase was

---

[41] *Poor's Manual of Industrials,* 1929, p. 82.
[42] Mr. W. B. Plunkett had died about ten years earlier.
[43] *Poor's Industrials,* 1931, p. 170.

followed in turn by a drastic 34 per cent reduction in the final year of the period under review.

Total expenditures pursued a somewhat similar course, rising to a high point in 1923, tapering off to 1928, and then advancing sharply to a maximum in 1932 which was about 380 per cent of the 1916 total. As in the case of current expenditures, there was a drastic reduction in the final year for which statistics are now available.

The rapid rise in total expenditures between 1916 and 1922 was accompanied by marked increases in all important types of current expenditures, but the lion's share of this advance was the result of increasing school and highway expenditures and an extremely large increase in the cost of operating the town police and health departments.[44] The bulk of the latter increase represents the cost of operating a hospital given to the town by Mr. Plunkett.

The reduction of current expenditures in 1923 was due almost entirely to a sharp curtailment of highway costs. The slow rise to 1928 was reflected mainly in the school, poor-relief, and public health accounts. It is striking, however, that the more rapid increase that followed was due mainly to the startling rise in poor-relief costs from $39,000 in 1928 to $220,000 in 1932. Apparently the free-spending policy which characterized the years following 1928 manifested itself very largely in the form of a liberally administered system of poor relief. This conclusion finds considerable support in the fact that when economy became inescapable in 1933 the town found it possible to reduce its welfare expenditures from $220,000 to $114,000.[45]

[44] Detailed statistics follow:

Year	Highways	Schools	Interest	Poor	Health	Police
			(In thousands of dollars.)			
1916	25.8	56.0	8.1	14.5	2.9	2.6
1922	83.6	120.9	19.8	27.3	25.1	25.5
1923	42.0	123.7	29.3	24.2	26.4	25.8
1928......	41.0	160.7	28.6	39.0	41.6	26.2
1930......	53.3	163.5	24.5	58.2	45.0	27.0
1932......	29.7	157.4	38.9	220.3	42.5	26.5
1933......	12.7	121.7	32.2	114.2	35.0	18.4

[45] It must be recognized that Adams received $20,945 in 1933 from the Federal Emergency Relief Administration, and that there was no income of this nature in

The economy program also served to bring highway costs to a level which was only 24 per cent as high as that of 1930. At the same time a 33 per cent reduction in the salaries of school teachers and a 20 to 50 per cent drop in those of town officers assisted materially in a sharp curtailment of school, police, and health-department expenditures. Yet the net effect of these heroic economies was considerably less than the 48 per cent reduction in the cost of maintaining the town's poor.

The years between 1917 and 1921, which, it will be recalled, were marked by rapidly rising current expenditures, are notable for substantial outlays on highway construction.[46] These costs continued to mount in succeeding years, but their advance was overshadowed by the size of the capital expenditure for schools, the bulk of the latter representing the expense of constructing a junior high school towards the cost of which Mr. Plunkett gave more than $100,000.

There was a distinct decline in capital outlays during the period following 1927, but the last two years of the period under review produced a striking increase in highway expenditures at a time when other capital outlays were at a very low level. This road construction was concentrated almost entirely in 1932.[47]

It is apparent that the first sharp impact of the depression was met by liberal, open-handed poor relief, and that this was supplemented in 1932 by a substantial road-building program. Together, these policies explain most of the rapid increase in total expenditures during the years following 1928. The sharp curtailment of highway outlays and the equally severe retrenchment in

---

1932. On the other hand the town's receipts from the state highway department for the maintenance and construction of town roads dropped from $37,000 in 1932 to $12,000 in the following year. In so far as fewer people could be employed with this highway money, a larger burden must necessarily be borne by the town's welfare organization. This added burden undoubtedly offset most of the new income received from the federal relief agency.

[46] Detailed statistics follow:

Period	Schools	Highways	Sewers	Misc.	Total
1917–1921		$104,048	$45,200	......	$149,248
1922–1926 ..	$451,030	275,374	89,226	$24,006	839,636
1927–1931 ..	21,987	102,938	93,079	20,533	238,537
1932–1933		154,891	27	5,922	160,840

[47] Only $15,245 was spent for road construction in 1933.

current expenditures, particularly in the cost of poor relief, account for the marked drop in total expenditures in 1933.

Let us turn to a consideration of the town's ability to bear the rapidly increasing burden of expenditures which characterized the period as a whole. The Tax Commissioner's estimate of total taxable wealth rose from $9,000,000 to $23,000,000 between 1916 and 1925, an increase of 259 per cent as compared with an advance of 264 per cent in total current expenditures. But the fact that the continued rise of the latter to a maximum in 1932 was accompanied by a 43 per cent drop in total taxable wealth[48] indicates that an increasingly onerous burden was being put upon the remaining taxable property in the town.

This, however, requires further elucidation. Let us consider the record of locally assessed valuations:

Year	Personalty	Real Estate Land	Buildings	Total
		(In thousands of dollars.)		
1916	2,852	1,089	3,149	7,090
1922	4,839	1,227	4,921	10,987
1923	6,092	1,652	6,461	14,205
1925	6,245	1,700	6,790	14,735
1928	5,143	1,741	6,646	13,530
1931	4,506	1,736	6,420	12,662
1933	2,580	1,725	6,547	10,852

It has already been pointed out that Adams' industrial character explains the relatively small importance of land values in its real-estate assessments, the dominant element in the total being the values placed upon the mills operating within the borders of the town. It has also been pointed out that the bulk of the personal property valuation in a community of this character is composed of the machinery and stock in trade of these same industrial enterprises, and that the failure of the personalty valuation to respond significantly to the removal of intangibles from the tax list by the income tax in 1916 is indicative of the relatively slight importance of this type of property in Adams.[49]

The latter's tax base expanded 55 per cent between 1916 and 1922, the bulk of the increase appearing in the personal property

---

[48] The total valuation for 1932 was $13,338,000 or $1,050 per capita as compared with $1,725 per capita in 1925.

[49] The personalty assessment in 1916 totaled $2,851,854; in 1917, $2,826,221.

and building assessments. This was far less rapid than the accompanying increase in expenditures and was followed in 1923 by a revaluation which was intended to produce a general 10 per cent rise in the assessed value of all property located in the town.[50] A period of slow development followed which brought the Adams tax base to a maximum in 1925 about 108 per cent above the 1916 total.

Although a decline began in the following year, it did not assume serious proportions until after 1928. The entrance of the Berkshire interests into Adams ended the paternalistic attitude toward the town previously maintained by the management of the chief industrial enterprise within its borders. The Berkshire Association immediately began to press for lower assessments. Its share of the local tax bill dropped from one third of the total in 1929 to one fifth in 1933. Finally, in the latter year the management of these mills flatly refused to pay any taxes until a satisfactory abatement had been made, and town officials went payless for a period of six weeks while this problem was being straightened out. Chiefly as a result of the consequent sharp drop in mill valuations the town's total tax base shrank nearly 20 per cent between 1928 and 1933, the decline being very definitely concentrated in the assessed value of personal property in the town.[51]

To this must be added the record of the town's receipts from state taxes:

Year	Income Tax	Corporation Tax*	Total	Per cent of Total Current Expenditures
1917	$6,486	$36,087	$42,573	25
1924	32,010	72,595	104,605	30
1930	67,638	51,992	119,630	27
1933	26,016	27,019	53,035	14

* Includes a negligible income from the tax on bank shares.

Adams' revenue from the state income tax in 1917 was rather small. At this time the state treasurer was paying to each town an

---

[50] This information was furnished by a town assessor.

[51] The removal of motor vehicles from the local tax lists by the Motor Vehicle Excise Tax of 1928 could not have been very important in a town of this character. The bulk of the decline is due to the drop in the machinery assessment from $4,100,000 in 1930 to $2,200,000 in 1933.

amount which was roughly in proportion to the amount of the town's loss by the removal of intangibles from the local lists as a result of the enactment of this tax in 1916.[52] However, legislation adopted in 1919 and 1920[53] providing for a gradual transition to a system of allocation according to the proportion of state taxes paid by the respective towns and segregating a portion of the receipts for use as grants in aid for educational purposes caused Adams' income to increase 395 per cent between 1917 and 1924, while the town's receipts from the state corporation taxes were rising to a level about 100 per cent in excess of that prevailing at the beginning of the period. As a result, Adams' revenue from state taxes in 1924 was sufficient to offset 30 per cent of its greatly increased current expenditures. Although receipts from the corporation tax began to decline in the years that followed, this decline was more than offset by an accompanying increase in revenue from the state income tax. The net increase, however, was not quite as large as that in current expenditures. As a result, state taxes were paying only 27 per cent of the current expenditures in 1930. The next three years brought an abrupt drop in receipts from both the corporation and income taxes, a drop which was far in excess of the accompanying decline in total current expenditures.

Although the town's income from these state taxes may be said to have assisted materially in financing the rapidly increasing burden of expenditures down to the beginning of the period of general industrial depression, it must be admitted that the catastrophic drop in this revenue after 1930 was an additional and very severe hardship to a town which was already hard pressed in consequence of its attempts to alleviate in a liberal fashion the social results of acute economic distress.

These changes in receipts from state taxes, in the scale of local expenditures, and in the base upon which the resulting property taxes were levied are mirrored in the record of the town rate which is presented below together with the average for the state as a whole:

[52] *Acts and Resolves*, 1916, c. 269.
[53] *Ibid.*, 1919, c. 314 and c. 363, part 1.

Year	Adams	Massachusetts
1916	$20.00	$19.14
1925	27.00	28.53
1927	30.00	29.51
1931	30.00	29.80
1933	36.00	30.02

It is clear that the increase in revenue from state taxes, and the sizable growth of the local tax base were not sufficient to prevent a 50 per cent increase in the Adams rate between 1916 and 1927, but it is also true that this increase was about equivalent to that shown by the state average.

In the face of rapidly rising expenditures and a substantial decline in its tax base, the town saw fit to maintain a stable rate of thirty dollars between 1927 and 1931. The following year, however, brought another upward spurt in expenditures, a further decline in valuations, and an abrupt drop in receipts from state taxes. The town rate rose six dollars in one year. The sharp curtailment of current expenditures in 1933 was not sufficient to allow any reduction in the tax rate, and Adams finished the period under review with a rate 20 per cent in excess of the current state average and 80 per cent above the rate which the town itself had applied in 1916.

Finally, let us turn to the record of the town's bonded debt, which is summarized below:

Year	Schools	Sewers	Highways	Misc.	Total
		(In thousands of dollars.)			
1916	60.0	9.0	60.5	18.8	148.3
1921	20.0	36.0	79.0	....	135.0
1922	360.0	32.5	122.5	50.0	565.0
1925	296.0	79.0	158.0	....	533.0
1931	202.0	127.0	108.5	17.5	455.0
1932	183.0	123.0	180.0	15.0	501.0
1933	165.0	115.0	143.0	199.0*	622.0

* Includes $185,500 in the form of a relief loan from the Commonwealth.

There was no substantial change in the town debt until 1922, when large school and highway outlays caused a 300 per cent increase in a single year. This abrupt rise was followed by a general downward movement to 1931, a marked increase in 1932 resulting from heavy borrowing to finance the large program of highway expenditures undertaken in that year, and a further increase in

1933 attributable to the floating of a large loan for relief purposes. The town's per capita debt rose from $13 to $49 between 1916 and 1933. Its indebtedness per $1,000 assessed valuation advanced from $20.91 to $57.31.

Once again we find that the years under review divide quite distinctly into sub-periods. The interval between 1916 and 1923 was marked by a general and rapid rise in current expenditures, a sharp increase in receipts from state taxes, and the rapid development of the base upon which local property taxes were assessed. However, the changes in these last items were not sufficiently important to prevent a sizable increase in the tax rate used by the town. Liabilities did not rise until 1922, when school and highway construction saddled the town with a very substantial debt.

Current expenditures rose slowly to 1928, the increases being due mainly to the rising cost of operating the school and health departments. Nevertheless, the curtailment in capital outlays which came after 1926 produced an abrupt drop in total expenditures to a level substantially below that prevailing in 1922. There was some shrinkage in the tax base after 1925, and this was accompanied by a substantial reduction in income from state corporation taxes, changes which are indicative of the declining prosperity of the industrial enterprises operating within the town. On the other hand, receipts from the state income tax continued to advance rapidly, and in 1928 Adams found itself with a tax rate that was not substantially in excess of the state average, and total liabilities which were very much lower than the previous maximum reached in 1922.

It will be recalled that 1928 was the year of Mr. Plunkett's death, and that one of the consequences of this event was the passing of the town's main industrial enterprise into the hands of "foreign" capital, a circumstance which soon destroyed the previously friendly relationship between the management of the mills and the town government. Moreover, it became apparent very quickly that the younger generation of Plunketts was not sufficiently interested to assume the role of benevolent despot which C. T. Plunkett had played in town affairs. Control of the latter reverted entirely into the hands of an electorate which was dominated by persons paying only the nominal tax on polls. It is true that this group no longer constituted an absolute majority of the taxpayers in Adams,[54] but, as in Maynard and Millville, the general failure of property owners to attend town meeting allowed the poll-tax payer to dominate town politics. As a result, the control of Adams' financial policy passed into the hands of a group peculiarly liable to inaugurate and pursue liberal spending policies.

There was an immediate speeding up of the rate of increase in current expenditures, an increase which was concentrated, until 1930, in the school and health department accounts. This it will be remembered, came in the face of a continued shrinkage in the town tax base and a further drop in receipts from the state corporation taxes. However, revenue from the state income tax continued to advance and the town meeting found it possible to get along without increasing the rate applied to property located within its borders.

The general economic collapse of 1929 produced an immediate rise in Adams' poor relief expenditures, a development which seems to have been favored by a liberal administration of the public welfare department. When really hard times set in in 1932,

---

[54] The following statistics summarize the situation:

Year	Poll-tax Payers (1)	Total Taxpayers (2)	Per cent (1) to (2)
1916	1,935	3,848	50
1928	1,913	4,983	39

It has been pointed out by a resident of Adams presumably well acquainted with town finances that the finance committee which drew up the appropriations submitted to the town meeting for consideration was not under the control of the poll-tax payers — that the latter group was not represented among the members of the committee at all. He has pointed out further that the town meeting usually accepted the recommendations which this committee advanced. These facts he considers sufficient to disprove the thesis that the poll-tax payers were running the town. It does not follow from this evidence, however, that control over town finances resided in the committee in question. That body would have been restricted in the character of its recommendations by its knowledge of the nature of the electorate which would pass upon its findings. The fact that the meeting usually accepted the proposals as advanced may indicate nothing more than an accurate judgment on the part of a conservative committee as to what the more "liberal" electorate would accept. That this hypothesis is probably the real explanation is suggested by the hearty agreement of other equally well-informed residents of Adams with the thesis advanced in the present chapter.

poor-relief costs leapt to a staggering total. This sudden increase came in the face of a further shrinkage in the town tax base and an abrupt decline in revenues from state taxes. It necessitated a six-dollar increase in the town rate. At the same time the Adams town meeting undertook a large program of highway construction which it financed with borrowed money. Consequently, the increase in the Adams rate was accompanied by a considerable advance in the town's total bonded indebtedness.

The next year brought conditions which were serious enough to enforce a rigid economy program even upon a town meeting of this character. There was another contraction in the tax base, a further decline in income from state taxes, and no substantial assistance from outside to alleviate the crushing burden of poor relief. There was a general recognition of the impossibility of meeting the welfare needs with further public-works expenditures financed by borrowing. Retrenchment was inescapable; expenditures were drastically curtailed, poor relief particularly being cut from $220,000 to $114,000 in a single year. The road-building program was halted. But even under these conditions the town avoided a further sharp rise in its tax rate only with the admittedly temporary assistance of a large loan from the Commonwealth, the proceeds of which were used for poor relief. In 1933 Adams had reached the point where not even a town meeting dominated by poll-tax payers could refuse to recognize the seriousness of its position and the necessity for rigid economy in town affairs.

This situation was of course not the result of any single cause. A large part of Adams' difficulty was the immediate result of widespread economic depression. Moreover, it is clear that the hospital and junior high school fostered by Mr. Plunkett had saddled the town with large operating costs which proved extremely inconvenient during the period of acute financial stringency. But it must not be forgotten that the Adams town meeting, when freed from the influence of Mr. Plunkett in 1928, saw fit to increase the corporate standard of living despite the fairly obvious economic decay of the town. As a result Adams went into the industrial depression with its finances badly strained. It then spent lavishly in an attempt to alleviate the social hardships which that depression brought to large numbers of its citizens, and by 1933 these policies had brought the town into extremely dangerous financial straits. This factor, the spending policies pursued by the Adams town meeting during the years following 1928, is probably the primary explanation for the acuteness of the financial discomforts which the town was combating at the time this chapter was being written.

The foregoing history of Adams' recent financial experience has presented evidence bearing upon a point of considerable theoretical importance. It has sketched a situation in which an urban democracy of the type most likely to spend in excess of its financial resources was held in check to a considerable extent by the influence of a single powerful and respected citizen, only to break loose when this check was removed and spend itself into an extremely precarious financial position. The evidence at hand points to the necessity of making proper allowance for despotic or oligarchical elements which may be present within the framework of the nominal democracy typified by the New England town meeting, a necessity often neglected by students of political theory when dealing with this type of governmental organization.[55]

[55] Readers of Aristotle's *Politics* will recognize the significance of this in relation to Aristotle's analysis of types of democracies.

PART II

MISCELLANEOUS STUDIES

CHAPTER V

THE FINANCIAL HISTORY OF BELMONT

THE financial history of Belmont also begins with a separation for this, like Maynard, is a synthetic town. Since, however, the date of Belmont's incorporation is too early to permit of satisfactory statistical treatment, chief emphasis has been placed upon the town's subsequent development, which is of general interest because Belmont furnishes a typical instance of the wealthy suburban communities found on the outskirts of most large cities in the United States. The influx of population has a striking effect upon the finances of these units, the benefits of new taxable wealth being accompanied by demands for services requiring an addition to the burden of town expenditures. The relationship between these two factors provides the central theme for the sketch that follows.

I

The area which Belmont now occupies formerly belonged to Watertown, Waltham, and West Cambridge.[1] When the Fitchburg railroad reached it in 1843, it contained not more than 700 inhabitants,[2] had no church, store, or post office, and included only two school districts.[3] Although the railroad brought a slow increase in population, the 1,004 inhabitants residing in the area in 1853[4] seem to have possessed little community of interest. "Ecclesiastically, politically, and socially they were identified with the towns in which they dwelt."[5]

Yet in 1854 residents of the area petitioned the General Court for incorporation as a separate town. Although this request was unanimously rejected by a committee of the Senate, similar bills

---

[1] Renamed Arlington in 1867.
[2] Hurd, *Middlesex County*, III, 682.
[3] Conklin, *Middlesex County*, II, 387.
[4] Hurd, *Middlesex County*, p. 682.
[5] *Ibid.*, p. 683. See also Conklin, *Middlesex County*, p. 388.

were presented in the following years, and in 1859 the area was incorporated as the town of Belmont.

The issues behind this movement are clearly recorded in the published speeches of three men who opposed the unsuccessful petition of 1857,[6] and in the argument of the counsel for Watertown.[7] It is apparent that the persons active in the movement for incorporation were the representatives of land companies, prominent land owners, developers, and speculators who held property in the Belmont section. They also appear to have been men of considerable wealth.[8] Both circumstances would make them desire good schools and highways, and they seem to have considered the facilities provided by the three parent towns inadequate, particularly since they believed that the population of the area was destined to experience a rapid growth. They charged that the region was depressed as a result of the poor services provided by the towns to which it belonged, and asserted that the only hope of obtaining services of the desired quality, services which they believed due them in return for the taxes they paid, was to incorporate as an independent town.

Their opponents did not fail to emphasize the personal gain which the land speculators would derive from the creation of the new unit, pointing out that the proposed town would be rich and that the resulting low tax rate would tend to raise the price of the land company's stock. It was charged that this was the real motive behind the petition.[9] The inadequacy of the schools and roads in the Belmont area was flatly denied,[10] and the depressed value of real estate in the region was attributed to high fares on

---

[6] Speeches of the Hon. Gideon Haynes, Hon. W. S. Brakenridge, and Hon. Hugh W. Greene, on the Question as to Incorporating the Town of Belmont (Boston, 1857).

[7] Ivers J. Austin, Argument of Ivers J. Austin, Counsel for the Remonstrants from Watertown against the Petition for the Incorporation of the Town of Belmont (Boston, 1857).

[8] Mr. Haynes pointed out that the average amount of property assessed for eight of the petitioners living in the Watertown section of Belmont had been almost $93,000 in 1856. But if the assessment of one man is excluded, the average drops to about $40,000 (ibid., p. 10).

[9] See the speeches by Brakenridge and Greene in Speeches . . . on . . . Incorporating the Town of Belmont.

[10] It was pointed out that Watertown had already planned a new school at Waverly, had purchased the necessary land, and had appropriated $3,500 to pay for it. Mr. Haynes also alleged that one of the petitioners had signed the petition

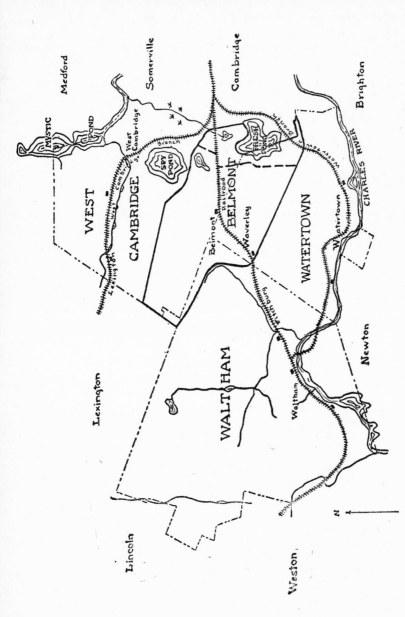

WATERTOWN—WALTHAM—WEST CAMBRIDGE

‧—‧—‧ ORIGINAL BOUNDARIES ———— BELMONT BOUNDARY 1859 ———— BELMONT BOUNDARY 1881

the Fitchburg railroad rather than to the financial policies of the parent towns. Finally, these men did not fail to emphasize the fact that the Belmont area did not contain even the skeleton of a village, that it had no manufacturing of any kind, and that it was not an independent unit from either a social or an economic point of view.[11]

Although the arguments used two years later were probably very much the same, it is likely that the struggle for incorporation had developed a considerable community of interest among the residents of the Belmont area.[12] Population had continued to increase, and in addition the petitioners had obtained the support of the outstandingly wealthy man of the neighborhood, whose influence must have been of considerable assistance in obtaining the incorporation.[13]

The new unit had an area of 3,648 acres,[14] a population of 1,175, and a total valuation of over two million dollars.[15] The per capita valuation was $1,733 as compared with $1,137 in West Cambridge, $756 in Watertown, and $695 in Waltham.[16] These

---

charging that the schools were inadequate at the same time that he was trying to sell his Belmont land and in his advertisement was stressing the point that "good schools" were located "quite near" to his property.

[11] "They have, as I have already stated, one small store, a shoe repairer who tends, and works in the depot at Waverly station, a blacksmith, who comes just within the lines, on the West Cambridge side, and who depends on the old town entirely for his support, and these constitute all the elements (excepting their wealth) upon which they ask for this new town." — Haynes, *ibid.*, p. 8.

[12] This is indicated by the construction of a meeting house in 1857 costing $13,000 (Hurd, *Middlesex County*, p. 683). This is significant in view of the fact that the construction of a meeting house was often the precursor of the earlier incorporations.

[13] This man, J. P. Cushing, paid taxes on an assessment totaling half a million dollars. His estate, "Belmont," furnished the name for the new unit. In 1857 the Watertown counsel had charged that the proposed boundaries were deliberately arranged so as to include the Cushing property, pointing out that the support of some rich man was necessary if the cost of the separation was not to become a prohibitive burden for the ordinary taxpayer.

[14] Conklin, *Middlesex County*, p. 387. Of these, 429 acres were taken from Waltham, 1,773 from West Cambridge, and 1,446 from Watertown.

[15] Hurd, *Middlesex County*, p. 682.

[16] That the difference shown is not offset by a divergence in per capita debt is apparent from the following data:

	Liabilities	Per Capita
Belmont	$13,600	$11.35
Watertown	35,325	11.72
West Cambridge	30,750	11.48
Waltham	57,950	9.00

figures are obtained by dividing the total valuation, as determined in 1859 for the apportionment of the state tax, by the population as of 1860. They show that Belmont's per capita valuation approached the amount specified by Dr. Chen, when dealing with statistics for the year 1919, as indicating an exceptionally wealthy town.[17]

The unusual wealth of the area is emphasized further by the receipts which were later obtained from the Massachusetts tax on corporate excess enacted in 1864. It will be recalled that the proceeds of this tax, so far as they were paid with respect to shares held by residents of Massachusetts, were distributed to the towns and cities in which the shareholders resided.[18] The inhabitants of a wealthy town would tend to own more than the average amount of stock in domestic corporations. In 1865, $3,887 was collected on shares held by residents of Belmont and this meant a distribution of $3.04 per capita to the town as against an average distribution of 91 cents for the state as a whole.[19]

The new town experienced something of a boom during the Civil War and immediately thereafter and by 1875 contained 1,937 inhabitants. The greater part of this gain disappeared with the annexation of a sixth of the town's area to Cambridge in 1880.[20] Yet, even when this is taken into account, Belmont shows little development during the decade following 1885, although a rapid advance in its population to 2,098 in 1890 produced a net increase of 78 per cent for the period as a whole.

Agriculture continued to be the chief occupation practiced in the town. The census for 1885 listed only eight establishments, employing nineteen persons, and turning out goods valued at $34,000 yearly. The census for 1895 classified Belmont as predominantly a residential town and this seems to have been its character during the entire period following the Civil War.

[17] *Op. cit.*, pp. 31–32.

[18] *Report of the Commissioners Appointed to Inquire into the Expediency of Revising and Amending the Laws Relating to Taxation* (1875), pp. 124–126.

[19] *Report of the Treasurer and Receiver General*, 1865, pp. 94–97.

[20] W. L. Chenery, *Some Statistics of the Town of Belmont, Massachusetts* (1890), p. 24.

Its total and total current expenditures are given for selected years in the following table:

Year	Total Actual*	Total Per Capita	Total Current Actual*	Total Current Per Capita
1860	23.3	$19.45	9.8	$8.20
1867	17.9	13.00	12.8	9.30
1874	42.9	23.05	28.7	15.45
1879	35.2	20.90	25.7	15.25
1884	33.5	20.45	26.3	16.10
1890	46.6	22.20	35.9	17.15†

* In thousands.
† Does not include deficit on operating account of the water works.

The large total expenditure for 1860 is due to the inclusion of the costs of procuring the incorporation.[21] If this amount is subtracted, a total of $15,500 remains, and it becomes apparent that the period is divided into three distinct intervals. There was a rapid rise to 1874, producing an approximately 90 per cent advance in per capita current expenditures, followed by a period of economy, which in turn gave place to a more moderate advance after 1884. Six years later Belmont's per capita current expenditures were 105 per cent in excess of those made at the beginning of the period.

The bulk of the advance in current expenditures to 1874 was the result of an increase from $2,800 to $8,500 in the cost of schools, and from $3,500 to $10,000 in highway maintenance charges. Subsequent economies reduced the cost of maintaining schools and highways to $7,500 and $6,700 respectively in 1884, and advances to $11,000 and $8,200 in these items, together with a rise in the cost of fire and police protection from $817 to $2,718, accounts for most of the increase in total current expenditures during the next six years.[22]

---

[21] The town meeting voted to assume these expenses, which amounted to nearly $9,000, and issued notes in order to meet this obligation. A group of residents filed suit in protest claiming that the town had no right to tax itself for such purposes. The plaintiffs were granted their claim and the money was ordered repaid to the town (*Jonathan Frost et al., In Equity, vs. The Inhabitants of the Town of Belmont et al.*).

[22] These are the kinds of expenditures which figured in the debates on the proposal to incorporate Belmont. The following table contains the per capita expenditures

Poor relief constituted a negligible burden throughout the period. Belmont's expenditure for this purpose was slightly lower in 1890 than in the first year of its corporate existence.[23]

The index of town expenditures furnished by the taxes levied upon polls and property is substantially inaccurate in this instance because of the importance of revenue from the state bank and corporation taxes in Belmont's finances. Hence the income from these sources has been added to the taxes levied on polls and property. The corrected index appears below:

Year	Belmont	Massachusetts
	(In thousands of dollars.)	
1861	15.9*	7,601*
1874	46.6	30,299
1884	45.2	30,652
1890	44.3	34,062

* Tax levy only.

The advance in Belmont to 1874 was apparently less rapid than in the state as a whole, and the decline to 1890 was not reflected

which Belmont and its parent towns made for current school and highway purposes at selected dates:

		Schools		
Year	Belmont	West Cambridge	Watertown	Waltham
1859..........	....	$1.76	$2.07	$1.24
1860	$2.34	1.38	2.19	1.42
1867	3.87	2.47	2.98	2.10
1874	4.60	5.57	4.78	3.35
1879	5.24	4.07	3.54	2.77

		Highways		
Year	Belmont	West Cambridge	Watertown	Waltham
1859	....	$4.50	$1.23	$ .51
1860	$2.93	1.97	.38	.65
1867	2.34	3.57	1.75	.89
1874	4.10	4.07	3.46	2.33
1879	3.40	2.10	2.30	1.77

In general these figures indicate that Belmont immediately began to spend more for these services than the parent towns had been doing, that it continued to spend more per capita throughout the period, and that the difference between Belmont's expenditures and those of the other towns was greater in 1879 than it had been in 1860. This tends to substantiate the claim of the petitioners for incorporation that the Belmont region was not getting the kind of schools and highways which its residents considered necessary for the proper development of the community, and due them in return for the taxes they were paying to the parent towns.

[23] The town spent $1,079 for the relief of its poor in 1860, $334 in 1874, and $1,048 in 1890.

in the Massachusetts total. It follows that the needs of this small but select residential community were not increasing as rapidly as those of the predominantly industrial state.[24]

Belmont's local valuation is summarized in the following table:

Year	Personalty	Real Estate (In thousands of dollars.)	Total
1861	940	1,207	2,147
1874	906	2,930	3,836
1879	624	2,489	3,113
1884	703	2,160	2,863
1890	841	2,343	3,184

Although the local assessments rose to 1874, the decline in subsequent years was accentuated by the loss of nearly one tenth of the total as a result of the annexation of the Strawberry Hill district to Cambridge in 1880. The advance during subsequent years failed to offset this decline, and as a result the local assessment at the end of the period was decidedly less than the maximum reached in 1874.

The personalty assessment showed a net drop of about 10 per cent for the period as a whole, owing largely to a sharp decline after the panic of 1873. Real-estate values, which had boomed in the early years, reacted less violently during the period of economy, and rose to a level in 1890 that represented a net increase of 51 per cent. It was this rise in the value of real estate which produced the advance of 48 per cent in the local assessment over the entire period under review. This, however, was very much less than the 150 per cent advance in the assessment for the state as a whole,[25] and the 266 per cent rise in Belmont's total current expenditures.

A considerable portion of the relatively slow growth in local valuations was offset by income received from the state taxes on bank shares and corporate excess. By 1874 these yielded $7,045,

---

[24] The possible objection that this discrepancy is the result of the loss of the Strawberry Hill district in 1880 can be met by pointing out that reduction to a per capita basis leaves a net rise for the entire period of less than 16 per cent in Belmont and nearly 25 per cent in the state.

[25] Personalty in the state at large advanced from $309,000,000 to $554,000,000; real estate from $552,000,000 in 1861 to $1,600,000,000 in 1890. The total assessment rose from $861,000,000 to $2,154,000,000.

which paid a fourth of Belmont's greatly increased current expenditures. This income rose to $10,127 in 1884, and a decline to $6,600 during the next six years left revenue sufficient to offset over 18 per cent of the town's total current expenditures.

The rapid advance in local assessments and in receipts from these state taxes brought the town's per capita taxable wealth from $1,733 in 1860 to $2,223 in 1876. In spite of the removal of the Strawberry Hill district in 1880, an area containing a sixth of the town's population but only one tenth of its local assessment, Belmont's per capita wealth declined to $2,101 in 1886, and then dropped sharply to $1,784 in 1890. Although it was still a very wealthy town, it was no longer as rich as it had been before the rapid increase of its population set in around 1885.

The result of the relatively rapid advance in town expenditures had been a rise in the tax rate from $7.20 in 1861 to $10.00 in in 1875. The rate applied in 1884 was two dollars higher, and the $11.50 rate used in 1890 represented a net advance of about 60 per cent for the period as a whole. However, the increase in Massachusetts was even larger, and as a result the rate applied to property in Belmont dropped from 81 to 78 per cent of the current state average.

The town had had liabilities of $13,600 in 1860 but this amount included an item of $9,000 borrowed to pay the expenses of the incorporation, for which the town was later reimbursed. Its debt rose with expenditures to $35,710 in 1874. Reductions during subsequent years were more than offset by the amount borrowed to finance the construction of a water supply, which raised the town debt to $60,750 in 1890.

Belmont had not developed with unusual rapidity during the first thirty years of its corporate existence. Its expenditures had risen somewhat less than in the state as a whole; yet the advance had been considerably in excess of the increase in the local assessment. However, sizable receipts from state taxes had offset a substantial portion of this discrepancy and the town rate had advanced considerably less rapidly than the average for Massachusetts. Although Belmont had gained financially by the removal of one sixth of its area,[26] its per capita wealth had dropped back to $1,784 in 1890. At this time it was still a small but wealthy residential community. Its financial position was still enviable, but the influx of population between 1885 and 1890 heralded the beginning of a new and less favorable era in the town's financial history.

II

Belmont's development continued at an accelerated pace down to the turn of the century, and a slower advance during subsequent years brought the number of its inhabitants to 4,360 in 1905.[27] The growth of its residential population was accompanied by the extension of the Boston Elevated Railway system into its borders, but since this was not accomplished until 1898, when Belmont's rate of growth had already begun to slacken, the street railway cannot be regarded as a cause of the development which came during the nineties.[28] However, its presence must have contributed substantially towards the slower growth experienced during the following years.

In 1886, the first date for which these statistics are available, there were 691 taxpayers assessed in the town, and 45 per cent of these had paid only the nominal levy on polls. The subsequent influx of suburban population failed to alter the position of the poll-tax payer in town meeting. While this group was far from being a political nonentity, it was apparently never in a position to control town appropriations, and hence the particular incentive to extravagance present in a town meeting dominated by this element was absent in Belmont during the period under consideration.

[26] A Belmont town clerk computed that the town had lost a sixth of its population, a third of its school children, and a tenth of its taxable property. — Chenery, p. 24.

[27] This was a net advance of 108 per cent or about three times the growth shown by the state total. The latter rose from 2,238,943 in 1890, to 3,003,680 in 1905.

[28] At any rate this is the attitude taken by the author of the selectmen's report for 1900 when he writes as follows: "New conditions and obligations are thus becoming almost daily more urgent and particularly is this true concerning transportation facilities. Certainly we are to be congratulated that, contrary to the expectations of many, the Boston Elevated Street Railway Co. *consented to* an extension of their system into our town." (Belmont Town Report, 1900, pp. 18–19; italics mine.)

The town's rapid growth is reflected in the record of expenditures presented below:

Year	Total*	Total Current†	Total non-Commercial Current‡
		(In thousands of dollars.)	
1890	46.6	39.0	35.9
1897	88.5	60.0	54.7
1900	109.2	72.4	65.9
1905	131.8	90.0	82.3

* Includes net payments on the town debt and all deficits on water, light, and sewer accounts.

† Total minus payments on the town debt, non-commercial outlays, and outlays on the water and light plants so far as they are not covered by a surplus in the corresponding operating account.

‡ Total current minus deficits on current account of the water works and electric light plant.

Total expenditures rose almost steadily to 1905, showing a net increase of 183 per cent, which was considerably in excess of the 108 per cent advance in population. Non-commercial current expenditures rose to 1897, declined in the following year, and then increased down to the end of the period. The continued rise after 1900, accompanied by a slowing down in the growth of the town's population, produced a net increase of 10 per cent in per capita non-commercial current expenditures for the period as a whole.

The more rapid advance in total expenditures was the result of increasing capital outlays. Large amounts were spent to install equipment for distributing electricity and water,[29] and considerable sums were paid out for sewers, although a large portion of this expense was met with special assessments.[30] The bulk of the non-commercial outlay went for schools and highways.[31]

Most of the advance in current non-commercial expenditures was the result of increases from $11,300 to $24,300, and from $8,200 to $20,500 in the cost of maintaining schools and highways

[29] Electric current was purchased from a private enterprise, and water was taken first from Watertown and then from the Metropolitan Water Board.

[30] Between 1897 and 1905 Belmont spent $62,833 laying sewers, including its portion of the expense involved in constructing private sewers. Of this total $28,136 was paid by means of special assessments and $1,735 out of miscellaneous receipts, leaving $32,962 to be met by the town itself.

[31] Between 1890 and 1905 Belmont spent $138,775 in capital outlays for schools, and $83,716 for the construction of highways. In the same period it had outlays of $1,730 for the fire department, $6,639 for playgrounds, and $1,254 for the town hall.

respectively. There was also an advance from $2,746 to $8,261 in the cost of fire and police protection, but the $2,989 spent for the relief of town poor in 1905 indicates that this burden was still a negligible one.[32]

The following table compares the resulting increase in Belmont's tax levy with the growth shown in the state as a whole, the tax levies having been corrected by the addition of receipts from the state taxes on bank shares and on corporate excess:

Year	Belmont	Massachusetts
	(In thousands of dollars.)	
1890	44.3	34,002
1897	78.9	44,533
1905	125.6	61,299

It is evident that Belmont's expenditures were advancing at far more than the average rate, but the unusually rapid rise in the town's population offset most of this discrepancy. The corrected tax levy in Belmont rose 37 per cent from $21 to $28.80 per capita, the state average advanced 34 per cent from $15.25 to $20.50.

Meanwhile, Belmont's local assessments had shown the following development:

Year	Personalty	Real Estate	Total
		(In thousands of dollars.)	
1890	841	2,343	3,184
1897	992	3,226	4,218
1900	1,376	3,836	5,212
1905	1,340	4,263	5,603

Personalty reached a maximum figure in 1901 of $1,396,000. Although the subsequent decline left a net advance of nearly 60 per cent, this was far less than the accompanying 108 per cent growth in the town's population. The result was a drop in the per capita personalty assessment from $400 in 1890 to $308 in 1905. Now the absence of manufactures and the decline of farming in the town indicate that the bulk of this personalty consisted of in-

---

[32] This is recognized in the selectmen's report for 1902 which states: "We are at the present time partially supporting twenty-eight persons. The appropriation for the support of the poor was two thousand dollars ($2,000) which has not been exceeded. We think Belmont is fortunate in not having many very poor within her limits." (Belmont Town Report, 1902, p. 14.)

tangibles. Although it is not possible to check this thesis directly on account of the absence of published data for the years in question, it is significant that the report of the special tax commission of 1897 cites Belmont as one of the towns in which intangibles dominated the personal property valuation.[33] Again, in the report of the commission of 1908 Belmont appears in a group of fourteen selected towns in which the chief items of tangible personalty made up only $2,300,000 of a total personal property valuation of more than $15,300,000.[34] Under these conditions the decline in Belmont's per capita personalty assessment is definite evidence of a falling off in the personal wealth of the residents of this area.

Although real-estate values had risen steadily to a level 82 per cent above that of 1890, it is apparent that the influx of suburban residents had failed to produce a proportional increase in the value of real estate situated within the limits of the town.[35]

The result of these changes was a 76 per cent rise in Belmont's local assessment. The rapid increase in population more than canceled this advance and brought the per capita assessment from $1,515 in 1890 to $1,287 in 1905. In combination with the substantial rise in per capita expenditures, these results point to a relative increase in the burden of taxation put upon property in this developing suburban town.

Receipts from state taxes are summarized below:

Year	Bank and Corporation Taxes	Street Railway Tax	Total Receipts	Per Cent of Non-Commercial Current Expenditures
		(In thousands of dollars.)		
1890	6.6	...	6.6	18
1897	9.1	...	9.1	17
1900	10.8	11.2	22.0	33
1905	11.8	8.2	20.0	24

[33] *Report of the Commission Appointed to Inquire into the Expediency of Revising and Amending the Laws of the Commonwealth Relating to Taxation* (1897), p. 50. This report shows that in eighteen selected towns (Belmont included) there was $3,100,000 worth of tangible personalty in 1896 and $52,600,000 worth of intangibles.

[34] *Report of the Commission on Taxation* (1908), p. 40.

[35] It ought to be pointed out that the building assessment had increased 114 per cent as compared with a 71 per cent rise in land values. Hence buildings had risen from 46 to 53 per cent of the real-estate assessment, a change characteristic of a developing suburban community.

These taxes paid about the same percentage of current expenditures in 1897 as in 1890. In the following year the street railway tax began to yield substantial revenue,[36] and although these receipts declined somewhat after 1900, Belmont was still obtaining sufficient revenue from state taxes in 1905 to pay nearly one fourth of its greatly increased current expenditures.

While this new income offsets a portion of the lag in local assessments, the fact must not be overlooked that the per capita receipts from the state bank and corporation taxes had fallen from $31.50 to $27.25 over the interval under consideration. Since this money was being distributed in accordance with the domicile of the owner of the capital stock, the decline is further evidence of the diminishing personal wealth of the residents of Belmont.

The estimated taxable wealth of the town itself dropped from $1,784 per capita in 1889 to $1,379 in 1898, and the increase to $1,440 in 1904 left a net decline of 19 per cent for the period as a whole. Belmont was beginning the transition from a select to a popular suburb. The new inhabitants were bringing with them a less than proportionate quantity of taxable wealth; and even before the turn of the century Belmont had dropped well below the criterion which Dr. Chen used to identify an exceptionally wealthy town.

The lag in valuations behind expenditures required a rise in the Belmont rate from $11.50 in 1890 to $19.90 in 1905. This was considerably more rapid than the increase in the state average.[37] As a result the town rate rose from a point 22 per cent below that average in 1890 to one nearly 16 per cent above in 1905.

Non-commercial debt advanced from $15,500 or $7.39 per capita in 1890 to $191,900[38] or $44.00 per capita in 1905. Of this

---

[36] Prior to 1898 these utilities were subject to the general tax on domestic corporations, and the receipts from this source were distributed to the towns in which the stockholders resided. In 1898 it was enacted that the entire franchise tax upon such companies was to be distributed among the towns and cities in which the tracks were situated. The lines in Belmont were those of the Boston Elevated Street Railway and it is probable that little stock was domiciled in Belmont. Hence the town must have benefited greatly by the change referred to above. See C. J. Bullock, *Historical Sketch of the Finances and Financial Policy of Massachusetts from 1780 to 1905* (New York, 1907), pp. 116–117.

[37] The state average rose from $14.84 in 1890 to $17.25 in 1905.

[38] After deduction of the par value of a sinking fund.

debt $105,000 was incurred for schools, $63,000 for sewers, and $58,500 for town roads. Clearly this rise in the tax levy had not enabled the town to pursue a pay-as-you-go policy in financing its non-commercial outlays. At the end of the period property in Belmont was not only subject to a greatly increased tax rate but was also burdened with a per capita non-commercial debt more than six times as large as that of 1890. This period of rapidly increasing population brought a distinct weakening in the town's financial structure.

Before turning to subsequent years, we must consider the record of the two commercial enterprises which Belmont acquired during the period now under consideration. The water-distributing plant, begun in 1887, seems to have been completed in 1889 at a cost of nearly $58,000. Service installation fees brought in $2,756 and a $54,000 loan made up most of the remainder. Another $66,000 was spent on extensions between 1890 and 1905, $6,000 of this being offset by service charges. By 1905 the total cost of the plant had risen to around $124,000, the town's investment to $115,178.

The operating account is summarized below:

Year	Current Receipts*	Current Expenditures†	Net Receipts
1888	$2,060	$3,445	$ − 1,385
1890	3,207	5,225	− 2,018
1895	4,718	4,795	− 77
1899	12,769	5,314	7,455
1905	14,659	10,235	4,424

* Rates plus miscellaneous receipts.
† Maintenance costs, interest charges, Metropolitan Water District Tax, and miscellaneous operating costs.

A decline in interest charges coupled with a gradual rise in receipts from water rates brought the operating deficit to a low point of $77 in 1895. A surplus in the following year gave place to two successive deficits, but thereafter receipts were always considerably in excess of the cost of operation. The net operating deficit of $10,600 incurred down to 1898 was more than offset by the surplus of $34,000 during the next six years. Again, this must not be considered a profit, since it takes no account of the interest on the money which the town itself invested in this enterprise, or the loss of the taxes which a private concern would have paid the town, and entirely neglects the physical condition of the plant. Yet the receipts obtained after 1899 were sufficient to offset all the construction costs incurred during these years; it is apparent that the enterprise had become something more than merely self-supporting.

The water board had begun to retire its debt in 1888 and by 1890 had reduced it to $45,000. The additional $40,800 borrowed down to 1905 was more than offset by debt repayment, and this fact, together with a sinking fund amounting to $5,000 in 1905, reduced the net debt to $38,900 at the end of the period. Since the cost of the plant had risen from $58,000 to $124,000, the town's equity had grown from 22 to 75 per cent of the total between 1890 and 1905 (cost of production being assumed to equal true value). As a result of the sound financial policies pursued by the water board, the enterprise was less of a burden in 1905 than in 1890,[39] a fact which serves to accentuate the significance of the rapid rise in the rate applied to property in the town.

Belmont purchased its electricity from a private company until it constructed its own distributing system in 1897. The new equipment cost about fourteen thousand dollars and was financed with borrowed money. No additions were made until 1906 and there was no reduction in the outstanding indebtedness.

The town had been paying between three and four thousand a year for street lighting just prior to 1898. The cost of operating the new distributing system rose from three to seven thousand during subsequent years.[40] The latter was far in excess of the $2,700 spent for street lighting in 1890, and it is clear that the new enterprise had placed an added burden upon the town, a burden which offset the greater part of the advantages derived from the sound financial policies pursued by the town water board.

[39] In 1890 the total expenditure on current and capital account exceeded the current receipts and the service installation charges by $8,300. In 1905 the corresponding excess was $2,968.

[40] Statistics follow:

Year	Current Receipts	Current Expenditures	Net Cost of Operation
1898	$934	$4,048	$3,114
1902	5,615	13,731	8,116
1905	7,126	14,400	7,274

III

The slow development marking the first five years of the twentieth century was followed by another period of increasingly rapid growth. By 1910 Belmont's population was 27 per cent larger than in 1905, and an even more rapid increase during subsequent years produced a population of around 8,600 in 1916. Since there was no appreciable development of industry or commerce, it is safe to conclude that this increase in the number of the town's inhabitants was the result of a second influx of suburban residents employed in Cambridge and Boston.[41]

As the first period of development was marked by the coming of the street railway, so this period is associated with the construction of a subway from Boston to Cambridge. The latter project, completed in 1913, connected with a trolley running out to Belmont and brought a considerable reduction in the time consumed by the trip between Belmont and Boston. It was no longer necessary to use the more expensive railroad facilities in order to obtain rapid transit to the business center of the neighboring city. The Town Report of 1911 indicates that Belmont's population had begun to increase well in advance of the completion of the Cambridge tunnel,[42] and it is highly probable not only that the latter was responsible for the extremely rapid growth after 1913, but that the prospect of its completion had also assisted Belmont's development during preceding years.

The same report pointed out that the character of the town was being altered by the new population, and commented upon the difficulties encountered in regulating building construction. By 1913 it had become apparent to the selectmen that a change was also taking place in Belmont's financial structure. Their report for that year comments upon "the very favorable and healthy

---

[41] The Census of 1915 states that out of 3,350 residents of Belmont who were gainfully employed, 1,293 or 38 per cent worked in Boston. However, the increase in the number of suburban residents did not prevent a rise in the percentage of the town's taxpayers who paid only the poll tax. In 1905 this element had constituted 46 per cent of the total number of taxpayers and by 1915 this percentage had risen to 49. There were in the latter year 3,548 taxpayers and 1,741 of these paid only the poll tax.

[42] Belmont Town Report, 1911, p. 42.

growth" which the town was experiencing, but also warns the voters that "the constant and insistent demands for improvements of all sorts should be met by restraint and conservatism in order to keep the balance of available resources on the right side."[43] Two years later these officials pointed out that the increase in population was forcing a very considerable extension of town services,[44] and that the school population was increasing so rapidly that new accommodations had to be provided.[45] By 1916 they were asserting that an excessive strain was being placed upon the town's resources,[46] that increased taxes were necessary if Belmont was to meet its obligations, and that the per capita base upon which these taxes had to be levied was not very large.[47] From the circumstances, the second wave of suburban population might be expected to produce financial results similar to those accompanying the development in the nineties, an expectation which is all the more logical because this second wave was associated with a drastic reduction in transportation costs which in itself would make the town more attractive to people of moderate means. To discover whether the results were similar, let us turn to the figures.

The record of town expenditures is given in the following table:

Year	Total	Total Current	Total Non-Commercial Current
		(In thousands of dollars.)	
1905	131.8	90.0	82.3
1910	136.6	117.2	111.0
1913	177.8	138.8	131.3
1916	363.4	174.5	167.2

Total expenditures moved erratically during the first five years, showing no substantial net increase in spite of the rapid growth of population. However, in the following year they began an almost

---

[43] Ibid., 1913, p. 74.

[44] "It is imperative for reasons of health and right living, that water supply, sewer service, drainage, streets and sidewalks, electric lighting, and other necessities be promptly installed and much work accomplished in a short time by the public service forces of the town."

[45] Ibid., 1915, p. 73.

[46] Ibid., 1916, p. 73.

[47] Ibid., 1916, p. 78.

unbroken advance to a total in 1916 which was 176 per cent in excess of the expenditure made in 1905. The result was an approximately 38 per cent increase in per capita total expenditures for the period as a whole.

Non-commercial current expenditures rose 35 per cent between 1905 and 1910, this increase being somewhat larger than the accompanying growth of population. Expenditures continued to rise to 1913, declined in the following year, and then rose to a level about 50 per cent above that of 1910. Although this increase was less rapid than the accompanying growth of population, the per capita current expenditure for 1916 was still slightly in excess of that made at the beginning of the period under review.

The discrepancy between the movement of total and total non-commercial current expenditures is of course due to the distribution of the capital outlays. The bulk of the $202,000 spent in this way between 1906 and 1910[48] had been paid out by 1908, and the outlays made during the next two years were relatively small.[49] Although the cost of highway construction was lower during the next six years, the extremely large amounts spent for sewers and for town schools produced a non-commercial capital outlay of $385,000. Over half of the $232,000 spent for educational purposes represented a payment made in 1916 on a new high school building necessitated by the growth of the town. It is the spectacular advance in these capital outlays during the latter portion of the period under review which accounts for the relatively rapid increase in Belmont's total expenditures.

Most of the advance in non-commercial current expenditures down to 1910 was the result of increases from $24,000 to $32,000 in school maintenance charges, and from $8,000 to $14,000 in the

[48] Statistics follow:

	1906–1910	1911–1916
Schools	$35,068	$232,194
Highways	85,318	26,117
Fire Dept............	5,498	9,000
Sewers	76,061	117,248
	$201,945	$384,559

[49] In 1906, $37,000 was paid out for capital purposes; in 1910 capital outlays totaled only $15,000.

cost of fire and police protection. The continued rise in these items to $62,000 and $21,000 respectively, together with a $6,000 advance in interest charges, explains the bulk of the increase in current expenditures during the next six years. The cost of maintaining roads was only slightly larger than at the beginning of the period and the town's poor relief expenditure showed no significant change.[50]

Although Belmont's total expenditures, as shown by the *Statistics of Municipal Finances*, dropped from $188,000 to $187,000 between 1907 and 1910, there was a rise to $476,000 during the next six years. This meant an increase of approximately 42 per cent in the town's per capita expenditure for the period as a whole.[51] The state total had increased from $90,700,000 to $134,000,000, or from $31.25 per capita in 1907 to $36.60 in 1916, a net advance of slightly less than 18 per cent. It is clear that the town's expenditures were moving forward at a pace far greater than the average, and that this discrepancy cannot be explained away by the unusually rapid growth of Belmont's population.

The accompanying changes in the local assessment are revealed by the following statistics:

Year	Personalty	Land	Buildings	Total
		(In thousands of dollars.)		
1905	1,340	2,018	2,245	5,603
1910	1,392	2,193	2,932	6,517
1913	1,681	2,442	4,121	8,244
1916	2,745	3,202	6,627	12,574

The substantial rise shown by the total during the first five years, due mainly to a rapid growth in the value of buildings, was

---

[50] Statistics follow:

Year	Schools	Highways	Fire and Police	Interest	Poor
			(In thousands of dollars.)		
1905	24.3	20.5	8.4	8.3	3.0
1910	32.4	22.0	14.3	9.5	3.5
1913	40.2	25.4	18.0	10.3	2.2
1916	62.1	26.1	20.7	16.2	3.1

[51] This was about $39 in 1907 and $55 in 1916.

dwarfed by a 93 per cent advance during the remainder of the period. This again was due in large measure to the continued increase in the building assessment which by 1916 made up no less than 67 per cent of the value of real estate in the town.

Down to 1913 personalty had increased much less rapidly than population. Hence the per capita assessment had fallen from $314 in 1905 to $238 in 1913. Although a spectacular advance during the next three years resulted in a personalty valuation of $318 per capita, this was not substantially higher than the assessment at the beginning of the period, and since the state average had risen from $237 to $336 over the same interval,[52] it is apparent that Belmont's new residents were bringing with them a relatively small amount of personal wealth.

Down to 1913 the advance in real estate values had also failed to equal the growth of population. As a result Belmont's local assessment had fallen from $1,280 to approximately $1,160 per capita. However, a sharp advance during the next three years brought the per capita local assessment to $1,460, and produced a net rise of about 14 per cent for the period as a whole. Since this was decidedly less than the 38 per cent advance in per capita total expenditures, it is apparent that the suburban population had failed to bring with it enough locally taxable property to offset the increase in expenditures necessitated by the development of the town.

Meanwhile, the latter had been adversely affected by the changes made in 1908 and 1910 in the method of distributing receipts from the state tax on corporate excess.[53] These changes represented a shift from a system of allocation according to the domicile of the owner of the capital stock to one in which the taxes paid with respect to shares held by residents of the state were transferred to the localities in which the business was carried on. Naturally the amount allocated to predominantly residential towns was seriously curtailed, a fact which helps to explain the decline in Belmont's receipts from the bank and corporation taxes from $11,800 to $8,600 between 1905 and 1916. Revenue from

[52] The state total rose from $712,000,000 in 1905, to $1,241,000,000 in 1916.
[53] Bullock, "The Taxation of Property and Income in Massachusetts," p. 41.

the street railway tax, after rising to $16,000 in 1911, dropped to $9,700 during the next four years. As a result Belmont's income from the three state taxes, which had paid 24 per cent of current non-commercial expenditures in 1905, offset only 10 per cent of the corresponding total in 1916.

Nevertheless, the large increase in local valuations had raised the Tax Commissioner's estimate of Belmont's total taxable wealth from $6,300,000 to $13,700,000. This was somewhat in excess of the accompanying growth of population, and hence the per capita total valuation, after falling to $1,240 in 1910, had been raised to $1,587 in 1916. It is apparent that the construction of the Cambridge subway had checked the decline in this index of the town's taxable wealth, but in 1916 Belmont was still considerably below the minimum valuation indicative of an unusually wealthy community.

Down to 1910 the rise in its local assessment had offset the decline in receipts from state taxes as well as the increase in town expenditures.[54] Hence the rate applied to property had dropped from $19.90 to $18.80. During the next three years expenditures rose more rapidly and the rate was moved up to $20.50. However, even though total expenditures advanced more than 100 per cent between 1913 and 1916, which was far in excess of the accompanying growth in the local assessment, the latter was nevertheless somewhat more rapid than the advance in non-commercial current expenditures. It is apparent that Belmont chose to finance its capital outlays with borrowed money, and that as a result it became possible to reduce the rate applied to property in the town to $18.60 in 1916. The latter represented a reduction from a level 15 per cent above the current state average in 1905, to one 4 per cent below in 1916.

This reduction, however, had been accomplished at the cost of a large addition to the town's non-commercial debt. The latter, which had fallen from $192,000 in 1905 to $157,000 in 1913, was

---

[54] Belmont met a large share of its sewer construction costs by means of special assessments. In 1905 the latter paid nearly 37 per cent of the cost of laying sewers; in 1913, 33 per cent; and in 1916, 35 per cent. Thus the burden put upon general property as a result of variations in the use of these assessments was only slightly larger in 1916 than at the beginning of the period.

raised to $386,000 during the next three years.[55] The consequence was an advance in the per capita non-commercial debt from a low point of $22.20 in 1913 to $45 in 1916. The latter was somewhat larger than the per capita burden of indebtedness resting upon property in the town at the beginning of the period under review. Moreover, by 1916 this increase, coupled with the substantial advance in commercial debt which will be discussed below, had brought Belmont to the point where it had to apply to the state legislature "for authority to borrow money outside the limit of indebtedness, for the purpose of providing funds for a new high school building."[56]

Meanwhile, a total of $116,800 had been spent between 1906 and 1916 in extending the town's water system. Service fees had brought in $14,500, leaving $102,300 to be paid by the town itself. By 1916 the total cost of this utility had risen to nearly $241,000, the town's investment to $217,000.

The operating record is summarized below:

Year	Current Receipts	Current Expenditures	Net Receipts
1905	$14,659	$10,235	$4,424
1914	30,727	15,871	14,856
1916	29,124	17,099	12,025

A rapid rise in current receipts brought the operating surplus to a maximum in 1914 and the decline during the next two years left a surplus nearly two and three-quarters times as large as that reported for 1905. There were no operating deficits, and the surpluses shown, totaling $99,600, could have paid all but $2,600 of the town's share in the cost of extending this equipment.

The water board had a net debt of $30,900 in 1905. Additional loans raised the gross debt to $50,500 in 1916, but the sinking

---

[55] Statistics of indebtedness appear below:

Year	Sewers	Schools	Streets	Other	Total*
			(In thousands of dollars.)		
1905	63.0	105.0	58.5	8.0	196.8
1910	83.0	97.0	24.0	7.5	168.4
1913	103.0	93.0	17.0	3.0	156.2
1916	131.5	323.5	22.0	.5	399.0

* Total less value of sinking funds.

[56] Belmont Town Report, 1916, p. 73.

fund had grown to $17,200 and hence the net debt was only $2,380 more than it had been at the beginning of the period. Since the cost of the plant had increased to $241,000, the town's equity had risen from 75 to 86 per cent, the cost of production being assumed to equal true value.

The record of the Belmont water works continues to reflect a sound financial policy. Rates were adjusted so as to yield an operating surplus which sufficed to pay almost all the construction costs incurred during these years. Moreover, since the total expenditures, over and above charges for installing service, had exceeded current receipts by $2,968 in 1905 and only $1,788 in 1916, it is clear that the water works were becoming an even smaller burden to the town during the period under consideration.

The electric light department had spent $32,700 for construction, raising the original cost to $47,537. The increase in current receipts from $7,000 to $36,600 had more than offset the rise in current expenditures, and as a result the cost of operation had fallen from $7,200 to $1,500. Although the burden of debt had risen from $14,000 to $29,000, the cost of the investment had increased much more rapidly, and hence the town's equity had risen from practically nothing in 1905 to 37 per cent in 1916. While the record is not a good one, it reflects a considerable improvement over the period ending in 1905. It is clear that the electricity system, as well as the water works, was a considerably smaller burden in 1916 than it had been at the beginning of the period under review.

The first five years of this interval had witnessed a falling off in capital outlays producing a decline in per capita total expenditures which was somewhat larger than the accompanying drop in Belmont's per capita local assessment. Receipts from state taxes had increased somewhat; hence the town rate had declined, and the non-commercial debt had been reduced by $33,800. Although Belmont's finances were in slightly better condition than in 1905, this was largely the result of a reduced scale of capital outlays, a condition which was bound to be reversed if the town continued to show rapid development.

The subsequent increase in current expenditures was equaled

by the growth of the town's population, and surpassed by its local assessment. Although receipts from state taxes declined sharply, the town saw fit to carry out a further reduction in the rate applied to property within its limits. But the increase in population forced Belmont to make large capital outlays, particularly for schools, and as a result total expenditures rose considerably more rapidly than local assessments, lifting the non-commercial debt from $158,000 to $386,000. The new equipment brought an immediate rise in interest charges and a sharp increase in the cost of operating schools. The town officers themselves recognized that the 1916 rate could not be maintained.[57]

In spite of a considerable increase in its per capita valuation, Belmont's financial status in 1916 cannot be considered a healthy one. The population streaming into the town had forced the assumption of a large non-commercial debt, and was threatening to produce a rising tax rate. It was beginning to appear obvious that the benefits, in the form of increased local assessments, which accompanied the new suburban population were soon to be outweighed by the burden which the town was being forced to assume. It is probable that by 1916 the balance had already swung in that direction.

IV

Belmont's rapid growth continued during subsequent years, and by 1930 the town contained 21,748 inhabitants. No substantial amount of industry had been attracted, and since a zoning law restricts entry to those plants willing to use electricity for power, there is no reason to expect an industrial development in the future. Some truck farms remain but these are being squeezed out of the Boston market by the competition of southern farmers. Belmont has become a thoroughly developed residential suburb. Although it retains one section which possesses considerable wealth, it is inhabited for the most part by suburbanites — wage earners, and salaried people who possess little wealth and belong to the "white collar" classes.

[57] Belmont Town Report, 1916, p. 78.

The continued increase in suburban population has finally put a check upon the growing importance of the poll-tax payer in town meeting. In 1915 this element had made up nearly half of the town's taxpayers, and the presence of so large a group constituted a real threat to the financial stability of the town. But the poll-tax payers were only one third of the total in 1920, and only 23 per cent in 1928, the last year for which statistics are available. It is clear that the new residents were a property-owning group, assuming a share in the increased burden of taxation which accompanies larger appropriations. A town meeting of this type may be expected to pursue relatively conservative financial policies.

Yet Belmont's expenditures showed the following development:

Year	Total	Total Current	Total Non-Commercial Current
		(In thousands of dollars.)	
1916	363	174	167
1918	308	234	232
1920	564	351	347
1929	1,269	888	879
1930	1,743	974	967
1931	1,451	1,099	1,090
1933	1,356	1,070	1,070

Total expenditures fell off sharply to 1918, as a result of the wartime curtailment of capital outlays, rose to 1920, and declined in the year of depression which followed. They then moved irregularly upwards to a maximum in 1930 which represented a net increase of 380 per cent over the 1916 level. A sharp curtailment during the years of depression left a total for 1933 which was still substantially in excess of that made in 1929, and which represented a net increase of 48 per cent in per capita total expenditure over the period as a whole.[58]

With the exception of a sharp decline during the depression of 1921, non-commercial current expenditures rose steadily to a maximum in 1931, and the slight reduction during the next two years left an expenditure nearly five and one half times as large as that made in 1916. On a per capita basis this meant an advance from $19.40 to $49.40 or 154 per cent over an interval of seventeen years.

[58] Per capita total expenditures were $42.25 in 1916 and $62.50 in 1933.

The nature of the capital outlays made during these years becomes apparent upon consideration of the following statistics:

	1917–1920	1921–1924	1925–1928	1929–1933
		(In thousands of dollars.)		
Schools	244.7	400.8	411.2	76.0
Highways .	33.5	62.4	403.4	428.4
Fire	10.3	32.2	64.9	35.0
Police	10.1	....	5.1	87.8
Sewers	44.0	207.8	329.8	326.2
Misc.	....	40.7	40.9	164.2
Total ...	342.6	743.9	1,255.3	1,117.6

School outlays remained the dominant item until after 1924 when large amounts began to be spent for highways and sewers. The latter items became increasingly important during subsequent years when school expenditures were tapering off. The yearly average outlay for the period between 1917 and 1920 was $85,800 as compared with an average of $64,000 during the previous interval when Belmont's rapid development was just getting under way. Although this average reached its maximum of $314,000 between 1925 and 1928, it is obvious that the curtailment indicated by the movement of total expenditures did not come until the very close of the period under review.

The larger items among current expenditures are presented below:

Year	Schools	Highways	Fire and Police	Interest	Poor Relief
			(In thousands of dollars.)		
1916 ...	62.1	26.1	20.6	16.2	3.1
1920 ...	147.5	64.1	42.0	20.4	6.0
1930 ...	390.1	123.2	154.8	58.1	9.2
1931 ...	421.5	115.9	158.8	63.4	24.8
1933 ...	418.3	98.6	171.7	76.4	70.3

The 550 per cent rise in the total between 1916 and 1931 was more than matched by violent increases in the cost of schools and fire and police protection. Interest charges had risen 290 per cent, and highway maintenance costs had reached a maximum in 1930 which was 370 per cent above the expenditure for 1916. Poor relief, still a negligible burden in 1930, had begun a precipitous rise which, together with an increase in the cost of fire and police protection, more than offset the decline in school and highway costs during the last years of the period under review.

Meanwhile, other services occasioning only small costs in 1916 had been expanded so that large amounts were being paid out upon them at the end of the period.[59] This extension of the scope of the town's functions, plus the rapid growth of the burden of poor relief after 1928, together with the mounting cost of operating schools and providing fire and police protection, is responsible for the major portion of the extremely rapid development in Belmont's non-commercial current expenditures.

The general expansion in local governmental services characteristic of the period under consideration is reflected in the rise of the total expenditure for the state as a whole from $134,000,000 in 1916 to $358,000,000 in 1931. But this 168 per cent increase was far less than the 425 per cent rise in Belmont from $475,600 to $2,020,100. Although this was more than offset by the relatively rapid growth of Belmont's population, the latter's per capita expenditure for 1931 was still 10 per cent higher than the average for the state as a whole.[60]

Meanwhile, local valuations had shown the following development:

Year	Personalty	Land	Buildings	Total
		(In thousands of dollars.)		
1916	2,745	3,202	6,628	12,575
1917......	849	3,410	7,505	11,764
1928......	2,313	6,878	26,138	35,329
1930......	1,128	11,827	32,213	45,168
1933	1,159	12,187	35,937	49,283

There was a decided drop in Belmont's assessment in 1917 due to the removal of intangible personalty from the local lists, the income from this property having become subject to the state income tax enacted in the previous year. Tangible personalty rose almost steadily to 1928, when the passage of the motor vehicle

---

[59] The more important of these were:

	1916	1931	1933
		(In thousands of dollars.)	
Library.........	4.9	19.8	19.4
Health	4.0	29.3	37.6
Parks	.3	13.9	16.2
Ash Collection ..	3.5	25.1	21.6

[60] Per capita expenditures were as follows:

Year	Belmont	Massachusetts
1916	$55	$36
1931	93	84

excise tax removed these vehicles from the local lists.[61] This brought another sharp drop in Belmont's personalty in the following year, and the slight increase to 1933 left a valuation only 42 per cent of that reported in 1916.

Although both land and building values rose almost steadily throughout the period, the building assessment showed an unusually sharp increase down to 1928, when it accounted for 79 per cent of the total value of real estate in the town. But in the following year a reviewing committee was appointed, consisting of the building inspector, a builder, and a real-estate operator, which conducted a thorough review of the land values. The result appeared in 1930. The assessed value of land was raised $4,600,000 in a single year, this being $400,000 more than the total increase shown between 1916 and 1929. A town assessor stated that the chief advances were suffered by land upon which the older houses in the town were constructed, on the theory that this property had fallen behind in the general rise of assessed valuations during the post-war boom. One result was a drop in the value of buildings from 80 to 75 per cent of the total real-estate assessment between 1929 and 1933. Nevertheless, at the latter date this ratio was still about 11 per cent above that existing in 1916.

A second peculiarity in Belmont's real-estate assessment is that both land and building values continued to increase after 1930 when the state totals were declining.[62] A town assessor pointed out that this phenomenon was due in part to the fact that the depression had not succeeded in halting building operations in the town, and in part to a policy pursued by the assessors when dealing with the property of citizens who were either welfare recipients or in danger of becoming such. Abatements were granted in these cases in lieu of a reduced property valuation, thus affording temporary relief and at the same time preventing a decline in the town's real-estate assessment. The procedure was

[61] It will be recalled that this tax was simply an administrative device installed to facilitate collection. The vehicles were certified by state registration officials to the town in which they were customarily kept and were taxed by the latter at the state average rate. (*Tercentenary Edition of the General Laws*, c. 60, A, sec. 1.)

[62] The total real estate assessed in Massachusetts was $6,403,000,000 in 1930, $6,039,000,000 in 1933.

admittedly based upon the theory that the current drop in the selling price of Belmont real estate was purely temporary.

The resulting changes in the value of land and buildings over the period as a whole dwarfed the decline in personalty, and as a result Belmont's local valuation for 1933 was nearly three times as large as that reported in 1916. This increase, however, was decidedly less than the 550 per cent rise shown by non-commercial current expenditures.

Part of this gap is closed by the receipts obtained from the state income tax. Under the original system of distribution which attempted to recompense wealthy towns for their loss of intangible personalty, Belmont received $37,000 in 1917. This had fallen to $32,700 in 1919 when the transition was begun to a system of allocation according to state taxes paid. Belmont's income rose subsequently to a maximum of $136,600 in 1930, but this increase was more than offset by the accompanying advance in current expenditures. As a result income from this tax paid only 14 per cent of these expenditures in 1930 as compared with 18 per cent in 1916. The violent decline in Belmont's receipts from the state income tax to $76,600 in 1933 left revenue sufficient to offset only 7 per cent of the non-commercial current expenditures. Hence the failure of this income to rise more rapidly may be added to the factors tending to increase the burden placed upon real estate in the town.

The receipts from other state taxes are shown in the following table:

Year	Bank and Corporation Taxes*	Street Railway Tax*	Total Receipts*	Per Cent of Non-Commercial Current Expenditures
1917	8.8	4.4†	13.2	6.5
1921	19.5	2.8	22.3	7.2
1924	8.9	4.0	12.9	2.2
1930	19.1	5.7‡	24.8	2.6
1933	11.3	...	11.3	1.0

*In thousands.   † Average 1917 and 1918.   ‡ Average 1930 and 1931.

Belmont's income from the tax on corporate excess must have been adversely affected by an act passed in 1916 completing the transition from a system of distribution according to the domicile of the shareholder to a system of distribution according to the place in which business was carried on.[63] Nevertheless, the receipts from the taxes on street railways, bank shares, and corporate excess rose 88 per cent between 1917 and 1930. However, this again was proportionately much less than the advance in current expenditures, and a sharp decline during the next three years left an income of really negligible importance. On the other hand $65,700 was received in 1929 from the motor vehicle excise, and although a decline after 1930 had reduced this to $48,000 in 1933, this revenue served to offset the decline in personalty during the years in question.

This new income, combined with increased receipts from state taxes and the violent rise in real-estate values, had brought the Tax Commissioner's estimated total valuation from $13,700,000 in 1916 to $48,600,000 in 1932. As a result, the per capita total, after declining from $1,587 in 1916 to $1,415 in 1922, rose to $2,250 during the next ten years. It is apparent that the new development had brought a substantial increase in the town's total taxable wealth.

Yet the advance in expenditures had been considerably in excess of the rise in local assessments, and the percentage of the new current expenditures which could be paid out of state taxes had fallen a great deal. Under these circumstances a substantial increase was to be expected in the rate applied to property in the town.

The probability of such a change was increased by the diminishing use of the special assessment in financing the cost of sewer construction. While such assessments had covered no less than 35 per cent of this outlay in 1916, they paid only 9 per cent in 1931, and apparently offered no assistance whatsoever in 1933, the $68,500 spent for sewers in this year being paid out of the general revenues of the town. On the other hand, street betterment assessments, which had played a negligible role down to 1925, were applied with increasing vigor during subsequent years. In 1933 no less than $42,000 was raised in this manner, which more than covered the amount spent in that year for the construction of new streets.[64]

---

[63] *Acts and Resolves*, 1916, c. 299.

[64] A total of $38,436 was paid out in this way in 1933. Belmont was also assisted

The result of all these changes was a rise in the Belmont tax rate from $20.00 in 1917 to a maximum of $33.25 in 1928, bringing the town rate to a level approximately 14 per cent above a greatly increased state average. Although current expenditures continued to rise, the sharp revision and continued increase in local assessments, coupled with the decline in capital outlays, brought the Belmont rate to $24.00 per thousand in 1933, while a decline in valuations over the state as a whole had raised the average rate applied to property in Massachusetts to $30.02, or 25 per cent more than the rate being applied in the town of Belmont. Nevertheless, the latter showed a net increase of 20 per cent over the period as a whole.

The rapid advance in borrowing, which had accompanied the completion of the subway and had raised Belmont's net non-commercial indebtedness to $386,000 in 1916, continued during subsequent years. A maximum was reached in 1930, when the non-commercial debt stood at $1,394,000. This was far in excess of the accompanying rise in population, and hence the per capita debt had advanced from $40.00 in 1916 to $64.40 in 1930. Up to this point the rise in the town levy had not sufficed to prevent a substantial growth in the burden of indebtedness borne by property in the town.

The subsequent decline in total expenditures which reduced the town rate so strikingly also brought a decline in the non-commercial debt to $1,062,000 or $49 per capita, which was only 22 per cent in excess of the per capita debt present at the beginning of the period under review.[65]

----

with grants of $27,000 and $13,400 from state and county authorities in 1933 and 1934 respectively. Income from this source had been sporadic. In 1917 and 1918 $15,700 was received; in 1925 and 1926, $57,500; and in 1928 there was an income of $27,800 from these sources.

[65] The gross debt is shown in greater detail in the following table:

Year	Sewers	Schools	Streets	Misc.	Total
			(In thousands of dollars.)		
1916..	131.5	323.5	22.0	.5	477.5
1920..	152.5	454.5	14.5	5.0	626.5
1924..	283.0	679.0	27.5	25.0	1,014.5
1928..	294.5	781.0	161.0	35.0	1,271.5
1930..	242.5	861.0	230.0	104.0	1,437.5
1933..	161.0	712.0	139.0	80.0	1,092.0

But before any conclusions are drawn from this evidence it is appropriate to consider the record of the town's commercial enterprises. Between 1917 and 1933 an additional $594,000 had been spent extending the town water works, raising the total cost and the town's investment to $835,000 and $716,000 respectively. The operating record follows:

Year	Current Receipts	Current Expenditures	Net Receipts
		(In thousands of dollars.)	
1916	29.1	17.1	12.0
1924	61.6	37.5	24.1
1926	63.7	58.8	5.0
1929	92.2	63.5	28.7
1933	106.7	105.7	2.0

A rapid advance in revenues had doubled the net receipts by 1924, but this was more than offset by a sharp rise in expenditures during the next two years. Operating charges again lagged behind the rise in income, and consequently net receipts rose to a maximum in 1929. However, a subsequent advance in expenditures had very nearly wiped out the operating surplus by 1933. There were no deficits during this period; the net receipts were sufficient to pay 53 per cent of the town's share in the cost of the extensions made between 1917 and 1933.

The water board debt dropped from $131,500 to $47,500 in the four years following 1916. It rose to $202,000 in 1927, and then declined to $148,000 in 1933.[66] Since the cost of the plant had increased from $241,000 to $835,000, the equity held by the town had risen from 46 to 82 per cent of the total.

Nevertheless, the large operating surpluses present during most of the period under review had paid a smaller proportion of construction costs than in the years before 1916, and at the close of the period income from water rates was being rapidly overtaken by the advance in current expenditures. By 1933 the enterprise threatened to fall short of being self-supporting, and seemed about to become a substantial burden to the town.

Outlays on the electricity distributing system totaled $366,000 for the years 1917 to 1933 inclusive, raising the total cost of the

[66] This is the net debt. The water-board sinking fund had been liquidated in 1930.

enterprise to $413,700. The operating results are summarized below:

Year	Current Receipts*	Current Expenditures	Net Receipts
		(In thousands of dollars.)	
1916	36.6	38.1	− 1.5
1924	113.7	89.0	24.7
1928	177.9	150.1	27.8
1933	232.6	229.2	3.4

* Does not include town appropriations.

Income exceeded current expenditures for the first time in 1917, and there were operating surpluses in all the remaining years. A considerable increase in expenditures after 1928 more than matched the accompanying growth in receipts; the result was a net receipt of only $3,400 in 1933, which was only slightly better than the operating record at the beginning of the period.

The debt on the plant had fallen from $29,000 to $6,000, which together with the concurrent advance in the cost of the equipment had increased the town's equity from 37 to about 99 per cent of the total. The financial position of this enterprise had improved appreciably during the twenties only to lose a large portion of this gain during the depression years which closed the period under review.

In 1916 Belmont's financial record had been such as to leave a possible basis for the view that the completion of the Cambridge subway had been financially beneficial to the town. However, the record for subsequent years casts considerable doubt upon such an opinion. It is true that real-estate values have risen very rapidly, and that this advance, together with increasing revenue from state taxes and from the excise on motor vehicles, has raised the estimated total valuation to well over $2,000 per capita. But a good portion of the rise in land values was the direct result of a revaluation conducted at the very peak of a boom period. These values, together with those placed upon buildings, have continued to rise throughout the subsequent depression, and it is highly likely that there has been at least a temporary over-valuation of some of the property in the town.

Belmont had also benefited by the vigorous policy pursued by its electricity distributing plant, but this must be set off against a substantial weakening in the finances of the town water board. Although increased use of the street betterment assessment had tended to relieve the burden placed upon property in general, this had been more than canceled by a decreased use of the special assessment for sewers, by a sharp drop in receipts from the income tax during the depression, and by a decline in the percentage of current expenditures which could be paid out of revenue obtained from other state taxes.

But these changes are of minor importance when compared with the record of town expenditures. The new population necessitated large outlays for the construction of schools, highways, and sewers. It brought an extremely rapid increase in the cost of operating town schools and supplying fire and police protection. Several minor functions have been expanded, and have come to require a substantial yearly appropriation. Since the resulting increase in total expenditures has outdistanced the advance in taxable wealth as well as the growth of population, it is not surprising to find the rate applied to property in the town rising to a maximum in 1928 which was 14 per cent above a greatly increased state average, and the town debt rising to a maximum in 1930 which was more than three and one half times the non-commercial debt outstanding in 1916.

Although Belmont's current expenditures showed a sizable advance during subsequent years, and although the town carried out a substantial reduction in the burden of its indebtedness, the sharp curtailment in total expenditures, the assistance received from the federal government, from state and county highway authorities, and from the contributions of the employees of the town itself,[67] combined with a continued rise in the real-estate assessment in the very teeth of an acute depression, had enabled the town to cut its rate to $24 in 1933.

It must be admitted that this evidence indicates that a rapidly developing popular suburb can meet the onslaught of an acute depression by curtailing the expansion of its capital outlays. In this instance the relief afforded by the policy was substantial, but too

[67] The town obtained a grant of $16,000 in 1933 from the federal government and $14,500 from the F.E.R.A. An employees' contribution of 5 per cent of their salaries was estimated to yield $37,600 in the same year.

much emphasis must not be placed upon the relatively low rate which the town was able to achieve. It is significant that no serious reductions were considered advisable in most of the current expenditures, the cost of operating the town being much larger in 1933 than in 1929. Moreover, the fact must not be overlooked that the low rate achieved in 1933 was the joint product of a number of rather special circumstances, of new and unusual sources of income, and of a striking advance in real-estate assessments during a period of acute economic distress. Finally, it seems likely that the drastic curtailment in outlays, which after all is the major factor in the decline of the town rate after 1928, is only temporary and will probably cease when the economic horizon begins to brighten. Fundamentally, it does not seem that Belmont's present financial position is as sound as in the years preceding the second rapid influx of suburban population.

During most of the period under review the burden of expenditures required by these new residents has clearly outweighed the benefits, chiefly in the form of increased real-estate assessments, which accompanied the development of the town. Since the improvement during subsequent years has been largely temporary, it may be concluded that the influx of suburban population resulting from the construction of a system furnishing rapid transportation between Belmont and Boston, while possibly of great profit to individual citizens, has not produced beneficial results in the finances of the town itself.

V

The story of Belmont's experience can be summarized as follows. During the first thirty years of its independent existence the extremely wealthy town set up by the incorporation of 1859 developed into a small, select, residential suburb. Its expenditures advanced rather slowly, and the town was favored by the existing method of distributing receipts from state taxes. Hence in 1890 it still possessed a very small non-commercial debt and a rate 22 per cent below the current state average. Its residents still possessed a large per capita wealth and the town itself was very well off financially.

But suburban population was beginning to flow in, bringing with it a rise in taxes that was considerably in excess of the accompanying advance in local assessments. In spite of increased receipts from state taxes and the use of the special assessment in financing the laying of sewers, a substantial town debt was accumulated, and the tax rate experienced a rapid increase. The new population had a distinctly bad effect on Belmont's finances.

The town's growth lagged somewhat during the early years of the twentieth century. The expansion of the school and highway systems was finally halted, and the increase in current expenditures slowed down. In spite of reduced income from the tax on corporate excess, and a continued decline in per capita taxable wealth, the town's finances had been improved considerably by 1910.

Then it became known that a subway was to be built between Cambridge and Boston and that this would greatly reduce the cost and consumption of time required to commute between Boston and Belmont. Population began to stream into the town. Its schools became inadequate and large outlays were inescapable. While the accompanying rise in real-estate assessments and the lag of current behind total expenditures made it possible to avoid an increase in the tax rate down to 1916, these things could not prevent a rapid growth in the town's non-commercial indebtedness.

Between 1916 and 1928 the threatened increase in Belmont's financial burdens became an actuality. The rapid rise in real-estate values was more than offset by the advance in total and current expenditures. The tax rate increased with unusual rapidity, and the non-commercial debt showed a large advance. Although there was a sharp decline in both the town debt and the tax rate during subsequent years, this was due mainly to the cessation of capital outlays enforced by the current industrial depression. The relatively low rate achieved in 1933 was the product of a number of peculiar circumstances. It did not indicate any real improvement in the financial structure of the town, for the cost of operating Belmont was greater in 1933 than in 1929. Hence the conclusion may be drawn that the Cambridge subway which so greatly stimulated Belmont's suburban development and hastened its transition to a "popular" suburb has brought financial burdens far outweighing the benefits received. Since this development took place under a town meeting which was at all times dominated by property-tax payers, the results obtained speak eloquently against the wisdom, from the point of view of the town's financial position, of booster publicity campaigns and well-intentioned attempts to reduce the cost of commuting to a wealthy suburban community.

CHAPTER VI

THE FINANCIAL HISTORY OF THE TOWN OF HOPKINTON, 1840–1905

THE previous chapter dealt with the financial results of a rapid influx of population into a wealthy suburban community; the present chapter contains a similar analysis of the results accruing to a small rural town with a rather low per capita wealth as a result of the growth and decay of a relatively important industry within its borders.

I

Hopkinton is located in the southwestern portion of Middlesex county. Although most of the area which it occupies is broken and rocky, there is considerable land suitable for farming, and until the 1840's agriculture was the chief occupation practiced in the town.[1] Lacking substantial commercial and industrial interests, its population had naturally grown less rapidly than that of Massachusetts as a whole,[2] and in 1840 there were only 2,262 persons resident in the town. However, a small boot and shoe industry had already sprung up within the borders of this predominantly rural community,[3] and the value of the footwear which it produced rose from about $150,000 in 1837 to over $1,000,000 in 1855. Five years later, one of the existing shops was converted into the third largest boot and shoe factory in the state.[4] While the number of these shops operating in the town dropped from eleven in the early fifties to seven in 1875, the value of the

---

[1] Conklin, *Middlesex*, II, 576, and Hurd, *Middlesex*, III, 780.

[2] Hopkinton's population increased from 1,027 in 1765, when reliable statistics begin, to 2,262 in 1840. This 120 per cent rise was far less than the 209 per cent increase in the state as a whole.

[3] In 1837 there were also three cotton mills in Hopkinton turning out goods worth $55,000. By 1845 their value product had fallen to $34,700; their decline continued during subsequent years.

[4] Conklin, *Middlesex*, II, 577.

goods produced continued to increase, although at a slower rate, until 1880, when the footwear turned out was valued at $1,980,000. The rapid development of this industry between 1840 and 1855 was accompanied by a 74 per cent increase in the town's population, and the slower development during subsequent years was reflected by a falling off in the rate of growth experienced by the town itself.[5] In the absence of other alterations in Hopkinton's economic structure it is obvious that this boot and shoe industry was the dominant factor in the town's development during the entire period 1840–1880, when both town and industry were rising to their peak.

What was the effect of the industrial development upon the finances of this small agricultural community? No record of expenditures is available for 1840 but the appropriations made in town meeting are shown by the town clerk's books, and these furnish a fair index of the approximate level of expenditures. The following appropriations were made in 1840 and 1850 respectively:

	1840	1850
Town Charges	$1,500	$5,000
Highways	1,000	1,250
Schools	1,000	1,075

It ought to be pointed out first that a portion of Hopkinton had been annexed to the new town of Ashland in 1849, and that therefore the appropriations for 1850 were for a town of smaller area than those made ten years before. Secondly, the school appropriations listed above are estimates. The records show an appropriation of $100 per district. There were ten of the latter in 1850 and it has been assumed that none were created during this decade. However, it is possible that the loss of the Ashland area might have reduced the number of districts in Hopkinton, and if this were so, the appropriation for schools would show a decline over the decade under review.[6] Finally, it must be observed that the

---

[5] Hopkinton contained 3,934 persons in 1855, 4,340 in 1860, and 4,601 in 1880.

[6] It is probable that the town appropriation does not represent the entire expenditure made upon the Hopkinton schools, for the town was still using the district school system. The latter had been authorized under the constitution of 1780. In 1800 the district had been given power to erect and maintain the schools within its borders, to levy a district tax, and to expend the money raised. The districts were

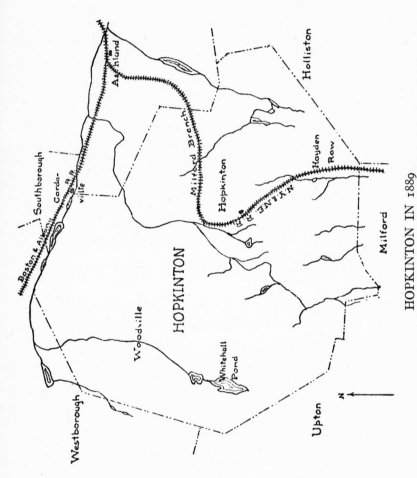

HOPKINTON IN 1889

SHOWING THE PORTION OF ASHLAND SET OFF FROM HOPKINTON IN 1849

total current expenditures for 1850, as recorded in the treasurer's books, were only $5,744, of which $1,093 was spent contesting the Ashland case. A new school was built at a cost of $1,328, producing a total expenditure of $7,126. This is only slightly less than the total appropriation made for that year. If the cost of the Ashland suit is excluded, Hopkinton's appropriations for current purposes must have been about $4,500 in 1850. Although the inadequacies of these data make their interpretation difficult, they seem to indicate that there probably had been a substantial increase in current expenditures during the decade under review.

Expenditures for the entire period during which the boot and shoe industry was rising to its peak are summarized in the following table:

Year	Total Expenditures		Total Current Expenditures	
	Actual*	Per Capita	Actual*	Per Capita
1840	3.5†	$1.55†	3.5†	$1.55†
1850	7.1	2.54	4.7	1.68
1857	19.5	4.75	12.4‡	3.10
1860	27.7	6.40	12.5‡	2.91
1867	45.0	10.09	24.0‡	5.85
1872	118.4	27.00	34.2	7.78
1876	48.8	10.80	48.1	10.65
1881	80.6	17.50	43.5	9.43

* In thousands.
† Estimated.
‡ Does not include interest charges.

It is apparent that total as well as current expenditures had advanced very rapidly between 1850 and 1857. Although the latter

made corporate entities in 1817, and a supervisory town committee was added in 1826. Under the *Revised Statutes* of 1835 the school districts were given power (c. 23, sec. 25) to choose a prudential committee which was to provide and maintain the school houses and select and contract with a school master for the district. The district was also given power (sec. 28) to raise money in order to carry out these functions. However, this system was not a mandatory one. The town itself was authorized to provide any of the district schools and could "raise such sums of money, for the support of the schools aforesaid (common schools), as they shall judge necessary" (c. 23, sec. 9). Under these conditions it is not possible to say just what the Hopkinton appropriation for the school account paid, although it is probable that this appropriation was supplemented by taxes levied by the individual school districts.

For a short history of the school district system in Massachusetts see J. W. Dickson, "The Educational History of Massachusetts," chap. cxxxvii in W. T. Davis, *The New England States* (1897).

item was checked during the next three years, it joined the upward surge of total expenditures during the Civil War and the period immediately following. Total expenditures reached a maximum in 1872, declined sharply during the next four years, and then rose to the end of the period under review. Current expenditures reached their maximum in 1876, and were only slightly lower in 1881.

This advance in expenditures had been far in excess of the accompanying growth of population. As a result the per capita total expenditure for 1881 was nearly eight times as large as that made in 1850, while the per capita current expenditure showed a net increase of 550 per cent over the same interval.

The advance in current expenditures to 1876 was largely the result of increases from $1,100 or 39 cents per capita to $11,300 or $2.50 per capita in the cost of operating town schools; from $700 to $8,400, or from 25 cents to $1.86 per capita for the relief of town poor; and from $500 to $6,100 in the cost of town roads, together with the addition of an expenditure of $12,700 for the payment of interest on borrowed money. The subsequent decline was due mainly to a drop from $8,400 to $6,600 in poor relief, from $6,100 to $3,200 in highway expenditures, and from $12,700 to $10,600 in interest charges. Over the entire interval between 1850 and 1881, the per capita cost of schools, highways, and poor relief had risen 575,400, and 550 per cent respectively.[7] It is apparent that this period of industrial development had witnessed a tremendous expansion in the cost of operating the town of Hopkinton, and that the increases in current expenditures had been far in excess of the accompanying growth of population.

Statistics of taxes levied become available in 1862 when the state document entitled *The Aggregates of Polls, Property, Taxes, etc.*, began to be published. Between this date and 1867, taxes levied on polls and property in Hopkinton rose from $18,400 to $31,200, or 69 per cent, which was far less than the rise from

---

[7] The per capita expenditures follow:

	1850	1881
Schools	$.39	$2.24
Poor	.25	1.24
Highways	.18	.72

$7,600,000 to $15,700,000 or 106 per cent in the state as a whole. Between 1867 and 1881 taxes levied in Hopkinton rose from $31,200 to $44,800, or 44 per cent, as compared with a rise from $15,700,000 to $24,800,000 in the state total. It is apparent that the Civil War had brought a comparatively small expansion in this town's expenditures, and that their subsequent development had also lagged somewhat behind the average for the entire state. However, it must not be forgotten that these statistics relate only to the second phase of Hopkinton's industrial development, to the period of slow expansion which had followed the first spectacular growth in what had become the town's chief industry.

The following table contains the record of property valuations during the period in question:

Year	Personalty	Real Estate (In thousands of dollars.)	Total
1840	...	....	502
1850	185*	607*	887†
1862	359	1,178	1,537
1872	659	1,362	2,021
1876	703	1,538	2,241
1881	772	1,652	2,424

* Values for personalty and real estate are for doomed property only.
† Given by state valuation of 1860.

By 1862 the rapid development of Hopkinton had raised its local assessment to a level which was 206 per cent above that of 1840. This was somewhat in excess of the accompanying advance in the total valuation for the entire state.[8]

It is significant that stock in trade assessed in the town had risen from $14,800 to $191,800 between 1840 and 1860, a twelve-fold increase during a period when the assessed value of this property in the state as a whole was doubling. Moreover, the value of bank shares listed in the town had risen from $3,400 to $28,200 during the forties, and had advanced to $112,500 during the next ten years. These were increases of 800 and 300 per cent respectively, and were far in excess of the 373 and 6 per cent advances in the state total. Moreover, the value of other corporate shares in Hopkinton had risen from $2,500 to $3,700 between 1850

[8] The latter rose from $299,900,000 in 1840 to $861,500,000 in 1861, a net rise of 188 per cent.

and 1860, when the assessed value of this type of security was declining from $27,700,000 to $15,600,000 in the state as a whole. The movement of these items, together with the rise in the town's total personalty assessment between 1850 and 1862, indicates that Hopkinton's personal property valuation had advanced with relative rapidity during the period under consideration, and that it was the increase in this type of property rather than the growth of real-estate values which explains the relatively rapid development shown by the town's total assessment between 1840 and 1862. These conclusions are in accord with the known facts of a rising industry in an otherwise slowly developing agricultural town.

Hopkinton's personalty assessment rose steadily from 1862 to 1881, showing a net increase of 115 per cent, again far in excess of the 52 per cent rise in the state as a whole.[9] This rise, however, was more than offset by the lag in real estate values, and as a result Hopkinton's total valuation fell considerably behind the 90 per cent rise shown by the state total between 1862 and 1881.[10] Consequently the 485 per cent increase in the town's local assessment between 1840 and 1881 was not as large as that shown by the total for Massachusetts as a whole.

A committee of the General Court had produced an estimated total valuation of about $220 per capita for Hopkinton in 1840. A similar estimate made in 1865 by the Commissioner of Corporations and Taxation amounted to $365, and by 1876 this had risen to $515 per capita. It is obvious that the new industry had been accompanied by a considerable expansion in taxable wealth, but that this increase had fallen far short of raising Hopkinton to the status of a wealthy community.[11]

The relatively rapid advance in town expenditures had raised the Hopkinton rate from about $6.97[12] in 1840 to $10.70 in 1862, when it about equaled the average for the entire state. By 1876 the continued advance in expenditures had produced a rate of $18.20 per thousand and this was 42 per cent above the current

[9] Personalty in Massachusetts rose from $309,000,000 to $469,000,000 between 1862 and 1881.
[10] The state total rose from $861,000,000 in 1862 to $1,648,000,000 in 1881.
[11] Chen, *op. cit.*, pp. 31–32.
[12] Estimated total expenditures divided by total valuation.

state average. A decline to $17.50 in 1881 coupled with a rise in Massachusetts as a whole brought it about that property in Hopkinton was being subjected to a rate only 18 per cent above the current state average. Nevertheless, this rate was 150 per cent higher than that applied in 1840 when the industrial development was just getting under way. It is obvious that the great increase in assessed valuations had failed to offset the rising level of town expenditures.

It is not unnatural that Hopkinton's net liabilities (after deduction of the par value of sinking funds) had risen with the tax rate from $33,000 in 1857 to $168,000 in 1876, a considerable portion of this advance being the result of investments in the capital stock of a local railroad which was later written off as worthless.[13] Although the net liabilities had been reduced to $125,000 by 1881, this was still 275 per cent in excess of those existing in 1857.

To sum up, the rise of the boot and shoe industry in Hopkinton was accompanied by a rapid increase in expenditures, particularly in the expenditures for schools, highways, and poor relief, all of these advancing far more rapidly than the accompanying growth of population. The new industry had also stimulated the growth of the local assessment, the advance in the personalty valuation being particularly striking. Yet large as these increases were, they failed to match the rise in town expenditures. As a result, Hopkinton not only acquired liabilities of $28.00 per capita, involving a per capita interest charge of $2.38, but also found it necessary to enforce a large increase in the town rate, an increase which brought the latter to a point considerably above the current state average. Since the greater part of the new liabilities was the direct result of a deliberate attempt to foster the industrial development of the town, and since the chief advances came in those types of expenditure most likely to react to the influx of an industrial population, it is extremely likely that the coming of the new industry had resulted in a net increase in the burdens borne by other property in the town.

[13] The town spent $80,000 in this way in 1872 and another $20,000 in the following year. The stock purchased was that of the Hopkinton railroad.

II

About 1880 when the boot and shoe industry was at its peak there were nine plants operating in Hopkinton, three of them being the property of a single organization.[14] Two years later a fire destroyed fourteen buildings, among them the largest of the shoe factories, which was rebuilt in the town of Framingham. With this event the rapid decay of the industry set in. By 1885 the state census listed only four plants, turning out goods worth $1,563,000 as against $1,981,000 in 1880, and employing 870 persons as compared with 1,076 "shoemakers" reported by the census for 1880. By 1895 only one plant remained, and ten years later the shoe industry had completely vanished. It is a striking fact that this abrupt decline is not to be accounted for by changing conditions of production or competition, but rather by the circumstance that most of the enterprises had been built up and operated by individual entrepreneurs, and when these men died there were no capable persons willing or able to carry on their work. As a result the enterprises were soon forced to stop operations and liquidate. In 1905 there were no shoe factories left and no new enterprises had come in to replace them.[15]

Hopkinton's population had dropped 11 per cent during the decade following 1880. It fell sharply to 1895, and declined more slowly during the next ten years. By 1905 the town contained only 2,505 inhabitants, or a little more than half of the population recorded for 1880. It is quite obvious that the town itself had declined as a result of the decay of its chief industry.

How were its finances affected by these developments? Expenditures are summarized in the table at the top of the next page. The third item, made necessary by the construction of the Hopkinton water works, consists of current expenditures minus the operating deficit of the water board. The construction costs of this enterprise, so far as they are not offset by operating surpluses, are included in total expenditures.

---

[14] For this information as well as for the general story of the shoe industry in Hopkinton I am indebted to Mr. E. M. Eldridge.

[15] The product of largest value in 1905 amounted to $19,000. This was the work of three plants with a total capital of $7,865 producing "Food."

Year	Total Actual*	Per Capita	Total Current Actual*	Per Capita	Total Non-Commercial Current Actual*	Per Capita
1881	80.6	$17.50	43.3	$ 9.43	43.3	$ 9.43
1887	71.4	18.00	54.4	13.75	54.4	13.75
1890	52.9	12.90	39.9	9.73	39.3	9.60
1895	76.1	25.55	44.5	14.90	43.2	14.50
1901	52.1	19.90	38.0	14.55	36.5	13.95
1905	44.4	17.75	38.5	15.35	37.5	15.00

* In thousands.

Non-commercial current expenditures rose to 1887. They dropped abruptly to 1890, but another rise during the next five years brought them to approximately the level prevailing in 1881. Although a sharp drop in 1896 was followed by a slow rise, the expenditures for 1905 were still 13 per cent less than those for 1881.

Total expenditures showed a slight decline between 1881 and 1895. They dropped sharply with current expenditures in 1896 but failed to advance during subsequent years, showing a net decline of 45 per cent for the entire period now under consideration.

Allowance for the growth of population by reduction to a per capita basis produces a 59 per cent rise in non-commercial current expenditures between 1881 and 1905 and wipes out the 45 per cent decline shown by the total expenditures.

There was relatively little change in current expenditures for schools, highways, and poor relief during this period of industrial decay. In 1905 the town was spending $10,800, $4,100, and $7,100 for these purposes as compared with $10,000, $3,200, and $6,600 in 1881. Naturally, the decline in population produced a substantial advance in the per capita statistics, the cost of operating schools rising from $2.24 to $4.17 per capita, the highway charges advancing from 72 cents in 1881 to $1.58 in 1905, and the per capita burden of poor relief increasing from $1.37 to $2.74 over the period under review.

Interest charges which had declined only slightly between 1881 and 1895 dropped from $9,000 to $2,600 in the following year. The rise to $3,100 in 1905 offset only a small proportion of the preceding decline. It is this reduction in interest charges which accounts for the drop in non-commercial current expenditures in 1896, but the decline in this item over the period as a whole was offset by increases elsewhere, and as a result current expenditures showed a net rise and per capita current expenditures an increase of 59 per cent. It is clear that the cost of operating Hopkinton had not diminished with the decline in population resulting from the decay of the town's chief industry.

The slow curtailment of total expenditures down to 1895 was accompanied by a slight drop in taxes levied from \$44,800 to \$42,700. However, the sharp drop in expenditures in 1896 brought the tax levy to \$33,600 in the following year, and the tax of \$32,800 levied in 1905 left a net decline of 27 per cent for the entire period under review. This is in marked contrast with the 137 per cent increase from \$24,000,000 to \$57,000,000 in the total for the state as a whole.

Meanwhile, local assessments had pursued the following course:

Year	Personalty	Real Estate (In thousands of dollars.)	Total
1881	772	1,652	2,424
1895	537	1,579	2,116
1896	386	1,525	1,911
1905	192	1,447	1,639

It is apparent that the total valuation dropped 32 per cent during the period under consideration and that the larger portion of this decline was the result of a slump in the personalty assessment. However, it is also apparent that the decline had not been a steady one. Personalty, after shrinking only 30 per cent between 1881 and 1895, was cut an additional 27 per cent in the following year, and declined rapidly to the end of the period. Although real-estate values fell more evenly, their decline was also more rapid after 1896.

As a result of this peculiar movement in local assessments, Hopkinton's estimated per capita taxable wealth rose from \$515 in 1876 to \$709 in 1895. However, it fell to \$690 during the next three years and reached \$674 per capita in 1905. Nevertheless, it is clear that the sharp decline in the local assessment after 1895 had failed to prevent a 28 per cent rise in the town's per capita wealth over the period as a whole. Valuations as well as expenditures failed to keep pace with the decline in the town's population.

The significance of the movement of local assessments as well as the sharp drop in expenditures between 1895 and 1897 is

brought out by the record of the town's indebtedness presented
below:

Year	Town Liabilities	Sinking Funds*	Net Town Liabilities†
		(In thousands of dollars.)	
1881	150	25	125
1889	180	82	98
1895	202	148	54
1896	66	15	51
1897	47	...	47
1902	41	9	32
1905	65	13	52

* Net after deduction of unpaid grants.
† Net after deduction of sinking funds only.

The growth of the sinking fund set up in 1887 for the retirement
of the town debt had much more than offset the subsequent increase in gross liabilities, resulting in a net indebtedness for non-
commercial purposes in 1895 only 42 per cent of that existing in
1881. In this and the following year the last payments were made
on the sinking fund. The latter was liquidated, and hence it was
no longer necessary to pay interest on the town securities held
by the trustees of the fund. These circumstances account for the
sharp drop in interest charges appearing in 1896, but because
the last payment to the principal of the fund was made in that
year, the corresponding drop in total expenditures did not come
until 1897.

It is striking that the liquidation of the fund was accompanied
by a marked reduction in local assessments. Apparently the substantial reduction in the local tax levy made possible by the
elimination of payments to this sinking fund had been considered sufficiently important to allow a substantial readjustment
in local valuations.

The total net liabilities in 1897 were largely the result of a loan
floated two years previously to build a new high school. A sinking
fund set up to retire this school debt assisted in the reduction of
total net liabilities to a new low point in 1902; but the construction of a town hall produced a substantial increase during the next
three years. Between 1881 and 1905 the town had built a high
school and a new town hall. Yet its total net indebtedness at the
end of this period was only 41 per cent as large as that existing in

1881. It is clear that Hopkinton had seen fit to curtail its liabilities during the years of its decline, and it is extremely significant that valuations had been kept up until the major portion of the liquidation had been completed.

By 1884 the town meeting had become convinced that it ought to provide fire protection for the area in which most of the boot and shoe factories were located, and began construction on a town water system.[16] By 1890 the original plant, representing a cost of $34,594, had been completed, but the equipment was already proving inadequate, and the water board recommended that arrangements be made for a larger source of supply.[17] This demand was not met until 1897, when new equipment was installed raising the cost of the plant to $57,175. There were no further outlays between 1897 and 1905. No less than 92 per cent of this investment was made out of borrowed money, the gross debt on the enterprise rising from $25,000 to $52,700 during the decade following 1887. However, the subsequent increase in the value of a sinking fund had produced a net debt of $19,600 in 1905. At the latter date the outstanding debt represented only 44 per cent of the cost of the existing equipment. This is a good showing for a town as hard pressed as Hopkinton must have been during this period. Yet it ought to be pointed out that the water board had paid less than $4,000 to the sinking fund through which the debt reduction had been carried out, while the town itself had contributed $19,590. In fact the town meeting had made a regular yearly appropriation of $2,000 to this fund beginning in 1899.

The operating account of the water board is summarized below. It will be observed that the first operating surplus, which appeared in 1889, was the result of a town appropriation paid nominally in return for water consumed by the town itself.[18]

---

[16] Permission to borrow for this purpose had been granted in 1877, the legislative act being amended in 1882 (*Acts and Resolves*, 1887, c. 183, and 1882, c. 182). According to the present engineer, the water system was intended primarily for fire protection. This opinion is substantiated by the fact that authorization came while the shoe industry was still in its ascendency, and the circumstance that actual construction was begun shortly after a serious fire had destroyed one of the largest factories in the town.

[17] Hopkinton Report, 1889, p. 33.

[18] The utility is exempt from local taxation under Massachusetts law. Since it derives both direct and general benefits from the operation of town government, the

Year	Current Receipts*	Current Expenditures†	Operating Surplus‡	Town Grant**	Net Operating Surplus††
1885	$1,166	$1,765	− $599	....	− $599
1889	2,105	2,205	− 100	750	650
1895	2,747	3,977	− 1,230	1,050	− 180
1897	3,121	2,420	701	1,350	2,051
1905	3,571	4,506	− 935	1,500	565

* Water rates, receipts from service installations, and miscellaneous receipts.
† Expenditures for labor, supplies, pumping, interest, and miscellaneous.
‡ Current receipts minus current expenditures.
** Town appropriation to pay for water used by the town itself.
†† Operating surplus plus town grant.

Moreover, it was only with the assistance of a still larger appropriation that the water board was able to show an operating surplus in 1905.

While the accounts of the enterprise show a substantial improvement during the period under review, it is clear that this was largely the result of the assistance granted by the town itself. In 1905 the latter was contributing a total subsidy of $3,500. It is clear that the water works added substantially to the burden placed upon property in the town during this period of its industrial decay.

Yet the failure of total expenditures to match the relatively slow decline in the town's local assessments down to 1895 had produced a rate 14 per cent higher than that used in 1881, and one third larger than the current state average. While the sharp drop in taxes levied during the next two years brought the Hopkinton rate to $17 per thousand in 1897, the continued decline in local

exemption of the utility is an improper procedure. In the words of Professor Lutz: "Such a charge is a proper element of cost which the industry should bear, whether it be publicly or privately operated" (*Public Finance*, 1929, p. 228). The amount which would be set off against the value of this *de facto* subsidy as a payment for water taken by the town itself and as a payment for the general benefits which non-takers of water would derive from the presence of the enterprise would be comparatively small. But even if these accounts are assumed to cancel one another there is little doubt but that the contribution which the Hopkinton town meeting made to its water board was an outright subsidy.

Since there were 240 families taking water in 1891 when 810 dwellings were assessed for taxation, and 386 taps on the mains as against 782 dwellings assessed in 1905, it is obvious that the above subsidy involved levying a property tax on a large group of individuals who received no direct benefit from the utility in question. The situation involved a manifest injustice to those of the property-tax payers who were not also consumers of the service provided by the town water board.

valuations had raised it to $19 in 1905. This rise, however, represents a net increase of less than 9 per cent over the period as a whole in comparison with a 17 per cent advance in the average rate applied to property in Massachusetts.[19] This lag behind the state average during a period when the town's only substantial industry was in process of complete liquidation reflects the decline in total rather than in current expenditures. With the exception of interest charges, the town's operating costs had not fallen with the drop in the local assessment. Hence it is clear that the debt-retirement policy enforced during the earlier portion of the period, which had made possible the decline in total expenditures, was the chief explanation for the town's ability to absorb a sharp reduction in taxable values without resorting to an unusually rapid advance in the rate applied to the remaining property within its borders.

It is significant that these praiseworthy efforts to adjust town finances to the community's decaying economic structure were made by a town meeting in which the poll-tax payers constituted a declining minority.[20] Since there seem to have been no extremely wealthy residents upon whom the major portion of the burden of increased taxation could be placed, it is clear that larger expenditures meant, to the majority of the voters in Hopkinton, a corresponding increase in their next tax bill. This is a condition favoring a conservative financial policy, and it goes far to explain the financial adjustment achieved by Hopkinton during its period of decline.

This record of diminishing indebtedness and reduced expenditures for poor relief and interest on borrowed money, together with the slower-than-average increase in the rate applied to property in the town, contrasts strikingly with the rising debt, the increasing cost of poor relief, schools, and interest charges, and the rapid advance in the local rate which characterized the period of

---

[19] The average had risen from $14.78 in 1881 to $17.25 in 1905.

[20] In 1887, for which year these statistics first become available, there were 631 persons in Hopkinton paying only the poll tax. This was 40 per cent of the total number of taxpayers. By 1900 there were only 354 of these poll-tax payers or 27 per cent of the total. In 1905 they numbered 464 and made up only 35 per cent of the taxpayers in the town.

Hopkinton's development as an industrial community. It is quite probable that the readjustment carried out during the subsequent period of decline left the town's finances in a sounder condition in 1905, when it had again become a small rural community, than in 1881, when the boot and shoe industry had brought the town to the peak of its industrial development. The evidence seems to indicate that the financial benefits accruing from that development were more than matched by the increased burdens placed upon the property in the town. We have again been dealing with an instance in which a development that undoubtedly would be labeled "progress" in the minds of most observers apparently brought with it a decided weakening in the finances of the locality in which the development took place.

CHAPTER VII

ON THE TAXATION OF ELECTRIC GENERATING STATIONS

ELECTRIC generating stations with their attendant equipment furnish another approach to the problem under consideration. Such property when taxed locally, as is the case in Massachusetts, brings to the community in which it is situated the benefits of a very large increase in taxable valuation. It will be demonstrated in the following pages that because of the semi-automatic nature of this equipment there is little if any corresponding advance in the burden of expenditures required of the town. Hence a clear discrepancy appears between the taxes paid, which fall ultimately on the consumers of the power generated, and the benefits which accrue to the generating station as a result of town expenditures. This chapter deals with two instances in which large generating stations have been constructed within the borders of a rather small town, each instance presenting a clear, though rather exaggerated, picture of the effect which such property has upon the finances of the community in which it is located.

A. FLORIDA

Florida occupies a portion of the eastern slope of the Hoosac range, a spur of the Green Mountains extending down into northwestern Massachusetts. When formed out of unorganized territory in 1815, the town contained about 400 inhabitants, and the subsequent agricultural development of the area had added 42 per cent to this total by 1855.[1] In the following year the Troy and Greenfield railroad began work on a tunnel through Hoosac Mountain, and although the railroad failed in 1861 the project

[1] This increase was about in proportion to that shown by Berkshire County but decidedly less than the accompanying increase in the state total:

Year	Florida	Berkshire	Massachusetts
1820	431	35,570	523,287
1855	612	52,791	1,132,369

was taken over by the state and carried to completion in 1873. The eastern portal of the tunnel was located in Florida, and a village was constructed at the tunnel entrance in order to house some of the laborers employed. This explains the rise in Florida's population to a high point of 1,322 in 1870. Population declined sharply with the completion of the project until in 1910 there were fewer people living in this area than there had been in the first decade of the nineteenth century.[2] The lumbering industry, which had once been quite important, was gone, and with the exception of the railroad laborers living in Tunnel Village Florida had become a purely agricultural community.

At that date the town had a local assessment of only $196,000. Land values made up about 63 per cent of this total; buildings accounted for less than 17 per cent; personalty something over 20 per cent. The town was receiving no assistance from the state taxes on bank shares and corporate excess, and hence the estimated total valuation prepared by the Commissioner of Corporations and Taxation revealed taxable wealth of only $487 per capita, an extremely low figure.

The meagerness of this valuation was offset for the most part by the moderate size of town expenditures, which, including capital outlays and net payments on debt, totaled only $5,868 in 1910. Of this sum, highway expenditures made up $2,563, poor relief $248, and school maintenance costs $2,316.[3] The smallness of these amounts, together with the absence of any sizable burden of debt,[4] made it possible for Florida to get along on a rate of $20 per thousand, which was only 13 per cent above the current state average.

Three years later an event occurred that revolutionized the financial status of the town. A dam was erected on the river forming its eastern boundary, the dam itself being located beyond the town's northern limits but the water being piped downstream for

---

[2] Florida contained 395 persons in 1910.

[3] The school and poor-relief items are current expenditures only. It is impossible to separate current from capital expenditures in the case of highways.

[4] In 1910 the town's net liabilities totaled $1,696. It should also be pointed out that the relatively small sums received in 1910 from the state highway department and from the state school fund ($565 and $1,064 respectively) were sufficient to cover nearly 28 per cent of the total expenditures.

about three miles to a generating plant with a capacity of 20,400 horsepower constructed in the town of Florida. As a result there was added to the valuation of the town not only the power plant itself, which is taxable locally as real estate, but also the water power generated. The latter is not a separate taxable entity in Massachusetts; its presence is taken into account in the assessment of land values, the value being allocated to the land on which the power is applied.[5]

Fortunately for the purpose of this study, no other alteration in the economic structure of the town has taken place. Population has continued to decline with the decay of agriculture,[6] reaching a total in 1930 about 28 per cent less than the total in 1910. The absence of complicating factors affords an excellent opportunity for observing the effects of the construction of an establishment such as this generating plant on the finances of a very small community.

Considering first the possible burdens which the generating plant may have placed on the town, let us look at the record of its expenditures. A substantial increase accompanied the beginning of construction on the power plant. Total expenditures rose from $5,900 to $10,300 between 1910 and 1916, a net increase of 76 per cent. A temporary halt during the war was followed by a rise to $30,700 in 1921. A small decline in the following year was succeeded by another rise to 1931,[7] and although the depression brought substantial reduction, total as well as current expenditures for 1933 were still seven and one half times as great as the total expenditures in 1910. They had risen from $5,900 to $44,100.

[5] Philip Nichols, *Taxation in Massachusetts* (1922), pp. 190–191. An exception occurs when the point of application is outside the state. In that event the value of the power is added to the land on which it originates.

[6] This decline is indicated by the following statistics taken from the *Aggregates of Polls, Property, Taxes, etc.*:

Year	Horses	Cattle	Sheep	Swine	Acres Assessed
1910	105	329	95	23	14,269
1930	60	195	48	4	11,098
1933	51	278	38	2	11,220

[7] At this date the town had total expenditures of $58,615 and current expenditures of $52,925.

The chief components of this total are of course the cost of highways, schools, and poor relief. Highway expenditures had risen from $2,600 in 1910 to $33,100 in 1931. They had dropped in the years which followed but retained a net advance of 670 per cent for the period as a whole. It should be pointed out that these statistics do not include money spent for the construction and maintenance of the state highway, which is the chief thoroughfare and the only hard-surfaced road in the town.

Current expenditures for schools had advanced from $2,300 in 1910 to $12,100 in 1933. Poor relief had risen from $248 in 1910 to something over $1,200 in 1927, and by 1933 the town was spending $5,822 for the relief of its poor.[8]

It is highly probable that a portion of this advance was due to the general expansion of local expenditures characteristic of this period, and the share of the increase that may reasonably be explained in this manner can be roughly estimated from data published in the *Statistics of Municipal Finances*. It is possible to compare Florida's expenditures directly with the totals for the state, the small towns within the state, and those in Berkshire County, of which Florida is a part. But a more effective comparison is possible if allowance is made for the disturbing element of population growth; and because of the small size of the town in question an even clearer picture is presented when attention has been limited to those services which are provided by all towns and cities in the state. The most important of these are of course roads, schools, and poor relief. Hence total expenditures for highways and current expenditures for schools and poor relief have

---

[8] The following statistics present a more complete record of these expenditures:

Year	Highways*	Schools	Poor
1910	$2,563	$2,316	$248
1916	4,773	3,675	685
1921	11,826	6,318	1,015
1927	29,891†	9,270	1,253
1931	33,089	12,058	3,540
1933	19,717‡	12,101	5,822

* No attempt has been made to remove capital outlays from this account.
† Includes $6,848 spent for the purchase of tractors.
‡ Includes $2,251 spent for road machinery.

been added together and reduced to a per capita basis. The results are as follows:

	1910	1927	1931
Massachusetts...................	$10.54	$30.14	$35.79
Small towns in Massachusetts*......	11.16	38.61	44.91
Towns in Berkshire County	9.45	28.16	34.06
Small towns in Berkshire County*...	12.01	40.40	53.96
Florida	12.86	115.93	169.35

* Towns under 5,000 in population.

Florida's expenditures for 1910 were about 22 per cent above the average for the state as a whole, 15 per cent above the average for the small towns in the state, and only slightly in excess of the average for the small towns in Berkshire County. By 1927 there was a tremendous difference between Florida's expenditures and the averages with which they are compared, and by 1931 the town was spending over four and one half times as much per capita as the state as a whole, nearly four times as much as the small towns in the state, and over three times as much as the average for the small towns in Berkshire County. In view of these great discrepancies it can be definitely concluded that some exceptional force was driving Florida's expenditures upwards at an unusually rapid pace.

To what extent can this be attributed to demands put upon the town by the presence of the generating plant? In 1933 the latter employed twenty-five men, most of whom lived in a village constructed by the power company. Since almost all were unmarried, there were only four families in this settlement and these had but three children. The latter attended school in Tunnel Village; their presence had put the town to no expense beyond the cost of transporting them to and from school.

Only one new road was required at the time the generating plant was built, a short stretch of gravel leading to the new village, and this was constructed by the power company itself. A town road passed the site of the generating station, and this has had to be maintained in somewhat better condition than might otherwise have been the case. The cost of maintaining this road, however, is the only addition to highway expenditures which can be

directly attributed to new demands arising from the presence of
the generating plant.

The abrupt rise in Florida's poor relief came mainly after 1927.
Per capita expenditure for this purpose rose from 35 per cent
below the state average in 1910 to slightly above that average in
1927, and then to a level nearly 60 per cent above in 1931. All
this came about in spite of an increase of 590 per cent in the state
average itself.[9] The power plant has caused no unemployment.
It had increased its staff during the current depression, and hence
was in no way responsible for the spectacular increase in the cost of
maintaining the town poor. It is obvious that no appreciable
portion of the extraordinary increase in Florida's current expenditures can be attributed to burdens put upon the town as a
result of the construction of this new enterprise.

Turning to the financial benefits which Florida may be said to
have derived from the presence of the generating plant, attention
should be given first to the record of locally assessed valuations.
The value of land in the town rose from $123,700 in 1910 to
$180,800 in 1933, a net gain of 46 per cent. Personal property
advanced from $41,500 to $139,400 during the period in question,
a net gain of 236 per cent in the face of the removal of intangibles
and motor vehicles from the local lists by the state income tax of
1916 and the motor vehicle tax of 1928.[10] But these large increases were of minor importance when compared with the tremendous advance in the assessed value of buildings. It should be
pointed out that in Massachusetts property is declared to be a
building for purposes of taxation if the object in question is
"affixed to the land." This definition has been construed to include the greater part of the machinery which makes up so large a
portion of the value of a hydroelectric plant. Hence the first
effect of the construction of the power station in 1913 was a 450
per cent increase in the town's building assessment. The rapid
increase of this assessment continued to 1920 and was followed by
a more gradual increase during the remainder of the period

[9] The per capita poor-relief costs given by the *Statistics of Municipal Finances*
were as follows:

	1910	1927	1931
Massachusetts	$1.07	$3.53	$7.38
Florida	.70	3.69	11.72

[10] *Acts and Resolves*, 1916, c. 259; *ibid.*, 1928, c. 379.

studied. As a consequence, the value placed upon buildings in Florida in 1933 was over 35 times as great as the value placed upon such property in 1910. Chiefly as a result of this tremendous increase, Florida's assessed valuation rose from $196,200 in 1910 to $1,415,157 in 1933, a net advance of more than 620 per cent for the period as a whole.[11]

Definite evidence that this increase in valuation was almost wholly the result of the addition to the tax list of the property of the New England Power Association is furnished by the assessor's report for 1930. At that date this company alone was assessed for $80,600 in personal property and $1,025,175 in real estate.[12] If its property is included in the town's total assessment, the latter rises 630 per cent between 1910 and 1930; if it is excluded, the remainder of the tax base increases only 67 per cent. The difference represents the minimum amount which can be attributed to the existence of the generating station; it neglects the effect which the presence of that station may have had on the value of other property in the town.

It will be recalled that the state income tax had been enacted in 1916, and that the receipts, so far as they exceeded the cost of collection, had been redistributed to the various local governments. For several years this had been done on the basis of the presumed loss suffered by the city or town as the result of the removal of intangibles from the local tax lists. In 1919, a gradual transition was begun to a system of distribution according to the proportion of state taxes paid by the respective towns, and this was further amended in the following year by an act segregating a portion of the receipts to be used as grants in aid for educational purposes. The alteration in method, which was completed in 1928, benefited Florida greatly. The town's receipts from the in-

[11] The statistics on which the above argument is based are summarized below:

Year	Personalty	Land	Buildings	Total
		(In thousands of dollars.)		
1910........	41.5	123.7	31.0	196.2
1912........	44.4	129.8	33.2	207.4
1913........	37.2	131.5	182.7	351.4
1920........	127.2	156.4	1,019.6	1,303.2
1930........	158.2	188.9	1,087.6	1,434.7
1933........	139.4	180.8	1,094.9	1,415.1

[12] The latter included $8,275 assessed to the New England Power Construction Company.

come tax rose from $553 in 1917 to $6,222 in 1930, and then dropped to $3,288 in 1932. A considerable portion of this new income must be attributed to the presence of the enterprise which in 1930 accounted for over three fourths of the base upon which the state tax was assessed.

The town obtained no substantial revenue from the corporation taxes until 1919, when it received $144. By 1930 this had grown to $641; in 1932 it had fallen back to $275. Most of this income is also due to the presence of the generating station, the only large piece of corporate property in the town.[13]

The rapid growth of local assessments, together with rising receipts from the income and corporation taxes, is reflected by the Tax Commissioner's estimated total valuation, which advances from $192,800 in 1910 to $1,715,600 in 1928 and then drops to $1,472,500 in 1932. The 1910 total meant a per capita valuation of about $487 as against an average of $803 in Berkshire County, and $1,188 in the state at large. By 1932 the town's wealth had risen to $4,796 per capita; the Berkshire average had become $1,380; the state average $1,765. Thus within a period of twenty-two years Florida had risen from the position of a relatively poor community to the third richest town in the state from the point of view of per capita taxable wealth.[14]

Florida received considerable sums from the state during the period under review for the construction and maintenance of town roads. Income from this source had averaged well below $1,000 a year between 1911 and 1915, but the average for the period 1931–1933 was well over $8,000 a year.[15] It is highly im-

[13] In 1930 three other public-service corporations were assessed for a total of $29,551, all of this being personalty. An enterprise serving the tourist traffic was assessed for $41,722.

[14] It was exceeded in 1932 by Hull with a per capita wealth of $9,160, and Manchester with $5,100. The significance of the Florida total is emphasized by comparison with the following per capita valuations for 1932: Boston, $2,580; Springfield, $2,135; Newton, $2,605; and Brookline, $3,810.

[15] The average receipts are given below:

Period	Average
1911–1915	$977
1916–1920	1,628
1921–1925	3,123
1926–1930	6,762
1931–1933	8,475

probable that this increase provided actual relief, since the grants made by the state had to be supplemented with town appropriations. It is more likely that money from this source was an incentive to increase highway expenditures and hence a partial explanation for the extremely rapid advance in the town's outlay for this purpose.

The net result[16] of the various factors affecting Florida's finances is reflected in her tax rate. The rapidly growing local valuation sufficed to bring the town rate from $20.00 in 1910 to $12.00 in 1918, when it was about 40 per cent below the current state average. Then expenditures began to outstrip the growth of the total valuation, and the rate started to advance. By 1931 it had reached $28.20, which was only $1.60 below the current state average. Reduced expenditures lowered the Florida rate to $23.20 in 1933, but this was still nearly twice the rate used in 1918, and substantially in excess of the rate applied prior to the construction of the generating plant.

To sum up, Florida was the recipient of an extremely large addition to its local assessment; the town benefited by substantial receipts from corporation and income taxes; and these receipts were chiefly due to the same cause which produced the great increase in the town's total valuation. Little, if any, additional expenditure had been required as a result of the construction of the generating plant responsible for the tremendous increase in the town's per capita wealth. Under the existing method of taxing this type of property, Florida received quite gratuitously an extremely valuable addition to her tax base. The ultimate bearer of the taxes levied, the consumer of the electricity generated, received from the town in return for the taxes paid by the company benefits so small as to be practically negligible. Here, then, is a clear instance of a failure to adjust local taxation to benefits received.

What was the town's reaction to the situation? For a time expenditures rose with relative slowness; then, in 1918, a spectacu-

---

[16] Florida had net liabilities of only $1,696 in 1910. These were wiped out in 1914. A similar debt, accumulated during the next two years, was paid off in 1917. During the years which followed the town's cash balance was always in excess of its current liabilities.

lar increase began which within thirteen years almost completely dissipated the condition of financial ease produced by the construction of the generating plant. Fortunately the town has been able to cut its expenditures during the depression, but this reduction is by no means in proportion to the rise that preceded it. It may with justice be concluded that Florida turned its back on a policy of moderate expenditures and a very low tax rate in order to indulge in a spending campaign of sizable proportions.

The town meeting which made this choice was one in which the poll-tax payer had little influence.[17] It was not a poorly attended gathering easily controlled by interested parties, but was well attended and dominated by the property-tax payers, in short, a town meeting which ordinarily would be expected to pursue conservative financial policies.

The explanation for its financial record is to be found in the high percentage of property in the town taxable to non-residents. In 1930, the latter were assessed for 84 per cent of the personalty, and approximately 90 per cent of the real estate taxed by the town.[18] Thus for every dollar of expenditures voted by the town meeting and paid out of local property taxes about 89 cents was collected from property holders not residents of the town.

This situation is particularly significant in connection with the extremely high level reached by Florida's poor-relief costs. It is not to be expected that relief will be strictly administered in a town where so large a portion of the resulting tax bill will be paid by non-residents possessing no voice in town meeting.

Another result is indicated by certain statistics relating to high-

---

[17] The following statistics make this point clear:

Year	Number Taxpayers (1)	Number Poll-Tax Payers (2)	Per Cent Column (2) to Column (1)
1910	193	52	27
1918	173	37	21
1928	187	32	17

[18] The statistics given by the assessor's report for 1930 are as follows:

	Personalty	Real Estate
Residents	$24,774	$136,231
Non-Residents	133,409	1,140,342
Total...............	$158,183	$1,276,573

way expenditures. The town reports publish them in such form as to make possible a fairly accurate determination of the recipients of the money spent. In 1927, out of a total expenditure of nearly $22,000,[19] 12 per cent was paid directly to eleven town officers and 28 per cent more to persons having the same family names. In 1931 a total of $5,963 was paid to a single contractor for the use of road machinery. Of the remaining highway expenditures 16 per cent went to seven town officers, and 18 per cent more to persons with the same family names. In 1933 there were fourteen individuals holding important town offices. These received 12 per cent of the money paid out, while 39 per cent more went to persons having the same family names. The size of these percentages indicates that a relatively large share of the money spent on the town roads had become one of the perquisites of town office. Such a situation is a threat to the political and economic health of a community. It makes financially profitable the holding of the town offices that are ordinarily more or less non-remunerative, and offers a distinct temptation to neglect farming for the temporarily more profitable task of working on the town roads.

Thus Florida's experience furnishes an instance in which a failure to make a reasonable adjustment between taxation and the benefits received from local expenditures produced results which not only were unsound financially but also threatened the political and economic welfare of the community. It will be illuminating to turn to a somewhat similar situation encountered in the finances of the town of Somerset.

B. SOMERSET

Somerset occupies a long, rather narrow portion of the west bank of the Taunton River opposite the famous cotton city of Fall River. There are two villages in Somerset and these accounted for the bulk of the 3,520 inhabitants reported by the census of 1920. Although the assessment rolls indicate that there were three small industrial enterprises operating in the town

---

[19] This figure does not include the cost of operating the town tractors, which was carried under a separate account.

at this time,[1] a substantial proportion of its population was made up of commuters employed in Fall River, Dighton, and Brockton.

In 1920 Somerset had total expenditures of $69,500 and current expenditures of $57,900.[2] Building values made up 48 per cent of a tax base of $2,884,000, land values and tangible personalty accounting for 32 and 20 per cent of this total respectively. Revenue of $7,943 from the state income tax and $3,762 from the taxes on corporations, banks, and street railways combined to offset nearly one fifth of the town's current expenditures. In combination with the local assessment these revenues produced a taxable wealth not greatly in excess of the $645 per capita reported by the Tax Commissioner in the preceding year. However, the relatively modest level of town expenditures[3] enabled Somerset to finance itself with a rate of $20.00 per thousand, which was slightly less than the average of $21.34 in the state as a whole.

There was a decided advance in town expenditures during the next three years, and in 1923 Somerset had total and current expenditures of $117,700 and $90,600 respectively. These represented advances of 69 and 57 per cent over the corresponding totals for 1920, the major portion of the increase in current expenditures being the result of a rise from $28,900 to $49,000 in the cost of operating the town schools.[4]

Chiefly as a result of the increase in revenue from the income tax from $7,900 to $10,900, Somerset's receipts from state taxes had advanced from $11,705 to $14,922. This had been accompanied by an addition of $264,000 to the town's real-estate assess-

[1] The Town Report for 1922 lists property of $75,000 for a shipbuilding company, $30,000 for a stove foundry, and $74,290 for a concern manufacturing shellac.

[2] The bulk of the latter is made up of the following: schools, $28,852; highways, $9,122; street lighting, $5,572; and poor relief, $4,674.

[3] The Statistics of Municipal Finances report maintenance costs, interest charges, capital outlays, payments on the debt from the sinking fund and from revenue, and net payments on temporary loans for Somerset of $73,771 or about $21.00 per capita. The same total for the state was $199,100,000 or $51.69 per capita.

[4] This rise accompanied the expenditure of $83,702 between 1920 and 1923 for the construction of two new school buildings. There is evidence that the accommodations had been inadequate, the Town Report of 1916 calling attention to the need for new buildings and pointing out that the town ranked 321 in the list of 353 towns in its per capita expenditure for schools. No capital outlays were made between 1916 and 1920. The pressure on schools was being increased by the influx of suburban population and in 1924 the school committee was again asking for more accommodations.

ment, producing a total valuation of $3,135,000, about 8 per cent above the corresponding total for 1920. These advances, however, were of small importance compared with the rise in expenditures, and as a result the town rate increased from $20.00 to $34.50 while the excess of the town's liabilities over cash on hand rose from about $32,000 to nearly $91,000.

Hence we find that in 1923 Somerset was in a rather strained financial position. Expenditures were advancing rapidly, chiefly as a result of the educational requirements of an expanding suburban population; there was no corresponding increase in receipts from state taxes; and since local valuations also failed to show a corresponding increase, the per capita wealth of the town remained small.[5] Its liabilities were rising in the face of a rapidly advancing tax rate, and by 1923 property in the town was being subjected to a rate which was well above the current state average.

In the following year construction was begun on the Montaup generating station, a steam plant with a capacity of 102,000 horsepower located near the village of Pottersville in the town of Somerset and supplying current for the cities of Fall River, Brockton, Pawtucket, and Woonsocket. Although the effect of this new property on the town's finances is clouded somewhat by the fact that Somerset was developing fairly rapidly as a suburb,[6] the value of the new power equipment was so large that significant repercussions in the finances of the town might readily be expected. The record of town expenditures is summarized in the table on the following page.

There was a rapid increase in the total to 1927, the year in which the town began to build a water system. A gradual decrease during subsequent years failed to offset the whole of this increase, and in 1934 Somerset had total expenditures which exceeded the 1923 figure by 136 per cent. Current expenditures did not reach their peak until 1932, and the slight decline during the next two years left a total which was 150 per cent greater than that existing

[5] In 1922 the Tax Commissioner reported a total valuation of $3,114,824. This was about $770 per capita.
[6] Somerset's population increased as follows:

1920	3,520	1930	5,398
1925	4,818	1934	5,752

in the year preceding the beginning of construction on the generating plant.

Year	1. Total Expenditures*	2. Total Current Expenditures†	3. Total Current Non-Commercial Expenditures‡
		(In thousands of dollars.)	
1923	117.7	90.6	90.6
1927	858.7	212.0	199.2
1932	289.0	249.5	232.5
1934	278.6	240.5	227.4

* Total including capital outlays, net payments on non-commercial debt, and deficits on both current and capital accounts of the water works.

† Item 1, minus capital outlays, net payments on non-commercial debt, and deficit on the capital account of the water works.

‡ Item 2, minus deficit on the operating account of the water works. Note: the deficit on the capital account of this enterprise includes payments on maturing serial notes.

This divergence between the movement of total and total current expenditures is due to the large capital outlays made during the early portion of the period under review. By 1931 Somerset had spent $220,000 on the construction of schools, had built a town house costing $50,000, and had spent $13,500 for new fire-fighting equipment. Highway outlays had reached $33,000 in 1927, and although they tapered off subsequently, the yearly town expenditure for this purpose averaged nearly $12,000 during the period 1925 to 1931. All this was in addition to the water works previously mentioned, which had cost Somerset $568,000. Although there have been very few capital outlays since 1931,[7] the persistent deficits shown by the water works have preserved a substantial gap between Somerset's total and total current expenditures.[8]

[7] Highway outlays averaged $3,639 between 1932 and 1934. A sum of $1,118 was spent in 1933 for police equipment.

[8] These deficits are as follows:

Year	Capital*	Current†
	(In thousands of dollars.)	
1927	496.8	12.8
1928	97.8	13.2
1929	32.3	27.6
1930	48.0	20.9
1931	47.3	17.1
1932	23.3	16.9
1933	23.0	13.7
1934	23.2	13.1

* Notes retired, cost of extensions, and construction expenses.

† Net revenue minus town appropriation.

The 150 per cent advance in current expenditures was in part the result of increases in the cost of schools, highways, fire and police protection, street lighting, and public health, all of these being services which would respond readily to the demands of an expanding suburban population. In addition there was an increase from $5,000 to $40,000 in the cost of maintaining the town's poor,[9] which was not unconnected with the distress experienced during this period by the city of Fall River.[10]

The net result of these movements was an advance in the town's total expenditures, as reported by the *Statistics of Municipal Finances*, from $28.09 per capita in 1924 to $60.21 in 1932 — a net increase of 114 per cent as compared with the 18 per cent increase shown by the per capita total for the state as a whole.[11]

While this increase was less rapid than that in the total expenditures of the town of Florida, it was decidedly in excess of the advance which could be called normal for the state at this time. Very little, if any, of the difference can be explained by demands put upon the town as a result of the construction of the generating plant. The latter required no new roads and has brought no increase in the town's highway maintenance costs since construction materials and supplies are brought in over a state-maintained highway. About a hundred men are employed at Montaup and some thirty of these live in Somerset. It is not likely that the children of the latter group account for any sub-

---

[9] The record of current expenditures is summarized below:

Year	Schools	Highways	Police	Fire	Light	Poor	Health
				(In thousands of dollars.)			
1923 ...	48.7	10.3	2.9	1.6	6.1	5.1	2.4
1927 ...	70.7	29.4	7.8	6.2	12.1	14.3	7.7
1932 ...	93.7	23.0	8.8	6.3	13.9	36.9	14.0
1934 ...	92.4	24.0	8.2	6.0	13.0	40.0	15.9

[10] For an account of this situation see *Causes of the Financial Breakdown of the Local Government of Fall River, Mass., and Means Taken by Massachusetts to Reestablish the Finances of that City* (1933).

[11] These expenditures were as follows:

	1924		1932	
	Actual*	Per Capita	Actual*	Per Capita
Somerset	135.4	$28.09	320.3	$60.21
State	274,362.8	68.40	344,414.1	81.04

* In thousands of dollars.

stantial proportion of the great increase in the cost of maintaining the town schools.

Although the power station required little in the way of increased expenditures, it added tremendously to the amount of property taxable in the town of Somerset. The latter's total assessment rose from $3,135,000 in 1923 to a peak of $13,903,000 in 1929, most of this advance being the result of a rise in personalty from $560,000 to $6,281,000, and an increase from $1,555,000 to $6,153,000 in the value of buildings assessed by the town.[12] A slow decline during subsequent years reduced the total valuation to $12,876,000 in 1934,[13] leaving a net advance of about 310 per cent over the amount taxable by the town in the year preceding the construction of the power station. The latter was assessed for $5,100,000 in personalty and $3,400,000 in real estate in 1934. The addition of this $8,500,000 to the Somerset tax base accounts for all but 13 per cent of the net increase in the total valuation. In 1934 this single piece of power equipment was paying two thirds of the taxes levied on property in the town.

Somerset's receipts from the state income tax rose from $10,900 to $49,200 between 1923 and 1930. Although they dropped to $23,000 in 1934, there was a net increase of 110 per cent over the period as a whole. This was due mainly to the tremendous advance in local valuations. The latter increased the proportion of the state tax paid by Somerset and hence the proportion of the receipts from the income tax which were allocated to this town. Since the expansion in taxable values was so largely the result of the addition of the power property, the bulk of the increased receipts from the state income tax must also be attributed to the construction of this enterprise.

Income from the corporation tax rose from $3,000 to $7,000 between 1923 and 1929 and then fell to $1,553 in 1934. The additional revenue received during the boom period must also be attributed to the presence of the power station.

---

[12] Land values increased less rapidly. They rose from $1,021,000 in 1923 to $1,469,000 in 1929.

[13] A portion of the decline in the value of personalty is again explained by the removal of motor vehicles from the local tax lists.

The decline in income from the corporation, street-railway,[14] and bank taxes[15] was more than offset by the increase in receipts from the state income tax. Revenue from the last-named source combined with the tremendous advance in local assessments to raise the Tax Commissioner's estimated total valuation to $13,800,000 in 1932. This gave Somerset a per capita wealth of $2,397 as compared with $770 in 1922. It may be concluded that the construction of the Montaup plant had raised Somerset from the status of a rather poor community to a position in which its per capita taxable valuation exceeded the current state average by 35 per cent.

These changes more than offset the unusually large increase in current expenditures, and as a consequence the town rate fell from $34.50 in 1923 to $21.00 in 1934, while the state average was rising from $27.07 to $33.87.[16]

In Somerset as in Florida the construction of a generating plant within the borders of the town has added tremendously to the taxable wealth. Although both towns have seen fit to use the new property as the basis for an unusually large advance in town expenditures, there seems to have been at least a difference of degree between the financial policies pursued. Somerset had been in a more difficult financial position. A considerable influx of suburban population brought a demand for a substantial expansion in the services provided by the town while bringing a comparatively small additional amount of taxable property. Somerset, like Belmont, was undergoing the financial difficulties which accompany the development of a town as a middle- or working-class suburb; its needs were running far in advance of its capacity to spend.

When such a town receives a large and almost gratuitous addition to its tax base, it is to be expected that it will attempt to

---

[14] The street-railway tax, which yielded $834 in 1923, ceased to bring in revenue after 1932.

[15] The yield of the bank tax dropped from $133 in 1923 to $55 in 1934.

[16] The large capital outlays made during the early part of this interval raised the excess of town liabilities over cash on hand from $90,800 in 1923 to $709,000 in 1928. This had been reduced to $465,000 in 1934. The bulk of the increase resulted from the construction of the town water works.

meet more fully the demands of its expanding suburban population. Somerset did provide itself with a great deal of new equipment, but the net advance in current expenditures that followed
the completion of these capital outlays was considerably less
striking than the advance shown in Florida, where no similar incentive to increased expenditures existed.

It is not possible to explain this distinction by the position of
the poll-tax payer in town meeting, since this element is in a distinct minority in both places.[17] The power property pays a
smaller portion of the total tax levied in Somerset, and there has
been less time for the influence of the presence of this property to
become apparent. But another, more powerful, factor must be
considered. The Somerset town meeting is peculiar; its sessions
are very short and are devoted mainly to a rather perfunctory
acceptance of the recommendations of its finance committee,
which in turn is dominated by a single individual who, by devot-
ing most of his time to town affairs, has achieved an almost dicta-
torial position. Although this man appears to be cordially dis-
liked by a considerable portion of the voting population, he
apparently has been able to interest most of the property-tax
payers in the maintenance of a low tax rate. It is highly likely
that the personal influence of this one man is responsible for the
fact that Somerset has avoided to a considerable extent the ex-
cesses appearing in the town of Florida. This being the case, it is
clear that Somerset's recent financial history has furnished
another instance in which the presence of despotic elements
within the nominal democracy of the New England town meeting
has vitally affected the financial policies pursued.

Yet it ought not be forgotten that in both the cases discussed in
this chapter the construction of sizable units of power equipment
brought very great increases in the taxable wealth of the towns
where that equipment was located. In both instances town ex-

---

[17] The Somerset statistics follow:

Year	Poll-tax Payers (1)	Total Taxpayers (2)	Per Cent Column (1) to Column (2)
1920	329	1,641	20
1923	402	1,968	20
1928	439	2,431	18

penditures increased rapidly, the power property being called upon to pay an extremely large proportion of the resulting advance in the local tax levy while the ultimate bearers of the tax in question, the consumers of the electricity generated, received services from the town which were negligible to an extreme. Hence it is clear that the existing method of taxing this type of property is capable of producing situations in which serious financial problems arise out of a failure to bring about a reasonable adjustment between the incidence of the burden of taxation and the allocation of the benefits provided by local governmental expenditures.[18]

[18] The Somerset and Florida cases are also valuable in another connection. Since the construction of the power equipment was not accompanied by an appreciable extension of the services required of the town, the revenue yielded by taxes upon this property constituted an almost gratuitous new income available either as a basis for increased expenditures or as a means of reducing the rate applied to other property in the town. Consequently the cases dealt with in this chapter bear directly upon an extremely important issue, namely, will new revenues available for use in relieving the burdens put upon real estate actually provide this relief or will they simply be absorbed by a further advance in local expenditures?

There is little doubt that the Florida meeting used its new revenue as the basis for additional spending, and even though the property holders in Somerset received considerable relief in the form of a lower tax rate, here too a large percentage of the new money was absorbed by increased expenditures. Unfortunately for our purpose these are the only outstanding examples of the situation in question within the state of Massachusetts. There are, however, a considerable number of similar cases in the state of Vermont, and six of these have been subjected to the same analysis applied to the finances of Somerset and Florida; for the results of this investigation see E. E. Oakes, "The Taxation of Public Utility Property in Vermont," *Bulletin of the National Tax Association*, December 1935.

CONCLUSION

SINCE the concluding paragraphs of most of the preceding chapters have been limited to a restatement of the course of events dealt with in the chapter in question, it is desirable to point out, by way of conclusion, certain details which possess general theoretical implications, and to draw some generalizations from those portions of the studies concerned with the division of towns.

The phenomenon of town division appears to be definitely associated with a failure to bring about what we have called a reasonable adjustment between the burdens of local taxation and the benefits yielded by local governmental services.[1] In the earlier divisions the failure to make this adjustment was based primarily upon geographical separation. While this influence was also particularly important in the division of the town of Adams, the later separations were more largely the result of social and economic diversification. The development of an industrial area within the borders of two predominantly agricultural towns led to the incorporation of Maynard. This is also the most logical explanation for the incorporation of the town of Blackstone in 1845. The growth of a wealthy industrial and residential community in a relatively poor town produced Hopedale. The development of unusually wealthy suburban communities split Wellesley off from Needham and brought about the incorporation of Belmont. Although the division of Blackstone is probably not to be explained by either geographical separation or social

---

[1] It is interesting to note that a division of the ecclesiastical parish often foreshadowed the older town separations. Milford, for instance, became an independent precinct before it was taken from Mendon; Wellesley was set up as a parish long before it broke with Needham. In both cases the source of discontent was an objection on the part of residents of communities remote from the town church to the fact that they were being taxed for the support of an institution the benefits of which they could not enjoy. This same objection was raised during the separation of Needham from Dedham, and during the quarrel leading to the annexation of the district known as Needham Leg to Natick. It is apparent that this argument is very similar to that put forward in most of the later divisions, namely, that the existing governmental structure did not permit a proper adjustment between taxation and benefits received.

diversification, this division, like the others encountered, seems the almost inevitable result of the failure of the Massachusetts town to provide the several groups which may reside within its borders with a scale of local governmental services which their members will consider adequately adjusted to the burden of taxation they are asked to bear.[2]

Sweeping generalization as to the results of the remedy applied in these situations, namely, the division of the town in question, is of course difficult. In three cases, Belmont, Wellesley, and Hopedale, the new units were extremely wealthy. For a considerable period after their incorporation these towns possessed enviable financial structures. Milford and the parent towns from which Belmont was taken were unfavorably affected, and the same was true also of Needham during the period immediately following the loss of the Wellesley area, but the independent development of the remnant of this community soon brought it back to a relatively favorable financial position.

The incorporation of the areas which became the towns of Maynard and Millville and the separation of the two industrial communities located at opposite ends of the old town of Adams eventually produced extremely unfavorable financial results. Maynard, Millville, and Adams became in effect single-industry towns with over-specialized economic structures little able to withstand a severe industrial depression. Millville became bankrupt; Adams was not far from the same fate; Maynard has twice been in a very precarious financial position.

While the Millville and Maynard incorporations seemed at first to have an unfavorable effect upon the finances of Blackstone and Sudbury respectively, there is little doubt that the parent communities benefited over the long run as a result of the removal of these highly specialized industrial areas.[3] It is clear that the town of Stow was greatly and immediately benefited by the incorporation of Maynard, and the favorable effect which the annexation of the Strawberry Hill district to Cambridge in 1881

[2] Direct evidence of the use of this argument appears in the cases of Hopedale, Needham, Wellesley, Maynard, and Belmont.

[3] This was also probably true of the removal of the Blackstone area from the town of Mendon in 1845.

had upon the finances of Belmont furnishes still another illustration of the fact that a town may lose a large portion of its area and population without damaging its financial structure.

In general it is safe to conclude that the practice of attempting to adjust differences between the various elements that may appear in a Massachusetts town by the process of dividing the town itself, while not necessarily harmful to either party, is capable on the one hand of setting up towns which find themselves in an excessively easy financial position, and on the other, of incorporating units whose finances are undermined by the over-specialized character of their economic life.[4] It ought also to be pointed out that the separation procedure is itself directly opposed to the modern tendency to consolidate local governments in an attempt to obtain more efficient and hence less expensive governmental machinery.[5]

Some of the studies contain evidence indicating that a rapid industrial development is not ordinarily beneficial to a town's finances. This is the chief implication of the short chapter dealing with the financial history of Hopkinton between 1840 and 1905. The same conclusion may be drawn from the statistics for Stow and Sudbury during the decade prior to the incorporation of Maynard, and it is fairly clear that the rapid industrial development which came to the last-named town after 1901, as well as during the World War and immediately thereafter, brought financial burdens considerably in excess of the benefits received.

It is apparent that industrial units of this type find it extremely difficult to adjust their finances during periods of acute depression. This can be illustrated by the experience of Maynard during the nineties and after 1929, by the collapse of Millville, and by the serious difficulties recently encountered by the town of Adams.

---

[4] In passing it ought to be observed that the experiences of Needham and Milford indicate that these towns would have been pursuing a more expedient course if, in recognition of the relatively large share of the burden of local expenditures borne by wealthy areas, they had provided these areas with somewhat more expensive services than those furnished in the rest of the town.

[5] For example of such consolidation one can cite the union school district, the metropolitan water, transportation, and park districts, the county grammar and high school, and the proposed amalgamation of county and city governments where the two units are nearly coterminous.

The experience of Hopkinton, however, during the years when its single industry was undergoing complete decay indicates that a proper financial policy, a process of courageous liquidation, will go far to alleviate the financial evils of an industrial decline.

Belmont's story bears upon a similar problem. Its experiences constitute a fairly clear-cut demonstration that a rapid suburban development may be distinctly injurious to a town's financial structure, that the new population may bring with it financial burdens which far outweigh the benefits received.[6]

The seventh chapter presented some spectacular results of the Massachusetts system of taxing electric generating stations. In the two outstanding instances in Massachusetts where large units of this type of property are taxed by relatively small towns, the power equipment added tremendously to the assessment upon which the local property tax was levied. Since there were no corresponding increases in the expenditures required of the towns, a large and practically gratuitous new income was made available for use either in financing increased expenditures or in alleviating the burden placed upon other property in the town. In both cases this condition of extreme financial ease was followed by a sudden increase in town expenditures. Consequently the experiences of Florida and Somerset provide interesting examples of another situation in which serious financial difficulties have resulted from a failure to bring about a reasonable adjustment between the burden of taxation and the benefits received from local governmental expenditures.

One of the chief by-products of these investigations has been a demonstration of the significance of the ratio between the number of poll-tax payers and the total number of taxpayers in a town. This point also has to do with the relationship between benefits and taxation in local finance, for the poll-tax payer shares in most of the services resulting from increased expenditures and bears no portion of the accompanying increase in taxation. In Hopkinton this type of citizen made up a declining minority of the town's voters during a period when a successful liquidation policy was

[6] Additional light is thrown upon this point by the financial decay of Blackstone during the twenties when it was developing as a working-class suburb.

being carried out. The poll-tax payer dominated the Maynard meeting after 1901, and was the controlling influence in the new town of Millville; the financial policies pursued by these units have not been particularly sound. When with the death of Mr. C. T. Plunkett the poll-tax payers of Adams came into a dominant position in town meeting, the finances of the town, already strained, were exposed to greater stress by the liberal manner in which the town attempted to combat the social evils of acute industrial depression. Thus the evidence at hand offers considerable support for the conclusion that the dominance of a town meeting by this type of citizen, whose tax bill will not respond to increases in town appropriations, will ordinarily lead to open-handed spending policies.

We hasten to add, however, that a mere numerical majority of such voters will not always produce these results. It is clear, for instance, that this type of citizen did not control the town of Adams during the period down to 1928, in spite of his numerical importance. His power was held in check by the personal influence of the family that dominated the political and economic life of the community, constituting a despotic element within the nominal democracy of the New England town, which was apparently strong enough to offset the numerical strength of the poll-tax payers.

The substantial difference between the policies of the Florida and the Somerset meetings, and the contrast between the record of the Maynard water works and that of the town itself, provide further illustrations of the effect of *de facto* changes in the political organization of a community upon the financial policies which it will pursue.

The foregoing studies also cast some light upon the proposition that the brunt of rising expenditures is borne by real estate. This theory finds substantiation in the record of Needham's valuations during the period preceding the incorporation of Wellesley, and a similar conclusion can be drawn from the Belmont statistics for the years 1860–1890, 1913–1916, and 1916–1931. On the other hand, Hopedale financed most of its large expenditures out of a rising personalty assessment, and to a great extent the same was true of Wellesley, while Sudbury's personal property valuation rose almost twice as rapidly as its real estate during the decade following 1861 when Assabet village was thriving. This tendency continued during the first period of Maynard's independent existence, but the new town's subsequent industrial development had a greater effect upon real estate than upon personalty. Finally, the rise in valuations accompanying the growth of the boot and shoe industry in Hopkinton was considerably more rapid in the case of personalty than in that of real estate. Apparently the tendency in question is not universal. Exceptions occur when a town is undergoing a rapid industrial development or is receiving a considerable accumulation of intangible wealth. The latter situation, however, will no longer be found in Massachusetts, since intangibles are now reached by the income tax and the proceeds of that tax are no longer distributed to the town of the taxpayer's domicile.

These financial histories have provided two opportunities for studying real-estate assessments in a rapidly developing suburban community. In Belmont the flow of population brought a more rapid advance in the building assessment than in land values. In Wellesley land values advanced about as rapidly as the building assessment. It is significant that the two towns differ substantially in other respects. Belmont is much more the "popular" suburb; transportation between Boston and Belmont is much cheaper than between Wellesley and Boston.

The preceding chapters also offer several good illustrations of the fact that capital outlays bring with them a more or less permanent rise in the cost of operating a government. This phenomenon explains the increase in Needham's school maintenance costs after the completion of the building program begun in 1870, and the failure of Sudbury's current expenditures for schools to drop with the removal of Assabet village in 1871. Moreover, a considerable portion of the difficulties experienced by the town of Adams during the recent depression were the result of the inflexible operating costs of the schools and the hospital constructed during the twenties. But the clearest evidence is to be found in the Belmont chapter. Attention should be directed particularly to the advance in school and highway maintenance charges which followed the construction necessitated by the suburban development of the nineties and that precipitated by the completion of the Cambridge subway.

Although several of the towns owned and operated local utilities, their experiences do not permit much in the way of generalization. This is mainly the result of the serious inadequacy of the accounting methods pursued. It appears from the published statistics that the Belmont utilities have fairly good financial records, but that among those investigated only the Maynard water works has enjoyed a conspicuous success. Yet it is highly doubtful whether even this enterprise has been clearly profitable in any really adequate sense of the word.

Finally, it must be emphasized that although these studies have led to a number of fairly definite conclusions bearing upon significant political and financial problems, they derive their primary importance from the fact that they constitute a rather thorough application of the case method to the relatively neglected field of local finance. It is hoped that these studies will stimulate a wider use of this type of analysis, particularly upon the finances of small communities where large problems may be viewed against a simple background, where the difficulties of interpretation are reduced to what is probably the lowest level obtainable in the pragmatic study of public finance. It is certainly true that a wider application of this method would not only broaden our knowledge of the specific problems encountered in the field of local finance, but would also make possible a more thorough and generalized interpretation of the evidence which is already at hand.

BIBLIOGRAPHY

BIBLIOGRAPHY

Most of the statistics used in these studies have been taken from the annual financial reports published by the several towns. These reports, which are not listed below, are to be found in the offices of the town clerks and for the most part in the Massachusetts State Library.

The following primary sources have also been used:

Abstract of the Census of the Commonwealth of Massachusetts, Taken with Reference to Facts Existing on the First Day of June, 1855 (Boston, 1857).
Abstract of the Census of Massachusetts, 1865 (Boston, 1867).
Acts and Resolves Passed by the General Court of Massachusetts (Boston, annual).
Aggregates of Polls, Property, Taxes, etc., as Assessed April 1, etc., Public Document No. 19 (Boston, annual).
Annual Report of the Commissioner of Corporations and Taxation for the Year Ending November 30, etc., Public Document No. 16 (Boston, annual).
The Census of Massachusetts, 1865 (Boston, 1867).
The Census of Massachusetts, 1875, 3 vols. (Boston, 1876–77).
The Census of Massachusetts: 1880, Public Document, 1881, Number 15, Supplement (Boston, 1883).
The Census of Massachusetts, 1885, 3 vols. in 4 (Boston, 1887–88).
Census of the Commonwealth of Massachusetts, 1895, 7 vols. (Boston, 1896–1900).
Census of the Commonwealth of Massachusetts, 1905, 4 vols. (Boston, 1908–10).
Documents Printed by Order of the Senate of the Commonwealth of Massachusetts during the Session of the General Court, A.D. 1886 (Boston, 1886).
Documents Printed by Order of the Valuation Committee during Their Session of 1850 (Boston, 1850).
Fifteenth Census of the United States: 1930, vol. I (Washington, 1931).
The General Laws of Vermont, 1917, Including the Public Acts of 1917, Published by Authority (1918).
Journal and Documents of the Valuation Committee of the Year 1860 (Boston, 1861).
Journal of the House of Representatives of the Commonwealth of Massachusetts (Boston, annual).
Journal of the Senate (Boston, annual).
Journal of the Valuation Committee of Massachusetts, 1840 (manuscript in the Massachusetts State Library).
Poor's Manual of Industrials (New York: Poor's Railroad Manual Company, annual).

The Public Laws of the State of New Hampshire, 2 vols. (Manchester, 1925).
Report of the Treasurer and Receiver General for the Year Ending November 30, etc., Public Document No. 5 (Boston, annual).
The Revised Laws of the Commonwealth of Massachusetts, Enacted November 21, 1901, 3 vols. (Boston, 1902).
The Revised Statutes of the Commonwealth of Massachusetts, Passed November 4, 1835 (Boston, 1836).
Statistical Tables: Exhibiting the Condition and Products of Certain Branches of Industry in Massachusetts, for the Year Ending April 1, 1837. Prepared from the Returns of the Assessors, by John P. Bigelow, Secretary of the Commonwealth (Boston, 1838).
Statistics of the Condition and Products of Certain Branches of Industry in Massachusetts, for the Year Ending April 1, 1845. Prepared from the Returns of the Assessors, by John G. Palfrey, Secretary of the Commonwealth (Boston, 1846).
. . . Statistics of Municipal Finances, for City and Town Fiscal Years Ending between November 30 . . . and April 1, etc., Public Document No. 79 (Boston, annual).
Tercentenary Edition of the General Laws of the Commonwealth of Massachusetts, Comprising the General Laws Enacted December 22, 1920 to Take Effect January 1, 1921, as Amended Prior to January 1, 1932, 3 vols. (Boston, 1932).

In addition the following secondary sources have been referred to in the text:

Austin, Ivers J., *Argument of Ivers J. Austin, Counsel for the Remonstrants from Watertown, against the Petition for the Incorporation of the Town of Belmont, before the Joint Standing Committee on Towns* (Boston, 1857).
Ballou, Adin, *History of the Hopedale Community, from Its Inception to Its Virtual Submergence in the Hopedale Parish* (Lowell, 1897).
Ballou, Adin, *History of the Town of Milford, Worcester County, Massachusetts, from Its first Settlement to 1881* (Boston, 1882).
Bates, Frank Greene, "Village Government in New England," *American Political Science Review*, VI, 367–385 (August 1912).
Benton, Josiah Henry, *The Draper Corporations against the People of Milford. Argument of J. H. Benton, jun., Esq., before the Committee on Towns of the Massachusetts Legislature of 1886, against the Division of Milford and the Incorporation of Hopedale* (Boston, 1886).
Bullock, Charles Jesse, *Historical Sketch of the Finances and Financial Policy of Massachusetts from 1780 to 1905* (New York, 1907).
Bullock, Charles Jesse, "The Taxation of Property and Income in Massachusetts," *Quarterly Journal of Economics*, XXXI, 1–61 (November 1916).
Causes of the Financial Breakdown of the Local Government of Fall River, Mass., and Means Taken by Massachusetts to Re-establish the Finances of That City, State of Connecticut — Taxation-Document No. 255 (Hartford, 1933).

Chen, Tsung, "The Relation Between Local Governmental Expenditures and Density of Population in Massachusetts," unpublished doctor's thesis, 1926, Harvard University.

Chenery, Winthrop L., *Some Statistics of the Town of Belmont, Massachusetts, for the First Thirty Years of Its Corporate Existence* (Belmont, 1890).

Clarke, George Kuhn, *History of Needham, Massachusetts, 1711-1911* (Cambridge, Mass., 1912).

Conklin, Edwin P., *Middlesex County and Its People*, 5 vols. (New York: Lewis Historical Publishing Co., 1927).

Crane, Ellery Bicknell, *History of Worcester County, Massachusetts*, 3 vols. (New York: Lewis Historical Publishing Co., 1924).

Davis, William Thomas, *The New England States; Their Constitutional, Judicial, Educational, Commercial, Professional and Industrial History*, 4 vols. (Boston, 1897).

Dewey, Davis Rich, *Financial History of the United States* (11th ed.; New York: Longmans, 1931).

Drake, Samuel Adams, *History of Middlesex County, Massachusetts*, 2 vols. (Boston, 1880).

Facts Concerning Town Divisions, Illustrating the Policy of the State (about 1890), pamphlet in the Massachusetts State Library.

Fairlie, John Archibald, *Local Government in Counties, Towns, and Villages* (New York, 1914).

The Fiscal Problem in Massachusetts (New York: The National Industrial Conference Board, 1931).

Fiske, Joseph Emery, *History of the Town of Wellesley, Massachusetts*, edited and enlarged by Ellen Ware Fiske (Boston: Pilgrim Press, 1917).

Gutteridge, W. H., *A Brief History of the Town of Maynard, Massachusetts* (Hudson, Mass., 1921).

Harding, Arthur Leon, *Double Taxation of Property and Income; a Study in the Judicial Delimitation of the Conflicting Claims of Taxing Jurisdiction Advanced by the American States* (Cambridge, Mass.: Harvard University Press, 1933).

A History of the County of Berkshire, Massachusetts (Pittsfield, 1829).

History of Worcester County, Massachusetts, 2 vols. (Boston, 1879).

Hopkinton (Boston: Edison Electric Illuminating Company, 1909).

Hudson, Alfred Sereno, *The Annals of Sudbury, Wayland, and Maynard, Middlesex County, Massachusetts* (Ayer, Mass., 1891).

Hudson, Alfred Sereno, *The History of Sudbury, Massachusetts, 1638-1889* (The Town of Sudbury, 1889).

Hurd, Duane Hamilton, *History of Middlesex County, Massachusetts*, 3 vols. (Philadelphia, 1890).

Hurd, Duane Hamilton, *History of Worcester County, Massachusetts*, 2 vols. (Philadelphia, 1889).

James, Herman Gerlach, *Local Government in the United States* (New York: Appleton, 1921).

Jonathan Frost et al., in Equity, vs. The Inhabitants of the Town of Belmont et al. (n.p., n.d.), pamphlet in Harvard College Library.

Lutz, Harley Leist, *Public Finance* (2d ed.; New York: Appleton, 1929).

Mill, John Stuart, *Principles of Political Economy* (Ashley edition, 1909; reissue, New York: Longmans, 1929).

Nichols, Philip, *Taxation in Massachusetts* (2d ed.; Boston: Financial Publishing Co., 1922).

Oakes, Eugene E., "The Taxation of Public Utility Property in Vermont," *The Bulletin of the National Tax Association,* XXI, 66–75 (December 1935).

Opening Argument of Nathan Sumner Myrick, Esq., Testimony and the Closing Argument of Hon. Selwyn Z. Bowman before the Legislative Committee on Towns, 1886, in Favor of the Incorporation of the New Town of Hopedale (Boston, 1886).

Pigou, Arthur Cecil, *A Study in Public Finance* (London: Macmillan, 1928).

Proceedings of the Twenty-Fifth Annual Conference on Taxation, under the Auspices of the National Tax Association (1933).

Proceedings of the Twenty-Sixth Annual Conference, etc. (1934).

Reasons Why Hopedale Should be Set Off from Milford (The Committee for Hopedale, 1886).

Report of the Commissioners Appointed to Inquire into the Expediency of Revising and Amending the Laws Relating to Taxation and Exemption Therefrom (Boston, 1875).

Report of the Commission Appointed to Inquire into the Expediency of Revising and Amending the Laws of the Commonwealth Relating to Taxation (Boston, 1897).

Report of the Commission on Taxation, Appointed Under the Provisions of Chapter 129 of the Resolves of 1907, To Investigate the Subject of Taxation and to Codify, Revise and Amend the Laws Relating Thereto (Boston, 1908).

Sly, John Fairfield, *Town Government in Massachusetts, 1620–1930* (Cambridge: Harvard University Press, 1930).

Some Reasons Why the Town of Milford Should Not Be Divided Replied to by a Committee Favoring Division (1886).

Special Report of the Millville Municipal Finance Commission Relative to the Finances and Future of the Town of Millville, House Document, 1881 (Boston, 1935).

Speeches of the Hon. Gideon Haynes, Hon. W. S. Brakenridge, and Hon. Hugh W. Greene, on the Question as to Incorporating the Town of Belmont (Boston, 1857).

Spengler, Edwin H., "Is the Real Estate Tax a Benefit Tax?" Memorandum Number Five appended to *Report of the New York State Commission for the Revision of the Tax Laws,* Legislative Document (1932) No. 77 (Albany, 1932).

Taussig, Frank William, *Principles of Economics* (3d ed.; New York: Macmillan, 1921).

Worthington, Erastus, *The History of Dedham, from the Beginning of Its Settlement, in September, 1635, to May, 1827* (Boston, 1827).

INDEX

INDEX

Ability, measurement of, 4, 4 n
Ability theory, 3–4
Adams, town of, incorporated, 107;
divided, 107; economic development,
107–110, 117, 124–125, 130–131; mis-
management discovered, 115 n; town
board altered, 116, 116 n; proposal to
incorporate as city, 116
American Woolen Company, 60, 65, 67,
67 n, 71, 74. *See also* Assabet mills
Aristotle, 141 n
Ashland, town of, 184, 186
Assabet Manufacturing Company, *see*
Assabet mills
Assabet mills, 43, 45–46, 46 n, 48, 49,
59–60, 63, 64, 65, 67, 67 n, 71–72, 74
Assabet village, incorporated as the
town of Maynard, 41, 43 n, 223;
economic development, 43, 48;
reached by railroad, 45 n. *See also*
Maynard; Assabet mills
Austin, Ivers J., 146 n

Ballou, Adin, 15 n, 17 n
Bank tax, distribution of, 26 n, 37, 69,
122, 158; receipts from: Adams,
114 n, 122, 128, 128 n; Belmont,
152–153, 158, 165–166, 175; Blackstone, 89; Florida, 200; Hopedale,
17 n, 26; Maynard, 56, 62, 69, 75;
Milford, 17 n, 21, 26; Needham, 38;
North Adams, 122; Somerset, 210,
215, 215 n; Stow, 56; Sudbury, 56;
Wellesley, 37–38
Bates, F. G., 7 n, 9 n
Bellingham, town of, 85
Belmont, town of, incorporated, 146;
economic development, 146–148, 149,
154, 161–162, 169
Benefit theory, 3–5, 10; a justification
for local property tax, 5 n
Benefits, a criterion for determining
taxable jurisdiction, 5, 5 n; measure-
ment of, 3
Benton, J. H., 18 n, 22 n
Berkshire Cotton Manufacturing Com-
pany, 125, 131

Berkshire County, 107, 202, 203, 206
Berkshire Fine Spinning Associates, 131,
135
Blackstone, town of, becomes precinct
of Mendon, 80; economic develop-
ment of, 80–82, 80 n, 83–85, 93;
proposal to change boundaries, 85;
loss of Millville, 85
Blackstone Manufacturing Company,
80, 84, 85 n
Board of Tax Appeals, 104, 105
Boot and shoe industry, in Adams, 108,
108 n, 110; Framingham, 191; Hop-
kinton, 183–184, 190, 191, 223;
Mendon, 82; Milford, 17, 17 n, 21;
North Adams, 118; Stow, 43 n, 51
Boston, city of, 169, 181, 206 n
Boston and Albany Railroad, 34 n
Boston and Providence Railroad, 34 n
Boston and Troy Railroad, 115 n
Boston and Worcester Railroad, 34 n
Boston Elevated Railway Company,
154, 154 n, 158 n; constructs subway
to Cambridge, 161
Boxborough, town of, 41 n
Brakenridge, W. S., 146 n
Bridgeport, Connecticut, 6 n
Brockton, city of, 210, 211
Brookline, town of, 206 n
Browne, W. B., 107 n
Building valuation, in industrial towns,
61 n, 75, 88, 88–89 n, 97, 104, 121 n,
127, 134; in suburban towns, 97,
157 n, 164–165, 173–174, 210; in
Florida, 204–205; in Somerset, 214
Bullock, C. J., 26 n, 69 n, 158 n, 165 n

Cambridge, city of, 149, 152, 219
Case studies, value of in local finance,
10–11, 224
Chen, Tsung, 38 n, 149, 158, 189 n
Chenery, W. L., 149 n, 154 n
Cheshire, town of, 107
Cities, incorporation of in Massachu-
setts, 8
Clarke, George Kuhn, 29 n, 34 n